THE GLOBAL FACE OF PUBLIC FAITH

MORAL TRADITIONS SERIES

JAMES F. KEENAN, S.J., EDITOR

The *The* GLOBAL FACE

of **PUBLIC FAITH**

Politics, Human Rights, and Christian Ethics

DAVID HOLLENBACH, S.J.

GEORGETOWN UNIVERSITY PRESS : WASHINGTON, D.C.

The illustration shown on the cover is *Allegory of Good Government*,
by Ambrogio Lorenzetti, c. 1337–40. Fresco, Palazzo Publico, Siena, Italy. The detail
shown on the front cover is the personification of Good Government guided by the virtues
Faith and Charity (partially obscured) above, and flanked on the left by Peace,
Fortitude, and Prudence. The citizens of the Republic are shown below.

Georgetown University Press, Washington, D.C.
© 2003 by Georgetown University Press
All rights reserved
Printed in the United States of America

10   9   8   7   6   5   4   3   2   1   2003

This book is printed on acid-free paper
meeting the requirements of the American National Standard
for Permanence in Paper for Printed Library Materials.

Design and composition by Jeff Clark
at Wilsted & Taylor Publishing Services

Library of Congress Cataloging-in-Publication Data
Hollenbach, David.
The global face of public faith : politics, human rights,
and Christian ethics / David Hollenbach.
p. cm.—(Moral traditions series)
Includes bibliographical references and index.
ISBN 0-87840-139-3 (pbk. : alk. paper)
1. Christian ethics—Catholic authors. 2. Christianity and politics—Catholic Church.
3. Human rights—Religious aspects—Catholic Church. I. Title. II. Series.
BJ1249.H579 2003
241′.042—dc21

To my colleagues in Christian ethics

at Boston College:

Lisa Sowle Cahill, John Paris, and Stephen Pope,

with much gratitude for their friendship,

wisdom, and encouragement.

CONTENTS

PREFACE

The question of the appropriate relation between religion and politics has been much debated in recent years in the United States. This debate has often been lively, at times acrimonious. Religious leaders have entered the public forum of political debate in the United States on issues ranging from abortion to economic justice for the poor, the environment, human rights, and U.S. policy in response to terrorism. This engagement has cut across the conservative-liberal spectrum, both religiously and politically. Some fear that the engagement of religious communities in public debates threatens the stability and freedoms of the American republic. Others see it as a needed restoration of core values on which the health of American democracy depends.

More recently, especially since the terrorist attacks in New York and Washington, D.C., on September 11, 2001, Americans have become deeply concerned with the role of religion in international affairs. They have become painfully aware of ways that religious motivations intersect with political action today, especially when the religion is fundamentalist Islam. Despite the attacks of September 11 and their aftermath, however, the role of religion in international politics is certainly not limited to the violent activities of certain Islamic fundamentalist groups. Other religious communities, including Christian ones, have historically played notable roles in stimulating or reinforcing political conflicts and they continue to do so. This has raised fears that the global politics of the post–cold war era could become a clash of civilizations marked by new wars of religion. In response to this hypothesis, it is essential to remember that religious communities play important roles as peacemakers and advocates of justice on the international stage. The examples of Pope John Paul II, Archbishop Desmond Tutu, the Dalai Lama, and numerous other religious leaders give testimony to this more constructive political role of religious faiths, as do the activities of large numbers of the laity in these same communities. Thus, the question of whether religious believers will be contributors to conflict and bloodshed or to peace and justice is of considerable importance in both international politics and in the domestic politics of United States today. The stakes in the interaction between religion and politics are high, for both the religious communities themselves and the politics they influence.

Much has been written in recent years on matters of religion and politics. Because these issues continue to generate serious religious, political, and intellectual concern, I have here gathered some of my recent reflections on the public role of religion previously published (with one exception) in disparate places. These essays explore a number of aspects of the way religious communities have interacted with politics and social life. They also present some conclusions on how, in my judgment, religious communities ought to behave when they enter the domains of public and political life.

The essays in part 1, *Fundamental Matters*, deal with matters that shape the overall perspective one brings to the interaction of religion and politics. They are concerned with matters of a more theoretical nature, raising questions in the domains of social theory, epistemology, and theology. Chapter 1, "Faith in Public," addresses the matter of whether and how Christianity can find common ground with other religious communities in a pluralistic setting. It argues that dialogue across the boundaries of diverse traditions is possible and that such dialogue is essential to a fruitful engagement between Christianity and public life today. The common ground it envisions for a pluralistic society is dynamic and always in need of being recreated through mutual engagement. Thus, common ground and vigorous public presence by religious communities are complementary, not antithetical. A public role for religion need not be divisive and, in fact, can be the source of much needed solidarity.

Chapter 2, "Tradition, Historicity, and Truth," spells out some of the demands that this kind of participation in public life will make on religious communities. In particular, it calls on Christianity to recognize that its moral tradition is dynamic and not given once and for all. Both the religious and the moral dimensions of the self-understanding of Christians are always *in via*—on the way to an adequate understanding both of God and of how human beings should live together. The essay argues, therefore, that both an adequate theology and an honest account of history show that Christian ethics should be understood as a pilgrimage that is not yet completed. Such an understanding is particularly important when Christianity intersects with the politics of a pluralistic society.

Chapter 3, "Virtues and Vices in Social Inquiry," makes a similar argument that social theorists and others seeking to understand our common life together are also always on the way to the understanding they seek. Therefore, they need to approach their intellectual tasks with the virtue of humility and with a spirit of genuine solidarity with the people they seek to understand. If such humility and solidarity are brought to the task of understanding the public role of religions, the possibility of constructive interaction between religious communities will be enhanced. Chapter 4, "Social Ethics under the Sign of the Cross," carries this argument for humility and solidarity to the theological level. It argues that attaining a more humane social life calls for deepened awareness of the scope of human suffering that mars our world and for responding to that suffering in a spirit of solidarity. The central Christian symbol of the cross of Jesus Christ is presented as a call to that awareness and solidarity. Thus, the most distinctive symbol of the Christian tradition is presented as a source of the kind of social ethic and politics needed to attain a more humane social life in the midst of the political and moral pluralism of the world today.

Part 2, *The Church in American Public Life*, turns explicitly to several aspects of the recent debates about the interaction of religion with the politics of the United States. Chapter 5, "Religion, Morality, and Politics in the United States," presents an overview of some of the main currents in the public engagement of the Christian churches in American politics over the past decade and a half. It also identifies some of the theological self-understandings that motivate these forms of engagement and assesses the adequacy of these theologies. Chapter 6, "Religion and Political Life: Theoretical Issues," turns to recent arguments in American philosophy and jurisprudence about the proper role of religion in public and political life. The work of the recently deceased John Rawls, of course, figures prominently in these philosophical discussions. Rawls's views on the matter of the public role of religion have been revised a number of times, though this essay does not give an account of these changes; rather, it treats Rawls principally in light of the views he advanced in the early 1990s. Because these views remain influential both among philosophers and in the larger U.S. culture today, it is useful to let the analysis contained in this essay stand as it is. Only minor changes have been made to this essay from its initial publication, to help eliminate direct conflicts with Rawls's later positions.

Chapter 7, "Freedom and Truth," addresses the public role of Christianity, and Catholicism in particular, in light of the understandings of religious freedom proposed by the Second Vatican Council and in the writings of both John Courtney Murray and Pope John Paul II. It further develops the argument that active engagement by religious communities in public life need not be a threat to freedom in a pluralistic society. This argument depends on interpreting religious freedom as a positive empowerment for participation in social life, not as a negative immunity that relegates religion to the private sphere. Chapter 8, "The Context of Civil Society and Culture," stresses that religious engagement in public life should occur principally through its influence in the broad domain of the social, rather than primarily through direct influence on the legislature or the courts. Thus, institutional separation of church and state is not the same as the removal of religious communities from social influence. Separation of church and state is not the same as the privatization of religion. Chapter 9, "Politically Active Churches and Democratic Life," argues that engagement of religion in the life of society can in fact strengthen the quality of public life by encouraging citizen participation, provided the engagement is of the right sort. In a context such as that of the United States today, where public life is itself becoming weak and attenuated, this could well be the most important contribution of religion to the culture.

Part 3, *Global Issues*, turns to international considerations regarding religion and politics. Chapter 10, "Christian Social Ethics after the Cold War," addresses the fundamental changes that have occurred in global society since 1989. It considers possible contributions of Christian ethics in the domain of political economy in the aftermath of the collapse of the Soviet Union. In particular, it raises questions about the direction of Christian ethical thought concerning private property and the role of the state in market economies. Such issues are of considerable importance to the engagement of Christianity in the global public domain of the post–cold war world. Chapter 11, "Human Rights and Development: The African Challenge," explores how Christians should understand the relation between human rights and the economic development of the poor countries of the Third World, with particular attention to Africa. The final chapter of the book, "Faiths, Cultures, and Global Ethics," is a new essay that expands consideration of the public role of religious communities beyond Christianity to other religious traditions, such as Confucianism and Islam. It returns to the question of whether common moral ground can be achieved in the face of religious pluralism, concluding that common ground on a set of truly basic human rights is achievable and that all nations and cultures can be required to respect this set of rights. A broad agreement on the full list of rights commonly taken for granted in the West will take longer to achieve and it must be sought by ongoing argument aimed at persuasion. This distinction between basic and broader sets of rights has important political implications. It could even have military consequences in circumstances where enforcement becomes an issue. It also has religious implications, because it implies that all religious communities can be required to respect the truly basic rights. The most basic rights both guarantee the fundamental religious freedoms for all persons and also set limits to the legitimate exercise of religious freedom. They establish key parameters for the interaction between religion and politics.

ACKNOWLEDGMENTS

All of the chapters in this book except chapter 12 have been published elsewhere. They were initially written for specific occasions, such as a conference or at the request of a journal editor. They have been revised only to reduce repetitions and in a few places to update references to unfolding historical events and the developing ideas of other authors. I am most grateful to the editors of the journals and books in which the chapters originally appeared for permission to revise and reprint them here. Bibliographical information on where the chapters previously appeared follows.

Chapter 1 appeared in *Faith in the Public Forum*, edited by Neil Brown and Robert Gascoigne (Adelaide: Australian Theological Forum, 1999), 1–27. Chapter 2 was published in *Christian Ethics: Problems and Prospects*, edited by Lisa Sowle Cahill and James F. Childress (Cleveland: The Pilgrim Press, 1996), 60–75; copyright Lisa Sowle Cahill and James F. Childress, revised by permission. Chapter 3 was published in *The Nature of Moral Inquiry in the Social Sciences: Essays by Clarke E. Cochrane, David Hollenbach, Alan Wolfe, and Robert Wuthnow* (South Bend, Ind.: Occasional Papers of the Erasmus Institute, no. 2, 1999), 45–61. Chapter 4 was originally delivered as the Presidential Address to the Society of Christian Ethics and was published in *The Annual of the Society of Christian Ethics 1996*, 3–18. Chapter 5 appeared in *Theological Studies* 49 (1988), 68–89. A somewhat different version of chapter 6 was published in *Theological Studies* 52 (1991), 87–106. Chapter 7 was published in *John Courtney Murray and the Growth of Tradition*, edited by J. Leon Hooper and Todd Whitmore (Kansas City: Sheed and Ward, an imprint of Rowman and Littlefield, 1996), 129–48. Chapter 8 appeared in the *San Diego Law Review* 30 (1994), 879–901; copyright 1994 *San Diego Law Review*, reprinted with the permission of the *San Diego Law Review*. Chapter 9 was published in *Religion and Contemporary Liberalism*, edited by Paul Weithman (Notre Dame, Ind.: University of Notre Dame Press, 1997), 291–306; copyright University of Notre Dame Press, used by permission. Chapter 10 appeared in *Theological Studies* 53 (1992), 75–95. A version of chapter 11 was published in *Journal of Religious Ethics* 26 (1998), 305–17.

PART ONE FUNDAMENTAL MATTERS

I

Faith in Public

The beginning of the twenty-first century confronts all religious communities with a fundamental challenge: how to relate their distinctive visions of the good human life with the growing awareness that all persons are linked in a web of global interdependence. The diverse communities of the world today are increasingly bound together by the world market, their mutual dependence on the biophysical environment that knows no boundaries, cultural interactions made possible by communications technology, migration and forced refugee movements, and the transnational transmission of threats to human life and health such as the AIDS virus, drugs, and weapons of war. In this interdependent world, the need for a clear vision of the common good of the whole human race is evident. An understanding of the good we have in common is essential if we are to avoid the fate of a "common bad."

In this interdependent world, however, we are increasingly aware of religious and cultural pluralism. Pluralism, by definition, means that there is no agreement about the meaning of the good life. Indeed the complexity of emerging world realities is leading many communities to seek re-

3

affirmation of the distinctive traditions that set them apart from others. This is evident in movements for political devolution or separation in Québec, Scotland, Catalunya, and northern Italy. More ominously, it has led to armed conflict in the Basque country, Sudan, Nigeria, on the border of India and Pakistan, and in the Middle East generally. In the former Yugoslavia, Rwanda, Burundi, and eastern regions of the Democratic Republic of Congo, these conflicts have descended to the depths of attempted genocide. Thus, we face a paradox: attaining a vision of the global common good is increasingly problematic precisely at a historical moment when the need for such a vision is growing.

The challenge of this situation is particularly acute for religious communities. In a much noted and controversial article in *Foreign Affairs*, Samuel Huntington conjectured that the conflicts in the world politics of the emerging post–cold war era would be driven by a clash of civilizations and cultures rather than ideology or economics. Huntington noted that civilizations are communities distinguished from each other by "history, language, culture, tradition, and, most important, religion."[1] Huntington's diagnosis raises the specter of religious conflict on a global scale. Regardless of whether Huntington's thesis is correct (I think it oversimplifies[2]), the realities that led him to propose it have been causing considerable confusion among those who have identified the direction of history with the triumph of secularity. The so-called secularization hypothesis projected that the future would be characterized by declining influence of religion in the public sphere. The church-state issue would be more or less automatically solved by the withering away of the church, or at least the elimination of the church's presence in the public square. It has become apparent that this interpretation of the direction of the trends is at least questionable today.

José Casanova, a sociologist of religion, addresses this question by providing several alternative models for the public presence of religion in our time. He distinguishes three possible meanings of secularization: (1) the *decline of religion* in the modern world, which will continue until religion finally disappears; (2) the *privatization of religion* (i.e., the displacement of the quest for salvation and personal meaning to the subjective sphere of the self, a displacement that renders religion irrelevant to the institutional functioning of modern society); and (3) the functional *differentiation of the role of religion* from other spheres of human activity, primarily the state, the economy, and science.[3]

4

Casanova argues persuasively that the first two meanings of secularization are contrary to fact. Worldwide, religion is not declining. Casanova argues that the thesis of the decline of religion is largely based on the experience of modern Western Europe and is not generalizable to other parts of the world. Secularization understood as the privatization of religion is also factually a questionable generalization, in light of the widespread visibility of religious dimensions to political movements ranging from the Christian Coalition in the United States to the role that the Islamic resurgence has played in generating Huntington's diagnosis of the future of world politics. Whether it is desirable to propose such privatization as a normative objective can be questioned as well. For where religion becomes a private preference alone, public life lacks the depth of meaning that can generate loyalty and commitment among citizens. The resulting anomie can create a vacuum into which fundamentalist forces insert themselves, almost certainly without civility and possibly with violence.[4]

One of the results of these developments is that the proper role of religion in public life has become a much-discussed topic among moral philosophers and political theorists. The strength of these fields is their careful analysis of important theoretical issues raised by the religion and politics issue. The recent work of John Rawls, for example, argues that public normative discourse in a pluralistic society must ultimately be accountable to the standards of what he calls "public reason"—a form of discourse in which religious convictions play no constitutive role.[5] This has led others to propose alternatives to the constraints Rawls would place on the public role of religion by proposing alternative theories of rationality.[6] Important as these discussions of the meaning of rationality and of moral epistemology surely are, they are several steps removed from the conflicts and possibilities that arise when religious communities actually enter the public square. Robin Lovin has observed that, even when a theory of rationality provides some space for engagement between religious belief and political activity, few believers find this "authorizes them to do something that they would otherwise have refrained from doing." Thus, these discussions in moral and political theory are often "curiously abstract and unrelated to the role that religious beliefs actually play in the thinking of many persons."[7]

Casanova's third meaning of secularization—the differentiation of religion from the other spheres of public life such as the state—looks more promising. This approach fully supports the modern Western achievements of respect for religious and personal freedom. It presupposes that any public role for religious communities must avoid a quest for hegemonic control of social, intellectual, and political life by religion. This raises questions that I take to be central in a consideration of the role of faith in public life today. Is it possible for religion to provide a sense of ultimate meaning and salvation that includes the meaning and hope we seek in political, economic, and intellectual activity? Can this happen without religious truth claims becoming legitimations of political authoritarianism and intellectual obscurantism? If this cannot be done, religious efforts to identify and pursue the public good will amount to attempts to negate the achievements of modernity.

Thus, we need to consider how Christians might relate their faith to public life while also affirming the importance of civility and respect for the religious convictions of non-Christians in our diverse world. This problem has, of course, confronted Christianity in Europe since the Reformation in the sixteenth century. Today, however, it raises a host of new questions for Christianity, for the clarification of the role of faith in the public life of an interdependent global society cannot presume the history shared by European Catholics and Protestants as its experiential basis. Christianity is now definitively a world religion, not a European one with branch offices or colonies elsewhere.[8] This new context demands that the public role of faith be considered in light of the deepening awareness of religious and cultural diversity of our world. This essay will ask how Christians can remain faithful to their conviction of the truth of the gospel while engaging others with the respect demanded if the common good is to have plausible meaning in today's new context. In doing so, it focuses particularly on ways this question confronts the Roman Catholic tradition, but with the hope that what is said will be relevant to other Christian communities as well.

COMMON VISION AND CHRISTIAN DISTINCTIVENESS

Throughout much of its history, the main lines of Catholic social teaching were based on a natural law ethic derived from the conviction that human reason is capable of discovering the basic outlines of the universal human good. From Thomas Aquinas in the thirteenth century, to Pope Leo XIII's encyclical *Rerum Novarum* in 1891, to Pope John XXIII's *Pacem in Terris* in 1963, Catholic contributions to social morality regularly appealed to human reason to discern the universal moral demands of human nature. Because human nature was created by God, and because human reason is one of the Creator's greatest gifts to human beings, this natural law approach to social morality was seen as fully compatible with Christian biblical faith. Indeed a reason-based social ethic was understood as a direct implication of Roman Catholic faith.[9] There are analogues to this approach in Lutheran and Calvinist understandings of the "ordinances of God" and "common grace" discernible in the structures of the created world, even though the followers of Luther and Calvin were less confident in our ability to discern these without the aid of revelation than were Catholics.

This natural law approach in official Roman Catholic social teaching reached its clearest expression in John XXIII's affirmation of a charter of universal human rights in *Pacem in Terris*. This encyclical declared, "Any human society, if it is to be well ordered and productive, must lay down as a foundation this principle, namely, that every human being is a person; that is, his nature is endowed with intelligence and free will. Indeed, precisely because he is a person he has rights and obligations flowing directly and simultaneously from his very nature. And as these rights and obligations are universal and inviolable, so they cannot be in any way surrendered."[10] Human rights, in other words, are founded on a dignity whose clearest manifestation is rationality and freedom, and these rights are discernible by all reasonable people, not only by Christians. John XXIII added that human rights will be esteemed more highly when considered in the light of revelation and grace, for Christian faith reinforces a sense of human worth through its belief in God's redemptive love for all people in Christ.[11] But it is clear that *Pacem in Terris* proposes ethical standards for all peoples and cultures. These standards can be known by those who are not Christian and all people can be held accountable to them independent of their religious or cultural traditions. Thus, John XXIII went on to present a list of human rights very similar to the United Nations Universal Declaration. This natural law ethic of human rights was seen as universal, transcultural, and suited to the promotion of the common good of a religiously pluralistic world.

This sort of natural law–based, universalist ethic has deep roots in the Roman Catholic tradition. St. Paul, in the letter to the Romans, and

Thomas Aquinas, for example, maintained that the most basic requirements of human morality can be known by Christian believers and unbelievers alike. Christian morality is not sectarian in the sense Ernst
Troeltsch used this term (i.e., it is not a morality for Christians only). The
desire to find common moral ground between Christians and non-Christians is a deep impulse in the Catholic tradition because of its belief that
one God has created the whole of humanity and that all human beings
share a common origin, destiny, and nature. This universalism has continued to be a strong emphasis in Catholic social teaching in the decades
since Vatican II.

The Second Vatican Council, however, introduced notable complexities
into the Catholic affirmation of universalist natural law. The Council was
an assembly of Roman Catholic bishops drawn from most of the diverse
cultures around the world and from societies where all of the great world
religions play significant roles. As Karl Rahner points out, Vatican II was a
unique event in the history of the Catholic community in that it was "in a
rudimentary form still groping for identity, the Church's first official self-
actualization as a world Church" rather than as a European religion to be
exported to the rest of the world along with European culture.[12] This historical and sociological fact has had considerable influence on the teaching of the Council, including its social teaching. It has led to heightened
awareness that the cultural and religious pluralism of the world has an effect on what people see as reasonable interpretations of the human good
and, thus, as the reasonable demands of social morality. Despite the growing sense of the unity of the human family and the heightened exchange
of ideas across cultural and religious boundaries, "the very words by which
key concepts are expressed take on quite different meanings."[13] This
broadening of the church's self-consciousness called into question the robust confidence that universal norms of social morality are readily evident
to all reasonable people.

Thus, one can discern in some of the texts of Vatican II an incipient
emergence of what has since come to be called the postmodern suspicion
of universalism. In fact, this postmodern critique in the West has been
aimed at the eighteenth-century Enlightenment's belief that reason is independent of social context and the inherited presuppositions of cultural
traditions.[14] In line with this suspicion of Enlightenment rationalism, the

Council called for the revitalization of the role of biblical faith and Christian theological conviction in the formation of a vision of the human good. Nevertheless, it did not abandon the universalist aspirations of the natural law ethic.

This renewal of the biblical and theological roots of Catholic social thought is evident in the entire first part of the Council's *Pastoral Constitution on the Church in the Modern World, Gaudium et Spes*, which provides the overarching vision of recent Catholic social teaching. The document's treatment of three fundamental topics—the dignity of the human person, the importance of community and solidarity, and the religious significance of this-worldly activity—is supported both by distinctively Christian theological warrants as well as by natural law warrants based on reason. For example, in line with the natural law approach of *Pacem in Terris*, the Council continued to affirm that the dignity of the human person is discernible in the transcendent power of the human mind, in the sacredness of conscience, and in the excellence of liberty. Thus, this dignity can be recognized by all human beings and makes claims upon all, both Christian and non-Christian. Nevertheless, human dignity is known in its full depth only from Christian revelation. The Bible uncovers this depth in its affirmation that human beings are created in the image and likeness of God and therefore possess a sacredness that is properly religious. Further, redemption and recreation in Christ mean that human dignity has a theological dimension that only Christian faith can see. In a significant passage, the Council argued that an explicitly theological perspective, formed by an understanding of and response to the person of Jesus Christ, is necessary for the attainment of an adequate grasp of the normatively human: "The truth is that only in the mystery of the incarnate Word does the mystery of the human person take on light. For Adam, the first human, was a figure of Him who was to come, namely Christ the Lord. Christ, the final Adam, by the revelation of the mystery of the Father and His love, fully reveals human beings to themselves and makes their supreme calling clear."[15] Such an affirmation challenges the rationalist idea that Christian ethical reflection can rely exclusively on philosophical reason and natural law. It shows that the church's social mission is a religious one that flows from the heart of Christian faith. This emphasis has been developed and refined in the post-Conciliar official social teachings and in movements such as liberation and political theologies, both of which have strong biblical roots. It shows that the church seeks to bring a distinctively Christian orientation to debates about social existence in a world increasingly conscious of itself as divided and pluralistic.

DIALOGIC UNIVERSALISM/INTELLECTUAL SOLIDARITY

Thus, the Council seemed to want to have it both ways. While it reaffirmed a universal ethic or common morality that is normative in all cultures and for all religious communities, at the same time it affirmed a distinctively Christian theological foundation for this ethic and an epistemology based on revelation through which this ethic can be known. The same dual approach is present in the recent writings of Pope John Paul II.[16] Is such a position coherent?

There are several interpretations of the relationship between universalist and particularist sources that could explain this two-fold approach. First, one could affirm that universal moral standards are in principle knowable by all persons but that in practice revelation is needed because of the weakness of the human mind and its further distortions by sin. In the concreteness of the actual existence of most people, revelation and grace are needed to know and live by the natural law. This position can be found in Augustine and Thomas Aquinas, in the Catholic tradition, and especially in the work of John Calvin in the Protestant tradition. The disadvantage of this approach is that it sometimes fails to attend sufficiently to the way the sinfulness of the Christian community itself casts doubt on strong claims that Christians have privileged knowledge of the universal human good. Second, one could argue, as the present pope has, that the authoritative teaching office of the Roman Catholic Church guarantees that the magisterium is capable of discerning and teaching the universally normative natural law in ways that are preserved by the Holy Spirit from sinful distortions. This stance, however, risks undermining the claim to provide a common morality for a pluralistic world by suggesting that only the teaching office of the Roman church can in practice know what that universal morality is.

I would propose a third approach, which can be called "dialogic universalism."[17] Following postmodern critiques of the Western Enlightenment, it acknowledges that reason is embedded in history. Rational argument is deeply shaped by the tradition within which the inquirer has been educated. Neither the questions addressed by rational discourse nor the thought patterns available to address these questions are the products of ahistorical or pure reason. For example, urgent questions arise from the anomalies that become apparent within an ongoing tradition of inquiry and responses to these questions are in part dependent on the resources provided by received traditions. This dependence of rational inquiry upon tradition is evident not only in ethics and theology, but in other domains of knowledge as well. For example, in physics the questions addressed by Newton were not the same as those that confronted the Greeks in classical times, and the questions that emerged within Newtonian physics led Einstein to recast the framework of the Newtonian world. Similarly, the new questions facing Newton and Einstein gave rise to new methods of analysis and modes of thought. Thus, the demands of reasonableness in physics led to different conclusions about the structure of the universe in the differing historical periods of Ptolemy, Newton, and Einstein.

But this historical change in the questions and methods of thought in differing periods in the history of physics does not mean that Ptolemy's, Newton's, and Einstein's theories are equally true and therefore equally false. Consciousness of the historical contexts of these questions and methods does not imply historical relativism. Einstein was compelled to raise new questions because of perceived inadequacies in the physics he had learned. Once these questions have been seen as necessary ones, Einstein's conclusions can be judged more adequate than Newton's and to lead to a truer picture of the physical world. A thoroughgoing relativism in physics is not a consequence of our awareness that physics has a history. Indeed, such a relativism would bring physical inquiry itself to a halt, for if all conclusions are judged of equal truth value there is no purpose in pursuing any inquiry at all.

This insight borrowed from the sciences may provide a clue to the deeper structure of recent efforts by the Christian community to combine fidelity to the particularistic vision of the human good rooted in the gospel with a commitment to discerning the common morality needed in a pluralistic but interdependent world. It is what I mean by "dialogic universalism." This orientation was incipiently present in the Second Vatican Council's stress on respect for the other and on dialogue across the boundaries of diverse communities as essential expressions of Christian fidelity to the gospel. In such an approach, the starting point for the church's effort to contribute to the pursuit of a common morality is the gospel and the Christian tradition. But these received convictions must be brought into active encounter with visions of the human good held by other religious communities, with other traditions and different, non-Western histories. This method of dialogue does not imply relativism, just as the recognition that physics has a history does not imply that Ptolemy's picture of the cosmos is just as true as Einstein's. In fact the commitment to dialogue and mutual inquiry suggests just the opposite—that there is a truth about the human good that must be pursued and that makes a claim on the minds and hearts of all persons.[18]

Thus, when the Second Vatican Council stressed the particularity of its theological understanding of the human good, this did not lead it to reject the Catholic tradition's pursuit of universal moral standards that apply cross-culturally and across religious traditions. But this universalism was conceived as the outcome of inquiry and dialogue, not as already in full possession by the church and simply to be proposed to or imposed upon others. As *Gaudium et Spes* put it, "Everything we have said about the dignity of the person . . . lays the foundation for the relationship between the church and the world, and provides the basis for dialogue between them."[19] It went on to commend dialogue with other traditions and modes of thought as potential sources for an ethic that would be more adequate both theologically and in its reasoned understanding of the normatively human: "Thanks to the experience of past ages, the progress of the sciences, and the treasures hidden in various forms of human culture, the nature of the human being is more clearly revealed and new roads to truth are opened. These benefits profit the Church, too, for from the beginning of her history, she has learned to express the message of Christ with the help of ideas and terminology of various peoples, and has tried to clarify them with the wisdom of philosophers, too."[20] This stance of dialogue with cultures and the sciences was broadened by other documents of the Council to include inter-Christian ecumenical dialogue and dialogue with the other great world religions.[21]

This commitment to dialogue is therefore both a demand of Christian faith and a requirement of reasonableness. It is simultaneously an expression of fidelity to the gospel and of respect for the other. Christian faith entails care and respect for all persons, and respect for their dignity means listening to their interpretations of the human good. Further, Christian love calls for the building of the bonds of solidarity among all persons, and such solidarity requires efforts to understand those who are different, to learn from them, and to contribute to their understanding of the good life as well. I have called this "intellectual solidarity."[22] It forges a bond among persons that goes beyond tolerance understood as leaving others alone to the positive engagement with others that true dialogue demands. Such intellectual solidarity expresses a reasonableness that avoids the rationalist dismissal of historical traditions and communal particularities by taking the diverse traditions and cultures of the world seriously enough both to listen carefully to them and to respond with respect. This is a reasonableness that expects both to learn and to teach through the give-and-take of dialogue. For Christians such dialogue, therefore, embodies a dynamic interaction between the biblical faith handed on to them through the centuries of Christian tradition and the reason that is a preeminent manifestation of the *imago Dei* in all human beings.

This dialogic and dynamic linkage of faith and reason has implications for a number of the substantive questions of public life today. The most obvious is in the broad area of an ethic of human rights. Freedom of speech, association, assembly, and political participation are among the concrete expressions of any ethic committed to genuine dialogue and intellectual solidarity. Where these freedoms are denied, dialogue is impossible and conflict likely. Where the rights to these freedoms are not respected, persons are treated neither as the Gospel requires nor as reasonableness demands. Thus, Vatican II could state that "the right to religious freedom has its foundation in the very dignity of the human person, as this dignity is known through the revealed word of God and by reason itself."[23] Indeed, the Council linked its support for the full range of human rights with both the very core of Christian faith and the continuing commitment to a public morality that can be universally known by all. For it declared both that "by virtue of the gospel committed to it, the Church proclaims the rights of the human person" and that the social nature and intrinsic dignity of human beings means that "the goal of all social institutions is and must be the human person."[24]

The location of this commitment to human rights in the context of an ethic of dialogue has important implications for the way these rights are understood. Religious freedom, for example, is sometimes understood in the more secularized sectors of Western societies in a way that would marginalize religion from active presence in the public life of society. In this view, religion will be tolerated as long as it remains a private matter within the individual's conscience or inside the sacristy. The vision of religious freedom that follows from a commitment to intellectual solidarity is quite different from such a privatized account. For the Council stated, "It comes within the meaning of religious freedom that religious bodies should not be prohibited from freely undertaking to show the special value of their doctrine in what concerns the organization of society and the inspiration of the whole of human activity."[25] The free exercise of religion is a social freedom and the right to freedom of religion includes the right to seek to influence the policies and laws by which a free people will be governed and the public culture they share. The dialogic ethic underlying this claim means that protection of active engagement of religious believers in public life, not privatization of religion, is part of the substantive meaning of the right to religious freedom. Equally important, it also means that such engagement in public life should be conducted with deep respect for those who hold differing beliefs. Thus, believers should "at all times refrain from any manner of action which might seem to carry a hint of coercion."[26] Persuasion through reasonable discourse is the proper mode of public participation by religious believers, especially when they seek to influence law or public policy. This means that commitment to ecumenical and interreligious dialogue is a concomitant of religious freedom today.

More broadly, such a dialogic or solidaristic understanding of the relationship between faith and public life has implications not only for religious freedom, but also for the meaning of the full range of human rights contained in the U.N. Universal Declaration.[27] In the days of the cold war, for example, the West was largely inclined to conceive human rights in individualistic terms and to give priority to the civil and political rights to free speech, due process of law, and political participation. These were often conceived as negative rights or rights "to be left alone." By contrast, Eastern Bloc nations and those nations in the southern hemisphere that adopted Marxist-inspired ideologies stressed social and economic rights such as those to adequate food, work, and housing. These were understood as positive rights or as entitlements to share in the social and economic resources of the community as a whole. An ethic of dialogic universalism not only suggests that these two traditions ought to learn from the strengths of the other, but also that the opposition between individual freedoms negatively understood on the one hand and mutual solidarity in society on the other is a false dichotomy. Persons can live in dignity only when they live in a community of freedom (i.e., a community in which both personal initiative and social solidarity are valued and embodied).[28] The give-and-take of dialogue is the intellectual manifestation of such a linkage of personal initiative and social solidarity. But this linkage has material dimensions as well. It will be made effective in practice only when persons have both political space for action (civil and political rights) and the material and institutional prerequisites of communal life that make such action possible (social and economic rights). Thus, both civil-political and social-economic rights are genuine human rights that should be respected in all societies.

This sets a large agenda before the nations of our interdependent world. It means that a genuinely solidaristic understanding of the human good demands that commitment to human rights must not be limited to the promotion of the political freedoms prized in the West but must also include a commitment to economic justice in global, regional, and national markets. Human rights must not be turned into a banner under which a battle between "the West and the rest" is fought today. From the perspectives of both Christian fidelity and respect for the other, human rights are the most basic requirements of genuine solidarity in the economic as well as the cultural and political fields. Despite its vast scope, such an agenda can give substantive guidance for social, political, and economic institutions that a one-sided emphasis on the pluralism of interpretations of the human good fails to provide.[29]

The challenge of today's pluralistic and interdependent world, therefore, leads to a new way of conceiving the ancient question of the relationship between faith and reason in the development of an ethic that can guide the church's action in society. This new relationship is a dynamic process of interaction between fidelity to the distinctive religious beliefs and distinctive traditions of Christianity, on the one hand, and the pursuit of an inclusive, universal community, on the other. Dialogue—the active engagement of listening and speaking with others whose beliefs and traditions are different—is the key to such dynamism. Where such dialogue is absent, the chances of obtaining a vision of the common good of the world we are entering will be small to the point of vanishing. The Second

Vatican Council launched the Roman Catholic community on this path of dialogue. Since the Council, there has been both progress and retreat. Addressing the future requires renewed commitment to the agenda set by Vatican II.

NOTES

1. Samuel P. Huntington, "The Clash of Civilizations," *Foreign Affairs* 72 (summer 1993): 22, 25. This is developed at book length in Huntington, *The Clash of Civilizations and the Remaking of World Order* (New York: Simon and Schuster, 1996).

2. For an alternative view that attributes ethnopolitical conflict to the weakness of states undergoing a transition to democracy rather than the intensification of the cultural-religious factor, see Ted Robert Gurr, "Peoples against States: Ethnopolitical Conflict and the Changing World System," *International Studies Quarterly* 38 (1994): 347–77. In his work *The Black Man's Burden: Africa and the Curse of the Nation-State* (New York: Times Books, 1992), Basil Davidson adopts a somewhat similar view, arguing that the lack of fit between the structures of postcolonial nation-state and traditional social patterns helps explain the rise of conflict in many parts of Africa. Jean-François Bayart stresses the role of straightforward desire for power and wealth as the deeper motivation behind apparently ethnic conflicts in Africa in *The State in Africa: The Politics of the Belly*, trans. Mary Harper (London: Longman, 1993).

3. José Casanova, *Public Religions in the Modern World* (Chicago: University of Chicago Press, 1994), chap. 1. My account neglects the theoretical richness of Casanova's account, for purposes of simplicity in this context.

4. See Gilles Kepel, *The Revenge of God: The Resurgence of Islam, Christianity, and Judaism in the Modern World*, trans. Alan Braley (University Park: Pennsylvania State University Press, 1994), 4–5 (French original: *La Revanche de Dieu: Chrétiens, Juifs et Musulmans à la reconquête du monde* [Paris: Éditions du Seuil, 1991]).

5. See John Rawls, *Political Liberalism* (New York: Columbia University Press, 1993), lecture VI, "The Idea of Public Reason." My views on this issue are developed as part of a symposium on Rawls's approach to the public role of religion. See Paul J. Weithman, "Rawlsian Liberalism and the Privatization of Religion," with responses by Timothy Jackson, "Love in a Liberal Society," David Hollenbach, "Public Reason/Private Religion?" and John Langan, "Overcoming the Divisiveness of Religion," all in *Journal of Religious Ethics* 22.1 (spring 1994): 3–51. Rawls has himself rethought the issue in light of his revised idea of public reason in "The Idea of Public Reason Revisited," republished in his *The Law of Peoples with "The Idea of Public Reason Revisited"* (Cambridge, Mass.: Harvard University Press, 1999), 129–80.

6. See, for example, Kent Greenawalt, *Religious Convictions and Political Choice* (New York: Oxford University Press, 1988) and *Private Consciences and Public Reasons* (New

York: Oxford University Press, 1995); and Michael Perry, *Morality, Politics, and Law: A Bicentennial Essay* (New York: Oxford University Press, 1988) and *Love and Power: The Role of Religion and Morality in American Politics* (New York: Oxford University Press, 1991). See also the symposium on "The Role of Religion in Public Debate in a Liberal Society," *San Diego Law Review* 30 (1993), which includes essays by Greenawalt, Perry, Robert Audi, and myself.

7. Robin W. Lovin, "Perry, Naturalism, and Religion in Public," *Tulane Law Review* 63 (1989): 1518, 1523.

8. For a bold proposal that this global situation marks a new epoch in Christian history, see Karl Rahner, "Toward a Fundamental Theological Interpretation of Vatican II," *Theological Studies* 40 (December 1979): 716–27.

9. I have treated the relation of faith and reason in modern Catholic social thought at greater length in my *Claims in Conflict: Retrieving and Renewing the Catholic Human Rights Tradition* (New York: Paulist Press, 1979), chap. 3. This relation is treated in a parallel though different way in Jean Porter, *Natural and Divine Law: Reclaiming the Tradition for Christian Ethics* (Grand Rapids, Mich.: Eerdmans, 1999).

10. John XXIII, *Pacem in Terris*, in David J. O'Brien and Thomas A. Shannon, eds., *Catholic Social Thought: The Documentary Heritage* (Maryknoll, N.Y.: Orbis Books, 1992), no. 9.

11. Ibid., no. 10.

12. Rahner, "Toward a Fundamental Theological Interpretation of Vatican II," 717.

13. Vatican Council II, *Gaudium et Spes* (The Pastoral Constitution on the Church in the Modern World), no. 4. All references to Vatican II documents are from Walter Abbott and Joseph Gallagher, eds., *The Documents of Vatican II* (New York: America Press, 1966).

14. It is clear that Catholicism had never accepted the presuppositions of Enlightenment rationalism. But some eighteenth- and nineteenth-century Catholic thinkers, including moral theologians and social ethicists, were subtly affected by this rationalism in their apologetic efforts to defend Catholic thought in the face of the challenges raised to it by Western European modernity. They adopted the methods of their rationalist adversaries to counteract the substance of rationalist arguments. For discussion of the effect of such apologetic efforts on theological responses to modern atheism, see Michael J. Buckley, *At the Origins of Modern Atheism* (New Haven, Conn.: Yale University Press, 1987).

15. *Gaudium et Spes,* no. 22.

16. See, for example, John Paul II's encyclicals *Veritatis Splendor* and *Evangelium Vitae*.

17. I originally used this phrase in *Claims in Conflict,* chap. 3, p. 131. What is said here is a development of that earlier discussion.

18. See Alasdair MacIntyre, *Whose Justice? Which Rationality?* (Notre Dame, Ind.: University of Notre Dame Press, 1988), chap. 18. See also MacIntyre, *Three Rival Versions of Moral Enquiry: Encyclopaedia, Genealogy and Tradition* (Notre Dame, Ind.: University of Notre Dame Press, 1990), chap. 10, which relates this treatment of how traditions develop to the task of the university.

19. *Gaudium et Spes*, no. 40.

20. Ibid., no. 44.

21. See Vatican Council II, *Unitatis Redintegratio* (Decree on Ecumenism) and *Nostra Aetate* (Declaration on the Relationship of the Church to Non-Christian Religions).

22. See my "Afterword: A Community of Freedom," in R. Bruce Douglass and David Hollenbach, eds., *Catholicism and Liberalism: Contributions to American Public Philosophy* (Cambridge: Cambridge University Press, 1994), 323–43, at 334.

23. Vatican Council II, *Dignitatis Humanae* (Declaration on Religious Freedom), no. 2.

24. *Gaudium et Spes*, no. 41 and no. 25.

25. *Dignitatis Humanae*, no. 4.

26. Ibid., no. 4.

27. For one effort along these lines see the *Declaration Toward a Global Ethic* issued by the 1993 Parliament of the World's Religions held in Chicago, in Hans Küng and Karl-Josef Kuschel, eds., *A Global Ethic: The Declaration of the Parliament of the World's Religions*, trans. John Bowden (New York: Continuum, 1993), and commentaries on this Declaration from representatives of many traditions in Hans Küng, ed., *Yes to a Global Ethic*, trans. John Bowden (New York: Continuum, 1996).

28. For a fuller discussion of this point, see my "A Communitarian Reconstruction of Human Rights" and "Afterword: A Community of Freedom," both in *Catholicism and Liberalism*, 127–50 and 323–43.

29. Contra the views of those who reject the idea of universal human rights altogether as incompatible with the acknowledgment of cultural and religious pluralism, for example, Alasdair MacIntyre, *After Virtue: A Study in Moral Theory* (Notre Dame, Ind.: University of Notre Dame Press, 1981), 67, and Richard Rorty, "Postmodernist Bourgeois Liberalism," in Robert Hollinger, ed., *Hermeneutics and Praxis* (Notre Dame, Ind.: University of Notre Dame Press, 1985), 219–20.

2

Tradition, Historicity, and Truth

The dialogue between church and world just discussed will be significantly influenced by the way the church understands the history of its own ethical discourse. As we reflect on the role of Christian faith in the moral life of a pluralist world, we would do well to recall an essay written by James Gustafson several decades ago. Gustafson pointed to the need to navigate the tricky waters between a historically naive absolutism regarding moral norms and a historical relativism that makes normative claims impossible.[1] Awareness of the historical and communal embeddedness of all human thought and judgment has considerable impact on recent discussions of the public role of religious communities. The historical conditioning of religious and ethical thought is often taken to imply that religion and ethics should be treated as private matters. This way of thinking reaches beyond the academic sphere to the larger culture, leading to a prevalent mood that Albert Borgmann has called the "sullenness" of the postmodern mentality. Borgmann hears this mood voiced in contemporary emphases on autonomy or freedom of choice as the preeminent or even only values that can be defended in public. There are surely good reasons for this emphasis in the face of the enslavements humans attempted to impose on each other in the twentieth century. But Borgmann suggests that "what sounds like the assumption of ultimate responsibility is usually the flourish of moral retreat, the refusal to discuss, explain, and justify a decision."[2] If the historicity of values is pushed to its limit, no discussion, explanation, or justification of a decision is possible, for value commitments come to be seen as those of the self alone. Autonomy can thus serve as a screen for sullen disengagement.

Gustafson's essay did not predict that we were moving toward this outcome, but he was clearly concerned that historical consciousness raised challenges for theological ethics that would not be easy to meet. He pointed out how Ernst Troeltsch's intellectual biography had gradually moved from a stress on "the relativity of all historical movements in relation to the Absolute" to a stance at the end of Troeltsch's life in which he "was almost plaintively seeking a framework for greater universality."[3] There is a similar plea in Gustafson's own statement that "the task of theological and ethical work becomes that of finding justification for religious belief and for moral decisions which do not deny the relativities of history, but which provide an objectivity short of absolute claims. In ethics the task is to find some degree of order, continuity, and structure within historical change. If the absolutist has morality conforming to an immutable order and thus has difficulty in coping with historical change, the relativist has an openness to change but a difficulty in developing the criteria of purpose and action to guide choices and give direction to moral activities."[4]

The pull toward each of these clear-cut options and the difficulties with them remain evident today. In particular, Gustafson was not at all confident that developments in Roman Catholic moral theology toward a more historically conscious, less absolutist approach were sufficiently aware of the disorientation that could follow in the wake of such a move. The historical turn could liberate from false absolutes. But to at least some Protestants who had appropriated this historical awareness generations ago, the challenge was that of overcoming what Paul Ramsey called the "wastelands of relativism."[5]

Gustafson saw the problem as a continuation of debates between nominalists and realists: Whether and how is it possible to retain some universal judgments in the context of historicity? Do human beings have a nature or only an open and ever-malleable history? Are there abiding, unexceptionable moral principles and rules or only individual intuitions that are bound to particular circumstances?[26] In what turns out to have been an understatement, Gustafson predicted that the debates about these questions would continue for the foreseeable future. Today the advantage in the realist/nominalist argument seems to have tilted strongly to the nominalist side, but there have also been strong rejoinders reaffirming the reality of moral absolutes, particularly by Pope John Paul II and, in a very different way, by evangelical and fundamentalist Christians. In what follows, I will sketch some of the issues that are shaping this current debate. I will concentrate on some of the arguments advanced in the Roman Catholic tradition. I will not attempt to deal with other traditions in Christian ethics or with an empirical description of the manifestations of this tension in contemporary culture.[7] The chapter will also briefly illustrate how an approach to historicity has had significant impact on a key determinant of the relation of faith and politics, namely, the affirmation of the importance of religious freedom.

REAFFIRMATION OF MORAL ABSOLUTES TODAY

One of the strongest recent affirmations that there are binding principles or rules in Christian ethics that transcend the relativities of history is contained in Pope John Paul II's 1993 encyclical *Veritatis Splendor*. Much of the technical discussion of the encyclical has focused on the pope's rejection of "proportionalism" and "fundamental option," both of which are aspects of Roman Catholic moral theory that have developed in the years since the Second Vatican Council. It appears, however, that the encyclical's rejection of these theories is based on a conviction that they will lead to a loss of the moral compass that can be provided only by absolute, timeless moral norms. Further, the pope suggests that such a loss of moral bearings is directly linked with a loss of religious conviction and even faith in a transcendent, provident God.

John Paul II is clearly distressed by recent developments in Catholic moral theology as he interprets them. It is well known that there has been widespread disagreement with aspects of church moral teaching on sexual ethics. Contraception was the initial flash point, followed by further disagreement regarding traditional norms on homosexual expression, remarriage after divorce, and broader issues connected with gender roles. These matters are surely important concerns in the encyclical and provide part of the explanation for why it was written. The central issue for the pope, however, goes deeper than dissent from traditional Catholic teachings on sexual ethics. As the pope sees it, moral and, ultimately, religious relativism have reached crisis proportions both within the Catholic community and in the larger culture as well.[8]

Thus, the pope states that his goal is to recall "certain fundamental truths" that are at the basis of "the whole of the Church's moral teaching," particularly those "regarding the natural law, and the universality and permanent validity of its precepts." This is necessary because within the church itself dissent is no longer "limited and occasional" but has become "an overall and systematic calling into question of traditional moral doctrine." In what I take to be the central motivation of the encyclical, John Paul II states that this crisis has been brought about by "certain anthropological presuppositions. At the root of these presuppositions is the more or less obvious influence of currents of thought which end by detaching human freedom from its essential and constitutive relationship to truth."[9]

The essential link between freedom and truth has been a major theme in much of the pope's teaching. It provides a key for interpreting his critique both of current Catholic moral theology and of important elements in its cultural context. For example, he argues that only commitment to the truth about the dignity and rights of the human person, the visible image of the invisible God, was capable of resisting the oppressive forces of totalitarian regimes in his native Poland and the former Soviet bloc generally. "Only upon this truth is it possible to construct a renewed society and to solve the complex and weighty problems affecting it, above all the problem of overcoming the various forms of totalitarianism, so as to make way for the authentic *freedom* of the person."[10] Historical relativism, the pope suggests, is powerless in the face of systems that would subordinate the dignity of the person to an ideology or, more relevant to the last days of the Soviet system, to the self-interest of ruling bureaucrats. He lists the following political conditions as dependent on commitment to the transcendent and permanent truth of human dignity: "truthfulness in the relations between those governing and those governed, openness in public administration, impartiality in the service of the body politic, respect for the rights of political adversaries, safeguarding the rights of the accused against summary trials and convictions, the just and honest use of public funds, the rejection of illicit means in order to gain, preserve or increase power at any cost." These social norms "are primarily rooted in, and in fact derive their singular urgency from the transcendent value of the person and the objective moral demands of functioning states."[11] Freedom that is not anchored in such truths about the person is not freedom at all. Here the pope goes beyond a facile distinction between freedom and license that is often heard in jeremiads directed by older generations at those who are younger. His point concerns the social and political consequences that in fact came to prevail in Eastern Europe under the ideology of historical materialism. This ideology produced cynicism, indifference, and, to use Borgmann's term, sullenness, all leading to acquiescence in unfreedom.

There is an unsurprising convergence of the pope's analysis with that of other leaders in the revolutions that toppled the regimes of the former Soviet bloc. The theme of "living in the truth," as opposed to coping with the lies of bureaucratic communism, appears repeatedly in Václav Havel's writings. Havel saw "living in the truth" as the power that enabled otherwise powerless people to bring about the velvet revolutions of 1989.[12] Similarly, the Czech philosopher Erazim Kohák wrote that the "the entire tenor of Czech dissent, whose most prominent figures are playwright-philosopher Václav Havel and priest-theologian Václav Maly, has been on *life in the truth*…. In word and deed, Czech dissidents have demonstrated their conviction that there is truth, that there is good and evil—and that the difference is not reducible to cultural preference."[13] Nor, they would suggest, is it merely historically relative.

Both the pope and Havel also have doubts about whether the West presently possesses the moral purpose and commitment necessary to sustain its own freedom. To Havel, it appears "that the traditional parliamentary democracies can offer no fundamental opposition to the automatism of technological civilization and the industrial-consumer society."[14] More than the procedures of parliamentary democracy are needed to secure and sustain freedom. The pope's reading of the West is similar. The fall of Marxism has not solved the problem of freedom. He maintains that in the post-1989 world there is a genuine "risk of an alliance between democracy and ethical relativism."[15] As he put it in his encyclical letter *Centesimus Annus*, "Nowadays there is a tendency to claim that agnosticism and skeptical relativism are the philosophy and the basic attitude which correspond to democratic forms of political life. Those who are convinced that they know the truth and firmly adhere to it are considered unreliable from a democratic point of view, since they do not accept that the truth is determined by the majority, or that it is subject to variation according to different political trends."[16] Truth, then, is the basis of freedom, not the other way around.

Both John Paul II and Václav Havel go so far as to make genuinely ontological claims about the basis of the moral consciousness needed in both East and West today. These claims are sure to offend many Americans today, especially American intellectuals. John Paul II: "It is by responding to the call of God contained in the *being of things* that man becomes aware of his transcendent dignity. Every individual must give this response, which constitutes the apex of his humanity, and no social mechanism or collective subject can substitute for it."[17] Václav Havel: "The only genuine backbone of all our actions—if they are to be moral—is responsibility. Responsibility to something higher than my family, my country, my company, my success. Responsibility to *the order of Being*, where all our actions are indelibly recorded and where, and only where, they will be properly judged."[18]

For the pope, then, with echoes in the writings of Václav Havel, there is considerable danger in the moral relativism that can be detected in contemporary culture and intellectual life. It can be doubted whether the pope is right in claiming that such relativism is to be found in the writings of the Catholic moral theologians against whom *Veritatis Splendor* is directed. Others have explored that matter elsewhere, and I will not review the discussion here.[19] It is clear, however, that he intends to challenge such relativism wherever it appears and especially to reject claims that it is an approach to ethics "having a basis in theory and claiming full cultural and social legitimacy."[20] In a way that leaves little doubt about what he intends, John Paul states that "the central theme of this encyclical" is the "*reaffirmation of the universality and immutability of the moral commandments*, particularly those which prohibit always and without exception *intrinsically evil acts*."[21]

What are the immutable norms, asserted to be always and everywhere binding? The encyclical does not attempt to give a systematic or exhaustive list. The enumeration it does provide is contained primarily in a passage quoted from the Second Vatican Council. This includes "whatever is hostile to life itself, such as any kind of homicide [perhaps better translated as 'murder'], genocide, abortion, euthanasia and voluntary suicide; whatever violates the integrity of the human person, such as mutilation, physical and mental torture and attempts to coerce the spirit; whatever is offensive to human dignity, such as subhuman living conditions, arbitrary imprisonment, deportation, slavery, prostitution and trafficking in women and children, degrading conditions of work which treat labourers as mere instruments of profit, and not as free responsible persons."[22] And in subsequent paragraphs, which have led a number of commentators to conclude rightly that reproductive and sexual ethics were very much in the John Paul II's mind despite the wider agenda I am suggesting here, Paul VI's condemnation of contraception in *Humanae Vitae* is repeated. Further, the encyclical states that, "from a theological viewpoint, moral principles are not dependent upon the historical moment in which they are discovered."[23] This suggests that the immorality of these practices is not only exceptionless but also immutable. In other words, there exist standards of morality that are above the flow of history in the mind of God. Failure to apprehend these standards is explained in light of human finitude and sin. For the pope, however, the gospel of Jesus Christ, as this is interpreted and taught by the magisterium of the church, provides guidance in the midst of these weaknesses. It would not be claiming too much, therefore, to read *Veritatis Splendor* as asserting that the immutable moral teaching of the church is the bulwark needed to stem the tide of relativism John Paul sees lapping at the shores of civilization and culture throughout the world today.

A LOOK AT ACTUAL HISTORY

Is this claim plausible? In an important essay, "Development in Moral Doctrine," John Noonan suggests it is not. Noonan's many books on the development of Christian thought on specific areas of moral life have surely been among the most important contributions to the study of the history of Christian ethics in our time.[24] In this essay, Noonan's goal is to draw some general conclusions about how we might sustain a sense of moral direction today in the light of what the study of history reveals about the variations that have occurred in the past.

25

Noonan indicates the nature of the problem by sketching how the Christian tradition has changed its teachings on several questions of practical morality.

On usury: "Once upon a time, certainly from at least 1150 to 1550, seeking, receiving, or hoping for anything beyond one's principal—in other words, looking for profit—on a loan constituted the mortal sin of usury." Today, however, "the just title to profit is assumed to exist." Noonan states that the change can be exaggerated, for the taking of profit without just title continues to be rejected. But in practices such as taking interest on bank accounts and in the institutions of the entire financial world, the earlier rule against usury has disappeared in Catholic moral teaching. Ideas once unanimously taught by the church "are now so obsolete that one incites incredulity by reciting them."[25]

On slavery: "Once upon a time, certainly as late as 1860, the church taught that it was no sin for a Catholic to own another human being." Slaves should be treated humanely, and manumission was regarded as good. From St. Paul through St. Augustine, Henry de Bracton, and Juan de Lugo down to the American Bishop Francis Kenrick in 1841, many of the practices associated with chattel slavery went unchallenged by ecclesiastical authority. But "again, all that has changed. . . . In the light of the teachings of modern popes and the Second Vatican Council on the dignity of the human person, it is morally unthinkable that one person be allowed to buy, sell, hypothecate, or lease another or dispose of that person's children."[26] It should be noted that John Paul II reiterates this condemnation of slavery, citing the Second Vatican Council, as does Noonan. The pope, however, makes no mention of the eighteen centuries during which it was tolerated if not endorsed.

On religious freedom: "Once upon a time, no later than the time of St. Augustine, it was considered virtuous for bishops to invoke imperial force to compel heretics to return to the Church." For a period of more than 1,200 years, "the vast institutional apparatus of the Church was put at the service of detecting heretics, who, if they persevered in their heresy or relapsed into it, would be executed at the stake. Hand in glove, Church and State collaborated in the terror by which heretics were purged."[27] Gradually, however, the religious wars in post-Reformation Europe, and, definitively, the persecution of Christians by Fascist and Communist regimes in the twentieth century, led to another shift in positions. In 1832, for example, Pope Gregory XVI had declared that the right to freedom of conscience is an "insanity (*dileramentum*)."[28] The dramatic change is evident if one juxtaposes this condemnation with the Second Vatican Council's declaration that "the right to religious freedom has its foundation in the very dignity of the human person, as this dignity is known through the revealed word of God and by reason itself."[29] Indeed, Vatican II linked its support for human rights with the very core of Christian faith when it declared that, "by virtue of the gospel committed to it, the Church proclaims the rights of the human person."[30] The affirmation of these rights is at the center of John Paul II's critique of relativism. In fact, he has called the right to religious freedom the "foundation" of all human rights.[31] That the church has denied this right through much of its history in both solemn teaching and institutional practice is passed over in silence.

The purpose of Noonan's rehearsal of these dramatic shifts is to provide a basis for developing a theoretical perspective on the conditions and limits of change within the Catholic moral tradition. What he says is also relevant, I think, to other religious-moral traditions. Noonan borrows some ideas from discussions of the development of doctrine that have been elaborated to account for shifts of a more directly doctrinal sort in areas such as Trinitarian theology and Christology.

THEORIES OF THE ROLE OF TRADITION

Noonan rejects accounts according to which change has been a matter simply of the expression given to moral principles rather than change in their substance. He also finds it implausible to claim that real advances occur only as the result of working out the logical implications of earlier normative stances in Scripture. More plausible is John Henry Newman's understanding of the development of moral understanding by analogy to the development of organic life or of personal identity as a child becomes an adult. The Second Vatican Council saw new moral understandings arising through a similar growth of insight into the reality of Jesus Christ. The explanation by analogy to organic growth, however, must be able to distinguish when new organic growth is appropriate and when it is more like the growth of a cancer. And, as Noonan observes, the claim that new insight into the reality of Christ has arisen must face the question of whether one is merely looking in a mirror and projecting one's own experience onto an image of Christ.[32] The issue, then, is how to distinguish between "true and false reform in the church" (to borrow the title of an influential book by Yves Congar).[33]

One response to this question is that advanced by the ecumenically influential Lutheran theologian George Lindbeck. Lindbeck's approach has notable parallels in the writings of Stanley Hauerwas, which have themselves had significant impact in the Catholic community. Lindbeck has proposed a "cultural-linguistic" theory of religion. This theory compares religion to a language or cultural system. Like language and culture, a religious tradition provides a framework that shapes the way those who have learned it perceive reality, speak about reality, and order their lives in action. For Christians, the canonical Bible as a whole, understood as if it were a "vast, loosely structured, non-fictional novel" tells the overarching story of the interaction of God with creation, especially with human beings. This biblical story is the normative standard in light of which the adequacy and fidelity of all subsequent developments of the tradition are to be judged. Because this story is centrally a rendering of who Jesus Christ is, it is the meaning of Jesus Christ as he is portrayed in the Bible that is the norm that distinguishes "true and false" reforms in subsequent tradition. The practical task of the Christian community, which is at once religious and ethical, is "to be conformed to the Jesus Christ depicted in the narrative."[34]

Noonan, I think, would agree with Lindbeck up to this point. He would not, however, fully accept Lindbeck's description of how the Christian community goes about relating the biblical portrayal of Jesus Christ to changing patterns of society and culture, in the process reaching novel ethical standards like the ones Noonan's historical work has identified. For Lindbeck, the portrayal of Jesus in the biblical story is a self-contained structure of meaning. It defines a world of meaning in light of which Christians are to shape their lives and form their way of acting. The relation between the biblical story and the form of life of postbiblical Christians is a one-way street: from the Bible to the ways of life of the later Christian community in different historical periods. As Lindbeck puts it, "Scripture creates its own domain of meaning and the task of interpretation is to extend this over the whole of reality." Thus, the task of the postbiblical community is to redescribe "reality within the scriptural framework rather than translating Scripture into extrascriptural categories. It is the text, so to speak, which absorbs the world, rather than the world the text."[35] The religious concern here is to avoid theories of interpretation that grant a normative role to contemporary experience, for such theories run the risk of losing touch altogether with the central realities of the Christian story. In Noonan's terms, they risk projecting contemporary needs and experience onto the mirror in which one claims to be seeing Christ.

In Lindbeck's theory, the scriptural story is *applied* to the novel social and cultural realities encountered by the postbiblical church. These realities do not, in themselves, contribute to the meaning of Christian faith. Such applications may differ as historical circumstances change. To use an example treated by Noonan, the Christian tradition shifted its understanding of the morality of slavery from acceptance in New Testament times and through most of the postbiblical tradition to rejection in more recent centuries. Lindbeck argues that this shift occurred because Christians had come to recognize through their historical experience that a stable social order without the institution of slavery was in fact possible. Thus, the Christian story could be practically applied in a new way. The meaning of the story itself remained as it had always been. The newness comes from the fact that the "self-identical story" has been fused with "new worlds within which it is told and retold."[36]

Noonan thinks the process by which such shifts occur is more complex, involving a *mutual* interaction between postbiblical experience and the biblical story. New experience, such as the possibility of a society without slavery, not only leads to a new application of the biblical story, but also to new insights into the meaning of the story of Jesus Christ. Noonan notes, for example, that the impulse toward the abolition of slavery arose among individuals who "were ahead of the theologians and the Church."[37] In Catholic France it was Montesquieu, Rousseau, and the revolutionaries of 1789 who brought about the new social and cultural framework that made the condemnation of the institution of slavery by Pope Leo XIII possible. Lindbeck's description of the process as one in which the story of Christ has been "applied" to new circumstances fails to capture the fact that new insight into the meaning of the story of Christ also occurred in this process. Only after much argument and social upheaval did the requirement of Christ become clear. So, although Noonan agrees with Lindbeck that the story of Christ in the New Testament is definitively normative for

Christian ethics, "it is evident from the case of slavery alone that it has taken time to ascertain what the demands of the New [Testament] really are."[38] The meaning of both poles in the interaction of biblical story and postbiblical society and culture are clarified by each other in an ongoing way. This interaction generates the dynamism of tradition, leading to the sort of changes that Noonan points out.

Alasdair MacIntyre's *Whose Justice? Which Rationality?* is quite helpful in showing how such dynamism is possible within a framework of continuity. Like Noonan, MacIntyre has been influenced by John Henry Newman on this matter. Indeed, MacIntyre acknowledges that his understanding of the functioning of a tradition owes a "massive debt" to Newman, even though he has judged it better for his philosophical purposes not to say much about what he has derived from Newman the theologian.[39] MacIntyre's theory, like Lindbeck's, can be called postliberal or postmodern in arguing that human experience and thought are thoroughly embedded in historical traditions. In his earlier work, *After Virtue*, MacIntyre argued that both virtuous living and philosophical theorizing about the moral life are impossible unless those who engage in them have been educated in the stories and ways of acting and thinking of a particular historical tradition. He wrote, "I can only answer the question 'What am I to do?' if I can answer the prior question 'Of what story or stories do I find myself a part?' "[40] His more recent work is directed at showing that the fact that moral virtue and reflection are rooted in historically contingent events, texts, and communities need not undercut the possibility of assessing the adequacy and truth of competing traditions. The historicity of moral thought and practice need not lead to relativism.

His argument rests on a recovery of the understanding of a tradition as a tradition of "enquiry." In a mature tradition, the process of "traditioning" is not simply a matter of retelling stories, citing and applying classic texts and authorities, and socializing young people into preexisting roles, as Lindbeck implies. These surely have an important place in any tradition that expects to remain intact. "Conservative action upon its past" was one of the criteria that Newman used to distinguish authentic developments of the Christian tradition from corruptions of it.[41] But a living tradition is also marked by its power to assimilate ideas originally discovered elsewhere. In Newman's words, ideas about human existence "are not placed in a void, but in the crowded world, and make way for themselves by inter-penetration, and develop by absorption."[42]

In line with these ideas from Newman, MacIntyre understands a work-ing tradition as dynamic, self-critical, and open to knowledge gained from elsewhere. His understanding of a mature tradition as a tradition of in-quiry demands this. Such inquiry begins with the stories, authorities, practices, and canons of rationality that have been handed on to one from the past. From this received starting point, critical reasoning can become necessary for a number of reasons: the received tradition finds itself inter-nally subject to a number of interpretations by its adherents that require adjudication; the tradition encounters new questions that its mode of in-quiry up to now has not prepared it to handle; or the tradition meets an al-ternative tradition that confronts it with an alternative account of how things are or ought to be.

AN ILLUSTRATION: RELIGIOUS FREEDOM

The hero of MacIntyre's account of this process is Thomas Aquinas, whose great achievement was overcoming the conflict between Augustinian and Aristotelian traditions in the thirteenth century. Another, more recent, ex-ample is that noted by Noonan: John Courtney Murray's successful effort to incorporate religious freedom as a demand of the dignity of the human person into the Roman Catholic tradition. The insight into the importance of religious freedom was discovered by the liberal tradition, which gave it individualistic and sometimes skeptical overtones. Initially, the Roman Catholic tradition's commitment to both the truth of biblical faith and a strong sense of solidarity and the common good led to a straightforward rejection of the modern assertion of individual rights, especially the rights of conscience. It was Murray's genius to have discovered intellectually compelling arguments that could incorporate the insights contained within both traditions and to do so on terms that could enable both Catholicism and liberalism to hold to their valid insights while learning from each other. The incorporation of the liberal defense of religious free-dom into the Catholic tradition at the Second Vatican Council is well known. The possible contribution to Western society and culture by con-tinuing Catholic insistence that fundamental truth claims about human dignity make sense only in the context of equally fundamental commitments to social solidarity remains an ongoing project. But the fact that such a possibility exists is due to the fact that Murray's argument for religious liberty was not simply a concession that the liberal tradition had it right and the past Catholic tradition had it wrong. Murray *developed* the Catholic tradition, he did not surrender it. Indeed, he claimed persuasively, I am convinced, that his interpretation of religious freedom not only solved problems the encounter with liberalism had revealed within the Catholic tradition, but it could solve problems internal to liberalism (chiefly its individualism and tendency toward skepticism) that liberalism was incapable of solving itself.[43]

Thus, Murray's approach to development of the Catholic moral tradition on religious freedom exemplified the criteria MacIntyre, following Newman, has set forth for a tradition's advance through inquiry. It solved problems internal to both Catholicism and liberalism; it could explain why these problems had arisen in the first place; and it advanced an interpretation of religious freedom that could claim continuity with core elements of the biblical story of Israel and of Jesus Christ. This achievement should give scant comfort to those in Christian ethics who adopt a purely narrative-based approach to their work or to theologians such as Lindbeck, who urge a cultural-linguistic theory of religion as backing for purely narrative-based Christian ethics.

But the achievements of Aquinas and Murray, understood in light of this understanding of how Christian moral tradition develops, will give equally little comfort to those such as John Paul II who stake so much on immutable norms in their case against historical relativism. This understanding of development makes claims in the face of the relativist mentality that are simultaneously concessionary and oppositional. It concedes that there are few, if any, practical moral rules that are in principle unrevisable. Fundamental Christian stances, such as love toward God and neighbor and discipleship to Jesus Christ, are of course permanent norms for Christian behavior. There can be no Christianity where they are absent. They play a role in the Christian religion much like the principle of noncontradiction in the domain of thought or the imperative to "do good and avoid evil" in the moral life. There can be no rationality where a person finds self-contradiction acceptable, and there can be no moral life if one knowingly chooses to do evil. Similarly, there can be no Christianity without love of God and neighbor and an effort to know and follow Jesus Christ. These fundamental orientations can be further specified by what Thomas Aquinas has called the most basic principles of the natural law and by very general orientations that follow from the gospel. What these principles and orientations actually mean in the conduct of life at a particular moment in history or in a particular culture, however, must be historically discerned and is subject to development and change. This is not merely a matter of "application" of principles whose meaning is already clear. I think it makes little sense to say, for example, that the Christian imperative to love the neighbor has been applied in one way by a slaveholder in one society and in another way by an abolitionist in a different time and place. Rather, it is the understanding of the meaning of Christian love itself that has shifted. Concrete action-guides such as "treat slaves kindly" or "never enslave a human being" are not simply diverse applications of a single general principle of love of neighbor. They represent differing understandings of the principle itself. Similarly, movement from an action-guide that calls for the burning of heretics to one that affirms the human and civil right to religious freedom is not simply a change in the application of a constant understanding of the meaning of the creation of human beings in the image of God. Rather, it manifests a genuine change in that understanding itself.[44]

On the other hand, this view of the development of tradition presents a strong challenge to a crude historical relativism. Crude relativism is itself incompatible with genuine inquiry. It has no reason to investigate the truth or falsity of interpretations of morality offered within a given tradition such as Christianity or in competing traditions such as Catholicism and liberalism in the days before Murray made his arguments. Inquiry is based on the supposition that intellectual investigation can actually get somewhere, including inquiry into diverse claims about the right way to live and the ultimate meaning of human life. As MacIntyre points out, a relativist would never have any reason to revise his or her beliefs, for in strict relativism there are no grounds to prefer one belief over another. The very possibility of revision depends on recognizing that there is a truth that can cause such a revision to be necessary.[45] Relativists do not have any reason to argue at all; the best they can do is agree to coexist or cooperate. But what shape such coexistence and cooperation should take then reemerges as a matter demanding inquiry. At some point, the choice becomes one between willingness to make a claim to truth and an acquiescence in some form of nihilism. John Paul II is right to fear the latter, which lurks beneath the surface of some postmodern "sullenness." In light of what is argued here, however, he need not appeal to the timelessness of moral absolutes to provide an alternative to this danger.

ETHICS *IN VIA*

John Finnis, one of the strongest supporters of the line of argument contained in the pope's *Veritatis splendor*, maintains that the encyclical is not primarily about sexual ethics. In Finnis's words, "Faith, not sex, is the theme of *Veritatis Splendor*."[46] I think this is quite right. I also think, however, the faith at issue concerns quite a different matter than Finnis does. For Finnis the issue is whether contemporary men and women have the capacity to accept that God, not they, is ultimately in charge of the universe. Acceptance of this means willingness to obey God's absolute moral proscriptions even when the consequences are a deeply countercultural form of life, or even martyrdom.[47] I agree that, *in extremis*, no other stance is compatible with Christian faith. I disagree, however, that the demands of God and the meaning of fidelity to Jesus Christ are given once and for all in the way Finnis believes to be clear. One of the dimensions of Christian faith is a trust that God is involved in history in a way that makes the process of inquiry-guided development itself worth trusting, at least to the extent of being willing to undertake such inquiry. As Avery Dulles has written, "The Christian is defined as a person on the way to discovery, on the way to a revelation not yet given, or at least not yet given in final form. . . . The Christian trusts that, in following the crucified and risen Christ, he is on the route to the one disclosure that will fully satisfy the yearning of the human spirit. This confidence is sustained by a series of lesser disclosures which occur on the way, and are tokens or promises of the revelation yet to come."[48]

Christian ethics, both as a form of life and as an intellectual discipline, is rooted in a trust that the God who transcends all history is also present in and with these quests of the human spirit. Indeed, it is the Wisdom and Spirit of God that makes human discovery possible. Thus, all attempts to understand how to live this life are themselves on pilgrimage, *in via*. The efforts of Christian ethics must therefore always be ready to welcome fresh discoveries of God's gifts of freedom and reconciliation. We will be able to recognize new ideas and forms of life as coming from the hand of the God of Jesus Christ only if we have been schooled in the story of that God, as Lindbeck and Noonan agree. When we have been so schooled, however, we will then be ready to recognize in new moral insights the lesser disclosures that anticipate the final and full gift that God intends to give us— God's own self.

NOTES

1. See James M. Gustafson, "The Relevance of Historical Understanding," in Gustafson, *Theology and Christian Ethics* (Philadelphia: Pilgrim Press, 1974), 177–95, at 191 and 194. This essay was originally published in Paul Deats, Jr., ed., *Toward a Discipline of Social Ethics* (Boston: Boston University Press, 1972), 49–70. Further references here are to the text in Gustafson's book of collected essays.

2. Albert Borgmann, *Crossing the Postmodern Divide* (Chicago: University of Chicago Press, 1992), 10.

3. Gustafson, "Historical Understanding," 188 and 194. Gustafson cites Troeltsch's essay "The Ideas of Natural Law and Humanity in World Politics," appendix 1, in Otto Gierke, *Natural Law and the Theory of Society* (Boston: Beacon Press, 1957), 201–22.

4. Gustafson, "Historical Understanding," 194.

5. Ibid., 191–92. The reference is to Paul Ramsey's *War and Christian Conscience* (Durham, N.C.: Duke University Press, 1961), chap 1.

6. Gustafson, "Historical Understanding," 195.

7. For description and interpretation of a sociological sort in the context of the United States, see Robert Wuthnow, *The Restructuring of American Religion: Society and Faith since World War II* (Princeton, N.J.: Princeton University Press, 1988); for the global picture, see José Casanova, *Public Religions in the Modern World* (Chicago: University of Chicago Press, 1994), and (somewhat tendentiously) Gilles Kepel, *The Revenge of God: The Resurgence of Islam, Christianity, and Judaism in the Modern World* (University Park: Pennsylvania State University Press, 1994).

8. John Paul II, *Veritatis Splendor* (Vatican City: Libreria Editrice Vaticana, 1993), no. 5, p. 10.

9. Ibid., no. 4, p. 8.

10. Ibid., no. 99, p. 148.

11. Ibid., no. 101, p. 151.

12. See, for example, an essay by Havel that had wide influence in Czechoslovakia and beyond in the years before the revolutions of 1989, "The Power of the Powerless," in Václav Havel, *Open Letters: Selected Writings, 1965–1990*, selected and edited by Paul Wilson (New York: Vintage Books, 1992), 125–214, passim.

13. Erazim Kohák, "Can There Be a Central Europe?" *Dissent* (spring 1990): 194–97, at 195–96.

14. Havel, "The Power of the Powerless," 208.

15. John Paul II, *Veritatis Splendor*, no. 101, p. 151.

16. John Paul II, *Centesimus Annus,* no. 46.

17. Ibid., no. 13, emphasis added.

18. Havel, Address to a Joint Meeting of the House and Senate of the U.S. Congress, February 21, 1990, *Congressional Record* 136, Feb. 21, 1990, p. H395; emphasis added. For one indication of the offense taken to Havel's language of "Being," see Richard Rorty, "The Seer of Prague," *New Republic* (July 1, 1991): 35–39.

19. For disagreement with the pope on this point, see, for example, the essays by Richard McCormick, Josef Fuchs, Nicholas Lash, Lisa Sowle Cahill, and Herbert McCabe, in John Wilkins, ed., *Considering Veritatis Splendor* (Cleveland: Pilgrim Press, 1994), and Richard McCormick, "Some Early Reactions to *Veritatis Spendor*," *Theological Studies* 55 (1994): 481–506.

20. *Veritatis Splendor*, no. 106, p. 158.

21. Ibid., no. 115, p. 172, emphasis in original.

22. Ibid., no. 80, p. 123. The citation of Vatican II is from the Pastoral Constitution on the Church in the Modern World, *Gaudium et Spes*, no. 27.

23. *Veritatis Splendor*, no. 112, p. 167.

24. John T. Noonan, Jr., "Development in Moral Doctrine," *Theological Studies* 54 (1993): 662–77. Noonan's studies include: *The Believer and the Powers That Are: Cases, History, and Other Data Bearing on the Relation of Religion and Government* (New York: Macmillan, 1987); *Bribes* (New York: Macmillan, 1984); *Power to Dissolve: Lawyers and Marriages in the Courts of the Roman Curia* (Cambridge, Mass.: Belknap Press of Harvard University Press, 1972); *Contraception: A History of Its Treatment by the Catholic Theologians and Canonists* (Cambridge, Mass.: Belknap Press of Harvard University Press, 1965); *The Scholastic Analysis of Usury* (Cambridge, Mass.: Harvard University Press, 1957). Also, Noonan, ed., *The Morality of Abortion: Legal and Historical Perspectives* (Cambridge, Mass.: Harvard University Press, 1970).

25. Noonan, "Development in Moral Doctrine," 662–63.

26. Ibid., 664–67.

27. Ibid., 667.

28. Gregory XVI, *Mirari Vos Arbitramur*, translated in J. Neuner and J. Dupuis, eds., *The Christian Faith in the Doctrinal Documents of the Catholic church*, rev. ed. (Staten Island, N.Y.: Alba House, 1982), no. 10007.

29. *Dignitatis Humanae* (Declaration on Religious Freedom), no. 2.

30. *Gaudium et Spes*, no. 41.

31. *Veritatis Splendor*, no. 31, p. 52. There is, unfortunately, an ambiguity in John Paul II's discussion of religious freedom. Most of the time, it is interpreted in a way that is compatible with Vatican II's statement that this right "continues to exist even in those who do

not live up to their obligation of seeking the truth and adhering to it" (i.e., the right exists for believers and unbelievers alike). See *Dignitatis Humanae*, no. 2. At other times, though, he suggests that religious freedom means the right to hold the truth, as when the pope says, "In a certain sense, the source and synthesis of these rights [all human rights] is religious freedom, understood as the right to live in the truth of one's faith and in conformity with one's transcendent dignity as a person." See *Centesimus Annus*, no. 47. I think the ambiguity here is a studied one. I have discussed it in relation to the clear positions of Vatican II and of John Courtney Murray in "Freedom and Truth," chapter 7 in this volume. For a much fuller discussion of the direction and the ambiguities of John Paul II's thought on religious freedom, see Hermínio Rico, *John Paul II and the Legacy of Dignitatis Humanae* (Washington, D.C.: Georgetown University Press, 2002).

32. Noonan, "Development in Moral Doctrine," 669–73.

33. Yves Congar, *Vraie et fausse réforme dans l'Église*, 2me. ed., rev. et corr. (Paris, Éditions du Cerf, 1968).

34. George Lindbeck, *The Nature of Doctrine: Religion and Theology in a Postliberal Age* (Philadelphia: Westminster Press, 1984), 120–21. The characterization of the Bible as a loosely structured novel is borrowed by Lindbeck from David Kelsey, *The Uses of Scripture in Recent Theology* (Philadelphia: Fortress Press, 1975), 48.

35. Lindbeck, *The Nature of Doctrine*, 117–18.

36. Ibid., 83.

37. Noonan, "Development in Moral Doctrine," 674.

38. Ibid., 676.

39. Alasdair MacIntyre, *Whose Justice? Which Rationality?* (Notre Dame, Ind.: University of Notre Dame Press, 1988), 353–54.

40. MacIntyre, *After Virtue: A Study in Moral Theory* (Notre Dame, Ind.: University of Notre Dame Press, 1981), 201.

41. John Henry Newman, *An Essay on the Development of Christian Doctrine* (Garden City, N.Y.: Doubleday Image Books, 1960), 200–204.

42. Ibid., 189.

43. On this reading of Murray and Vatican II, see R. Bruce Douglass and David Hollenbach, eds., *Catholicism and Liberalism: Contributions to American Public Philosophy* (Cambridge: Cambridge University Press, 1994), especially my own essays in the volume.

44. This understanding of the relation between principles and applications reflects the discussion of "applicatio" in the hermeneutics of Hans-Georg Gadamer, without claiming to follow him in detail. See Hans-Georg Gadamer, *Truth and Method*, translation edited by Garrett Barden and John Cumming (New York: Continuum, 1975), 289–305.

45. MacIntyre, *Whose Justice? Which Rationality?*, chap. 18. See also MacIntyre, *Three Rival Versions of Moral Enquiry: Encyclopaedia, Genealogy, and Tradition* (Notre Dame, Ind.: University of Notre Dame Press, 1990), chap. 10, which relates this treatment of how traditions develop to the task of the university.

46. John Finnis, "Beyond the Encyclical," in John Wilkins, ed., *Considering Veritatis Splendor* (Cleveland: Pilgrim Press, 1994), 69.

47. Finnis, *Moral Absolutes: Tradition, Revision, and Truth* (Washington, D.C.: Catholic University of America Press, 1991), 12–16, 105–106 and *passim*. See also Finnis, Joseph M. Boyle, Jr., and Germain Grisez, *Nuclear Deterrence, Morality and Realism* (Oxford: Clarendon Press, 1987), 371–88. One is led to wonder whether Finnis's discussion of martyrdom has had a direct influence on the treatment of the same matter in *Veritatis Splendor*, nos. 90–94.

48. Avery Dulles, "Revelation and Discovery," in William J. Kelly, ed., *Theology and Discovery: Essays in Honor of Karl Rahner* (Milwaukee: Marquette University Press, 1980), 27.

3

Virtues and Vices
in Social Inquiry

This chapter will explore the importance of several of the moral virtues for intellectual inquiry that seeks to contribute to political and social life by advancing our understanding of human well-being. In particular, it will make some suggestions about the roles of the virtue of humility and the commitment to solidarity in the social inquiry of both engaged citizens and professional social scientists. What is said here is influenced by the retrieval of the importance of the virtues and vices in recent moral philosophy and theological ethics. This recovery of "virtue ethics," however, has not been much concerned with methodological issues such as the relation between morality and social inquiry. Rather, recent discussion of the virtues has dealt either with the place of the general notion of virtue in the overall moral life or with the influence of specific virtues in areas of activity such as the sustaining of relationships or the practice of medicine. This latter, practical, focus deals with virtues as discrete character traits that are conducive to particular kinds of action, as the virtue of courage leads to steadfastness in the face of adversity or the vice of intemperance leads to eating too much.

The notions of virtue and vice I will deal with here, however, go deeper than such isolable traits of the personality. I will be using the ideas of virtue and vice to point to what Iris Murdoch describes as "a person's general conceptual attitude and day-to-day 'being.'" This attitude includes a person's "meditation upon and conception of his own life, with its selective and dramatic emphases and implications of direction."[1] The focus here is on the way this deeper attitude and conception of self influences the inquiry of both engaged citizens and social scientists, whether for good or for ill. This more global orientation in social inquiry cannot be identified with separable predispositions to specific kinds of action. Nevertheless, some specific virtues and vices will be discussed as indicators of how more global personal orientations shape the style and tenor of social inquiry. These orientations have notable influence on the way such inquiry is carried out and the uses to which inquirers hope to put it. Thus, this orientation has important moral implications.

I will consider several virtues and vices that are simultaneously moral and intellectual. In particular, I will argue that a rethinking of the classical virtues of humility and reverence can add much to our understanding of the relation between morality and social inquiry. I will also argue that a virtuous kind of solidarity sheds light on the moral stance that should energize social inquiry. These virtues stand in contrast with excessive desire for social control, skepticism about the possibility of knowing anything significant about what is normatively human, and ironic detachment that treats all claims to normative understanding as naive. These orientations impede inquiry that can be expected to contribute to the overall good of the human community—the common good. So I will argue that they can be counted as vices.

SITUATING THE QUESTION HISTORICALLY

A rather sweeping historical note can set the context for my proposal. Premodern thinkers understood the social world as essentially static. The structures of the social world were seen as simply *given*, not as malleable by human agency or subject to transformation for human betterment. In much Greek and Roman thought, genuine knowledge could concern only the things that were changeless. "Science" sought to identify with certitude the necessary principles that explain why things are as they are. For this reason, only the changeless dimensions of social life could be the subjects of knowledge in the strict sense. A "science" of the contingent aspects of society was, strictly speaking, impossible. Premodern efforts to understand social life, therefore, sought to identify those social patterns that could be relied upon to remain constant. Similarly, the moral norms governing social life were regarded as changeless. Things would go well as long as persons lived up to changeless principles; departure from them would bring disorder and harm.

From our point of view today, this worldview placed an excessively high value on moral virtues that encourage passivity in the face of the way things are. Hierarchical social order was not to be challenged; one's "place" in society was to be accepted humbly. It also encouraged excessive respect for authority by those subject to it and paternalistic attitudes by those who exercised it. Authority was viewed as "ordained of God" and, when exercised correctly, as partaking analogously of God's fatherly care for his children. Social transformation, human betterment, and historical progress did not play a prominent role in this classical worldview.[2] The virtues it encouraged were not those that lead to such transformation. For us, this worldview gives a bad name to the virtues I argue we need today: humility and reverence. This raises the question of whether these virtues are necessarily tied to this premodern worldview. I argue they are not.

The framework of modern Western thought, by contrast, encourages precisely those virtues suited to activist efforts to make things happen in history and to change society for the better. As the modern West was being born, René Descartes drew a sharp distinction between the knowledge we could have of the inner human self and the knowledge we could have of the outer world of nature.[3] Descartes reintroduced an appreciation of the importance of inward subjectivity that St. Augustine had discovered more than a millennium earlier. This turn to subjectivity bore fruit in Kant's categorical imperative that we must always treat human beings as ends in themselves and never as means only.[4] It also led to the conviction that human selves could become "the masters and possessors of nature."[5] The development of Newtonian physics made it possible to apply this quest for mastery to the physical world. It was then a relatively short step to the conclusion that society too can be "worked on" and changed for the benefit of human beings. This conviction led to Marx's conviction that the real point of philosophy is to change the world, not simply to interpret it.[6] The dignity of the human person thus became the cornerstone of the whole edifice of subsequent moral theory, and the malleability of nature and society opened the doors for activist efforts to change society in ways that make human flourishing possible for all. These ideas indicate how the social sciences became linked to the rise of distinctively modern contributions to humanism.[7]

MODERN VIRTUES IN TROUBLE

In this humanistic vision, the key qualities of personality are independence, self-determination, suspicion of tradition and authority, and activist commitment to progressive social change. These same virtues, I think, play a significant role in the moral stance guiding the social sciences that emerged in the nineteenth century. In no way do I wish to deny the importance of these virtues or to suggest a return to premodern worldviews, with their ready acceptance of social stasis. One can, however, question whether the modern virtues are adequate to address the problems we face today.

The modern pursuit of mastery of the world has formed a corresponding discourse of prediction and, above all, control.[8] The autonomous self envisioned in this discourse seeks to find its own way through the entanglements of history and society in accord with a freely chosen life plan. Such a framework leads to thinking of the "real self" as a kind of demigod. It envisions freedom as unconstrained and unconditioned by what is already given in nature or society. When a choice is genuinely free, it resembles divine freedom, creating its own outcomes from nothing.

It is here, I think, that the virtues most prized by modernity run amok. The aspiration to independence cannot be sustained in the face of the increasing interdependence of social existence that is the result of growing economic interconnection, new technologies of communication, and recognition of the embeddedness of human beings within the web of the biophysical environment. These realities make the autonomous self of modernity less and less plausible. The breakdown of this plausibility has in turn led to declining confidence in the goals held out by modern humanism itself and by the humanistic aspirations of the social sciences.

Vices in Social Inquiry

For example, the hope tha... reason can shape nature and society
in ways that are truly beneficial... der suspicion. Human freedom an... quality of human life has come un-
instruments of raw power. We increas...ledge are viewed as likely to be
rogance will lead to a quest for dominatio...spect an anthropocentric ar-
In the same vein, claims to know norms of... inevitably pollutes nature.
pected of being expressions of cultural hubri...od human life are sus-
what is universally desirable for the well-being of a... than insights into
...sons.

The breakdown of the illusory transcendence of the...esian self thus
threatens to undermine the possibility of humanism it... for it often
leads to skepticism about the possibility of knowing what s...ld count
as truly human from a normative standpoint. In the face of t... loss of
confidence, the virtues that have emerged as the best we can hope f...are
a live-and-let-live tolerance and a knowing irony that comes from livi...
at a certain distance from one's own beliefs.[9] Postmodern thinkers such
as Richard Rorty celebrate this mood of irony as the mark of a liberal culture that has learned not to take itself and its hopes too seriously. Its crit-
ics see it as nihilism. I think this goes too far, for Rorty's irony still contains
enough of the humanistic aspiration to remain critical of the dangers of
domination and oppression. Albert Borgmann is more on target when he
calls it the "sullenness" of the postmodern mentality—the sense that the
best we can do is cope.[10] But however we characterize it, this mood is the
antithesis of the modern self-confidence that sufficiently enlightened human beings could bring the conditions of their social existence under the
control of human reason and direct social life to a more humane existence
for all. Social inquiry pursued by persons who have internalized this mood
is likely to be intent on showing how convictions about the normatively human are dangerous and need to be debunked. It is also likely to assume
that cultural relativism is the advisable normative posture and to undercut
any universalist claims about how human beings should live together.

This stance easily leads to disengagement from the pursuit of an enhanced quality of public life and a retreat into privacy. This retreat is far
from confined to the domain of postmodern theoretical discourse. Alan
Wolfe has pointed out how a live-and-let-live attitude has displaced belief
in the modern quest for a more just and equal society. Wolfe has concluded that the American middle class has added a new commandment to
the decalogue: "Thou shalt not judge thy neighbor."[11] One can ask: is it pos-

sible to sustain any form of humanism j...y only be a way of imposing
people are so suspicious that moral n... one group's perspective on others?...er, is increasingly evident. The di-
The paradox of this situation...day are increasingly bound to one an-
verse communities of the w...eir mutual dependence on a biophysical
other by the global mark...boundaries, by cultural interactions made
environment that kn...technology, by migration and forced refugee
possible by commu...nsnational transmission of threats to human life and
movements, by t...IDS virus, drugs, and weapons of war. But affirmation
health such as...and diversity go all the way down means there can be no
that plural...govern all this de facto interaction that cuts across cultural
norms...ries and links diverse social groups together. If we lack such trans-
bou...úral norms entirely, the likely outcome will be reaffirmation of the dis-
tinctive traditions that set each community apart from others. This is evident in movements for political devolution or separation in Québec and Scotland, in armed conflict in the Basque country, India and Pakistan, the Middle East generally, and in wholesale slaughter in the former Yugoslavia and Rwanda. Thus, we face a paradox: attaining a vision of transcultural norms is held to be increasingly problematic precisely at a historical moment when the need for such a vision is growing.

RETHINKING THE VIRTUES FOR SOCIAL INQUIRY TODAY

In this context I want to suggest that several virtues that have been downplayed in the modern West need to be retrieved, both in the lives of citizens and in the practice of the social sciences. Consider humility. The negative meaning of this virtue in contemporary usage is evident from the fact that dictionaries list "obsequiousness," "subservience," "submissiveness," and even "self-abasement" among its synonyms. Such qualities hardly count as virtues in a culture that values self-reliance and independence as highly as ours does. But humility can also be characterized as absence of pride or arrogance, two quite negative qualities in our cultural gestalt. Thus, I think it is fair to say that contemporary American culture is confused about how to relate its desire for independence with its aversion to arrogance. This confusion is also evident in the presuppositions of a social science rooted in the modern humanistic pursuit of human betterment that at the same time is skeptical about all judgments concerning what counts as better.

Perhaps we might find a way out of this apparent cultural and social scientific conundrum by noting that there are both similarities and differences between the classical virtue of humility, on the one hand, and postmodern skepticism and irony, on the other. Thinkers who have lost faith in the rational mastery of nature and the control of social processes reject the stance of the modern self, which they see as distorted by pride of intellect and arrogance of freedom. But they leave a void when their skepticism and irony displace the intellectual and volitional self-aggrandizement of modernity. Humility, however, does not leave such a void. As I propose to characterize it, humility leads to paying attention to the reality of other persons and the world of nature. It is the awareness that one is not the center of the universe precisely because one feels reverence for the inherent worth of realities beyond the self.

In other words, humility is a relational virtue. One can be humble only in relation to the world of nature, another person, or another society with a different culture and historical tradition. Humility is a bond of a certain kind with reality beyond the self. It forms the kind of connection with reality that is appropriate for persons who are finite and limited rather than demigods. Skepticism and irony, on the other hand, are qualities that put one at a distance from the objects of one's regard. Indeed skepticism and irony encourage distance even from oneself, one's beliefs, one's projects, and one's goals. On one level, irony seems to dissolve arrogance, but it also exalts the self as an observer who can view all lesser beings from the slyly knowing heights of self-satisfaction. By contrast, authentic humility requires acceptance of one's dependence on and vulnerability to what is beyond oneself. It is a stance toward the world that regards relationships with nature, other persons, society, and indeed with God as essential to authentic personhood. The "decentering" of the self expressed in humility puts one in a position to learn from others, to depend on others, and to make contributions to the well-being of others without attempting to control or dominate them. Authentic humility is not misguided self-abasement. It values the self for what it is, neither more nor less.[12] Through such humility, those who lose their arrogant selves will find themselves through relationships with nature, other persons, and society–relationships that befit beings who are not God (see Matthew 16:25).

Humility, understood this way, is a desirable virtue in both citizens and social scientists. Among citizens, it is a sine qua non for the formation of nondominative relationships among members of particular cultures and across the boundaries of diverse cultures. For social scientists concerned with moral inquiry, it has an intellectual dimension that I have elsewhere called "epistemological humility."[13] This is a cognitive stance that begins with the acknowledgment that one does not have ready answers to all questions of how people ought to live together. Nor does it presume that a moral orientation that seems reasonable or even necessary to the inquirer is evidently desirable to all other reasonable people. It acknowledges that one can attain genuine knowledge only through receptivity to the world beyond the mind of the inquirer.

This receptivity begins in a kind of wonder. Wonder is the beginning of all social inquiry, just as Plato said it was of philosophy.[14] By wonder I mean more than a puzzlement of not knowing what is happening or a quizzical uncertainty about how to explain what one observes. Wonder exists on the border between an unanswered question sensed to be answerable through further investigation and an experience of awe or reverence in the face of an inexpressible good.[15] Epistemological humility embodies this double sense of wonder. This makes such humility fundamentally different from skepticism. The inquirer who possesses this virtue does not simply affirm that persons and cultures are different from one another and leave the matter at that. Rather, epistemological humility is a cognitive stance that expects growth in knowledge to occur when one pays attention to, and forms the appropriate kinds of relationships with, others. It is not a virtue like temperance, which primarily orders one's relation with oneself and one's inner appetites. Rather, it principally concerns the proper ordering of one's relation to the realities one is trying to understand.

In efforts to understand human beings in their social interaction, epistemological humility presupposes that the inquirer and the subjects of inquiry are *fellow* human beings. Appreciation of this cohumanity is essential if acknowledgment of difference is not to become a pretext for distancing or indifference, on the one hand, or for domination and control, on the other. The experience of cohumanity evokes reverence for, and engagement with, the other. This reverence draws the inquirer both to seek to know the other more fully and to acknowledge that the other has a surpassing value that always escapes control by any sort of science human beings are capable of attaining.

In social inquiry, therefore, cognitive humility enables the inquirer to see cultural differences as expressions of different ways of being human. Differences of culture are not like the differences among biological species. For example, social inquiry into the lives of the Kikuyu and Maasai peoples in Kenya will reveal how very different they are both from each other and from Westerners. But anyone who confuses the Kikuyu and Maasai with nonhuman animals has not paid attention to rudimentary evidence. Kikuyu, Maasai, and Americans all have certain needs and capabilities in common, even though we may pursue and realize them in somewhat different ways.[16] A stance of receptivity that allows people and cultures to speak for themselves is a consequence of this sense of common humanity, and it leads to a deepened appreciation of what is common in the midst of the differences.

Thus, epistemological humility is simultaneously cognitive and moral, a matter of both the head and the heart. Greater appreciation of this kind of linkage between the cognitive and moral spheres could go a long way toward healing the rift between facts and values in social research. Such appreciation is a mark of inquiry conducted with intellectual humility. It leads to inquiry that begins with careful attention to and even reverence for the actual lives of those whose lives are being investigated. This attention and reverence will, in turn, lead to a deeper appreciation of commonality with other persons and groups. These virtues can make possible a kind of moral understanding that the skeptic and ironist have given up hope of achieving. They can also lead to normative proposals that are not simply power plays aiming at greater control of others.

Because of this hope in the possibility of deeper knowledge of diverse ways of being human, epistemological humility generates another moral virtue relevant to social inquiry that I like to call "intellectual solidarity."[17] This virtue is a readiness to take other persons or cultures seriously enough to engage them in conversation about their vision of what makes life worth living and how they live out this vision day by day. Such a stance presupposes a commitment to equality, for attentive listening to the self-understanding of others cannot occur from a posture that seeks mastery or control of those being studied. Normative conclusions drawn from such inquiry will also reflect the commitment to equality the inquiry presupposes. This does not mean, of course, that normative conclusions are possible only where unanimous consensus already exists. Indeed, investigation conducted in a spirit of intellectual solidarity will sometimes conclude that extant forms of domination of some persons or groups by others should be firmly opposed on normative grounds. Such opposition to domination emerges from the virtue of solidarity itself.

Intellectual solidarity also presupposes a commitment to *mutual* listening and speaking. In social scientific research, such mutuality or reciprocity should be present whether the research takes place in face-to-face interviews or through remote survey instruments. In the latter case, it implies that the instruments have been carefully designed to let the subjects of research say what they really mean. Developing research tools of this sort requires not only a spirit of reciprocity with those studied on the part of the researcher, but likely also calls for selective in-person exchange in the design process. Or, on the rather different level of social theory, these values will be evident from the start in the selection of kinds of phenomena the theories seek to explain.

In other words, the virtues of epistemological humility and intellectual solidarity mean that the goals and methods of social inquiry will be marked from the start by the moral values of equality and mutuality. For this reason, the spirit guiding such inquiry will be quite different from the skepticism and irony that often follow the collapse of the aspiration to be an intellectual master who looks down on nature and society from the lofty tower of Cartesian selfhood. These virtues presuppose that social researchers are not demigods but fellow travelers with other human beings through the course of history. Researchers can even be described, in biblical and Augustinian language, as fellow pilgrims on the earth along with those whose lives, societies, and cultures they study.

The very commitment to serious inquiry through listening and speaking with other persons across cultural borders depends on the hope that understanding might replace incomprehension. It even goes so far as to hope that some mutual agreement about what it is to be human could result. Inquiry of this sort is essential if we are to discover ways to live together on a planet that is at once increasingly aware of its pluralism, more tightly connected through economic interdependence, and more vulnerable to conflict among those who are different.

To address these new conditions, we need to get beyond both the pursuit of control that leads to domination and the ironic skepticism that leads to disengagement. I think that epistemological humility and intellectual solidarity can start us down this path. They counter the excessive desire for control, for in some ways they resemble the virtue of nonjudgmental tolerance so highly valued in American culture today. But epistemological humility and intellectual solidarity are crucially different from a live-and-let-live tolerance based on skepticism about all claims about what human beings have in common.

The similarity to tolerance is due to the fact that epistemological humility and intellectual solidarity are virtues of those who take equality and mutuality among humans seriously. Genuine solidarity is impossible among those who are not really equal. And humility is a condition for hearing what others have to say about themselves. It requires respect for the freedom of others to say what they really mean. So these virtues take seriously the skeptical ironist's warnings against the use of normative discourse as a tool of social control or domination. Nurturing such humility and solidarity requires a social atmosphere in which equality and freedom are valued and institutionalized. In this sense, they are "liberal" virtues, and they require the building and strengthening of the institutions of constitutional government, free speech, free exercise of religion, and so forth. Because epistemological humility and intellectual solidarity are fundamental orientations toward engagement with the other, however, they will not be found among people or societies who aspire to a life in which everyone leaves everyone else alone to the maximum feasible degree.[18] Persons do not and cannot live alone, so it is a fundamental mistake to presume that isolation or noninterference is the way to protect equality and freedom.

Similarly, conducting social research is not like viewing the world from the top of a high mountain. Humility and solidarity are virtues of people who live on a human scale, not on the scale of demigods. They are virtues needed by social scientists as well as citizens. This does not mean, of course, that only work that is immediately "relevant" to the solution of social problems should be pursued. Work that seems abstracted from pressing issues may in fact be essential to human betterment. But even apparently "ivory tower" research, when rooted in the virtues of epistemological humility and intellectual solidarity, will not delude the inquirer into thinking that he or she has left behind the vulnerabilities and interdependence of the human condition. Where research of any sort is grounded in an acknowledgment of these limits, it can become research that serves a *community* of mutual equality and freedom. Thus, the very method of social research embodies the norms that moral inquiry is in search of in an incipient way.

VIRTUE AND THE GOOD WE SHARE IN COMMON

Let me conclude by suggesting that the virtues of the social inquirer are those that enable his or her work to serve the common good. This, of course, assumes that there is such a thing as the common good in the pluralistic world in which we live. I am not going to try to support that assumption with argument here, or to lay out what I think the idea of the common good means today. I have attempted this elsewhere.[19] Here I will simply stipulate that the common good can be understood to include the good of being a community at all. Such a good comes into existence only when free and equal people enter into moral solidarity with each other. This solidarity is a stance that takes up shared *moral* responsibility for the de facto realities of interaction and interdependence that exist among people.

These interactions occur in a host of different kinds of relationships, from personal friendships, to family, to the workplace, to politics. Interdependence occurs on diverse scales, ranging from intimate relationships to global political economy. The common good is therefore an ensemble of goods existing on multiple scales, just as human relations are of different kinds and sizes. But each of these interactions is among human beings who are alike in fundamental and identifiable ways, such as needing food and shelter for their bodies, being capable of communicating with each other and of forming friendships and families, being sexual beings and capable of procreation, having the capacity for thought, association, work, politics, and—very important, I think—having the capacity for a relationship with a transcendent good, namely, God.[20]

These common characteristics, of course, are not realized in the lives of all people or all cultures in the same ways. For example, family life and political leadership will look very different among the Maasai or Kikuyu of Kenya and among the middle class of the United States, just as the conditions necessary for work to be conducted in a human way will be different today in the West than it was in preindustrial Europe. What is required in family life, politics, and work that respect the shared dignity of those who participate in them arises as a normative concern when solidarity guides intellectual inquiry. Such questions arise among both social scientists and ordinary members of the societies in question. For this reason, the list of needs and capabilities common to all human beings is itself open to revision. Such revisions are worth making only if they are in some sense more adequate descriptions of what it is to be human. Discovering that this is the case requires that investigation be conducted in a spirit marked by epistemological humility and intellectual solidarity.

In all such investigations, the social inquirer, whether citizen or social scientist, is a participant in the shared human venture of being on the way toward understanding what it is to be human at all. Because the social researcher is not outside or above this shared venture, he or she needs the virtues of humility and solidarity. Because the work of inquiry is a cognitive undertaking, these virtues will be manifest in the epistemological and intellectual presuppositions brought to the task. Inquiry done by men and women possessing these virtues is certainly not guaranteed to attain the full truth about the human good. To claim this would hardly be a sign of humility. But I think a case can be made that such virtues are considerably more likely to lead to an understanding of the goods human beings hold in common than are the efforts of one who peers down on society from on high. Pursuing an understanding of human relationships with these virtues for guidance will lead to better empirical research, more adequate social theory, and more humane normative proposals. The social inquiry of citizens guided by these virtues will help them make the lives of their communities better by undertaking this work along with their fellow citizens, not over against or from above them.

Such inquiry, then, will actualize the ancient Aristotelian insight that all virtues are finally directed to fuller attainment of the common good. This link is not simply an imperative directing the individual to contribute to the common good. It is also an assurance that the individual's good is supported by bonds of relationship with the community. By accepting the need for intellectual and moral support from beyond their own resources, both citizens and social scientists will in turn be able to make greater contributions to the good they share in common with their fellow humans.

Humility and solidarity, therefore, go hand in hand, both morally and intellectually. When this is recognized, moral inquiry and social research appear as inseparable aspects of an integral, humanistic undertaking.

NOTES

1. Iris Murdoch, "Vision and Choice in Morality," in Ian T. Ramsey, ed., *Christian Ethics and Contemporary Philosophy* (London: SCM Press, 1966), 206.

2. For a description of this "classical" world view and of the modern alternative to it, see Bernard Lonergan, "Dimensions of Meaning," in F. E. Crowe, ed., *Collection: Papers of Bernard Lonergan, S.J.* (New York: Herder and Herder, 1967), 252–67.

3. See René Descartes, *Discourse on Method,* in *Discourse on Method and Meditations,* trans. Laurence J. Lafleur (Indianapolis: Bobbs-Merrill, 1960), 8.

4. Immanuel Kant, *Foundations of the Metaphysics of Morals,* trans. Lewis White Beck (Indianapolis: Bobbs Merrill, 1959), 47.

5. Descartes, *Discourse on Method,* 45.

6. Karl Marx, "Theses on Feuerbach," XI, in Lewis S. Feuer, ed., *Marx and Engels: Basic Writings on Politics and Philosophy* (New York: Doubleday, 1959), 245.

7. See Charles Taylor, *Sources of the Self: The Making of the Modern Identity* (Cambridge, Mass.: Harvard University Press, 1989), 152.

8. Albert Borgmann, *Crossing the Postmodern Divide* (Chicago: University of Chicago Press, 1992), 2.

9. The term "irony" is used here to describe what Eric Gans calls "romantic irony," (i.e., "an attitude toward life that consists not so much in anticipating the opposite of one's expectations as in a knowing superiority to the ironies of fate that await us in the real world"). Eric Gans, *Signs of Paradox: Irony, Resentment, and Other Mimetic Structures* (Stanford, Calif.: Stanford University Press, 1997), 64.

10. See Borgmann, *Crossing the Postmodern Divide,* 6–12.

11. Alan Wolfe, *One Nation After All: What Middle-Class Americans Really Think about God, Country, Family, Racism, Welfare, Immigration, Homosexuality, Work, the Right, the Left, and Each Other* (New York: Viking, 1998), 54.

12. For a discussion of this point in the thought of Thomas Aquinas, see Stephen J. Pope, "Expressive Individualism and True Self-Love: A Thomistic Perspective," *Journal of Religion* 71 (1991): 384–99.

13. See my *Claims in Conflict: Retrieving and Renewing the Catholic Human Rights Tradition* (New York: Paulist Press, 1979), 131. I am indebted to several conversations with Margaret A. Farley for much of the way the idea of epistemological humility is further developed in these reflections, especially how it relates both to the desire for a godlike universal viewpoint and to the alternative of skepticism. See also Reinhold Niebuhr, *The Nature and Destiny of Man,* vol. 2 (New York: Scribner's, 1964), chap. 8.

14. Plato, *Theaetetus*, 155d. In *The Collected Dialogues of Plato,* Edith Hamilton and Huntington Cairns, eds. (New York: Random House, 1963), 860.

15. See Philip Fisher, *Wonder, the Rainbow, and the Aesthetics of Rare Experiences* (Cambridge, Mass.: Harvard University Press, 1998), esp. 120. Helpful as Fisher's analysis is, it shortchanges the perduring presence of reverence for the inexpressible that I intend by "wonder" here.

16. See Martha C. Nussbaum, "Human Functioning and Social Justice: In Defense of Aristotelian Essentialism," *Political Theory* 20 (1992): 202–46.

17. See chapter 1.

18. Richard Rorty says he shares this view with John Dewey: "[Dewey] assumed that no good achieved by earlier societies would be worth recapturing if the price were a diminution in our ability to leave people alone, to let them try out their private visions of perfection in peace." See Rorty, "The Priority of Democracy to Philosophy," in Merrill D. Peterson and Robert Vaughan, eds., *The Virginia Statute for Religious Freedom: Its Evolution and Consequences in American History* (Cambridge: Cambridge University Press, 1988), 273. This, however, is only one aspect of Rorty's (and Dewey's) public philosophies, for they both have strong commitments to human solidarity in the context of democracy. The tension in Rorty's position seems to me to end up being a self-contradiction.

19. See my *The Common Good and Christian Ethics* (Cambridge: Cambridge University Press, 2002).

20. For fuller development of these characteristics see my *Claims in Conflict*, 95–100, and Nussbaum, "Human Functioning and Social Justice." Nussbaum limits her consideration of religion to the need for religious freedom. I think much more can and should be said about the religious dimension as the root of humility and solidarity. Here it is perhaps enough to point out that all human beings have the capacity to recognize that they are not themselves God.

4

Social Ethics under the Sign of the Cross

The practice of social ethics is facing something of an identity crisis as we begin the twenty-first century. In the United States, this crisis is evident in the anxiety that has gripped Americans in the aftermath of September 11, 2001. The problem, however, goes considerably deeper than the ebb and flow of popular opinion. The present shaky identity of the field of social ethics is due to a loss of self-confidence by the Western tradition of humanism. By *humanism*, I mean here an orientation in thought and action that is guided by a central concern with the integral well-being of human persons and a hope that they can develop in such well-being.

The relation between humanism and Christian belief has of course varied considerably over the centuries in the West. It has ranged from a close connection between the two that Jacques Maritain called "integral humanism" to the deep oppositions described by Henri de Lubac as the "drama of atheist humanism."[1] The uncertain self-understanding in social ethics today is not due simply to a new version of the conflict between humanistic aspirations and Christian faith, whether that conflict is based on a challenge raised by humanism to Christianity or one raised by Christianity to humanism. It stems from a contemporary crisis of humanism as such, in both its Christian and secular forms.

These doubts about humanism can be described this way: many of us have lost confidence in our ability to develop an adequate normative description of what human well-being is, and many have lost hope in our practical ability to shape a society that enables human beings to develop in that well-being. There are currents of thought in our culture, in the academy, and in the churches, of course, that do not share this pessimistic mood. Nonetheless, the loss of confidence in the humanism of much past Western civilization is widespread enough in all these venues to be regarded as a sign of the times, perhaps the characteristic sign of our postmodern moment in history. To the extent this is true, social ethics finds its identity diffused and its future uncertain.

This crisis of humanism represents the surfacing of deep conflicts that have been present in the social and intellectual life of the West for several centuries. Near the dawn of the modern epoch, René Descartes gave expression to one of the tensions of modern consciousness that has now approached a breaking point. In the face of the uncertainty of philosophical opinion, Descartes proposed a practical philosophy based on knowledge that "I might find within myself, or perhaps in the great book of nature."[2] Under this impulse, the self and the mechanical world of nature became the twin foci of modern thought. By granting centrality to the inner resources of the rational self, this move gave expression to the most important of modernity's distinctive contributions to humanism. The modern interpretation of the dignity of the human person arose out of Descartes's turn to inwardness.[3] At the same time, the Cartesian agenda sought to make human selves into "the masters and possessors of nature."[4] The impact of this pursuit of mastery went far beyond the domains of the sciences, engineering, and technology, where it has been most evident. The overarching discourse of modernity has been a discourse of prediction and, above all, control.[5]

The uncertain identity of Western humanism and of social ethics today is due to a simultaneous loss of plausibility of the Cartesian self and loss of confidence in the possibility of the control of nature Descartes sought. The modern supposition that knowledge can lead to mastery of nature, social life, and history is under fundamental challenge. Indeed the pursuit of such mastery increasingly appears in the late twentieth century as a destructive, even demonic, force. This raises basic questions for an ethic based on pursuit of knowledge that leads to power over nature and society. It rejects the view that the use of the appropriate social scientific tool or technological implement will secure the humane goals we seek. Today, advances in understanding increasingly reveal how little control over events we really have, whether in society or the natural environment. Things, even fate, seem increasingly to be in the saddle. This amounts to a kind of crisis of faith—a loss of the belief that we are able to shape social life in accord with the values we hold. And if we lack such a faith, what is to become of social ethics?

Nearly a century ago, Ernst Troeltsch concluded *The Social Teaching of the Christian Churches* with a dire prediction about the impact this loss of control would have on social ethics in the Christian tradition. Troeltsch's historical analysis had convinced him that only the church-type theological ethics of medieval Catholicism and ascetic Protestantism stood a chance of bringing Christianity into some sort of coherent synthesis with modern civilization. At the same time, he believed that, in spite of great historical achievements, these two traditions "have now spent their force"—"the main historic forms of the Christian doctrine of society and of social development are to-day, for various reasons, impotent in the face of the tasks by which they are confronted." In Troeltsch's reading, the rise of historical consciousness and its accompanying relativization of all normative models of society implied that any ethic could only be an "adjustment to the world situation" based on a "desire to achieve what is practically possible." This called for an acknowledgment that, however noble Christian ethical ideals might be, only "doctrinaire idealists or religious fanatics can fail to recognize" that these ideals can never be realized. The truth of the matter, Troeltsch argued, is that the Kingdom of God is within us and cannot be given definitive expression in social interaction and institutions.[6]

Since Troeltsch wrote these somber words, much has happened in social ethical reflection. In the Christian churches, we have seen the rise of the social gospel, of Christian realism, of Catholic social thought represented by papal and episcopal teachings, and most recently of liberation, black, and feminist theologies. In social thought more broadly, Marxism, structural-functional sociology, neoclassical economics, and neoliberal, communitarian, and ideal-discourse moral/political philosophies have waxed and waned. There are important insights in all of these movements that are surely valuable today. But underlying the contemporary appreciation of all these variations in the theory of social existence there is the same dour mood present in Troeltsch's writing. It is the sense that the best we can do is "cope." This is the antithesis of the modern self-confidence that human beings, if sufficiently enlightened, could finally bring the conditions of their social existence under the control of human reason, thus placing social life at the service of a more humane existence. This contemporary self-distrust has both theoretical and practical dimensions.

Theoretically, for example, in 1918 Max Weber characterized modern intellectual life in the West as marked by a loss of confidence in the reliability of "grandiose" reason.[7] Where Descartes had disenchanted nature by viewing it mechanistically, Weber disenchanted the self by relativizing all normative self-understandings, even his own as a social scientist. In Weber's analysis, modern intellectual inquiry has lost the ability to answer ultimate questions about the purpose of human life. Rationality is instrumental; it deals with means, not ends. Thus, whatever knowledge of the social good we can gain does not "partake of the contemplation of sages and philosophers about the meaning of the universe" thought to be possible in earlier epochs. Weber, however, went further than a critique of metaphysics and religion. The forces of disenchantment challenge the ultimate worth of social scientific inquiry itself. Whether the work of a social scientist has any final truth or significance is not in the end a matter of intellectual judgment.[8] It is an issue to be settled by a decision about which "demon" one will grant functional divinity in one's way of life. Thus, Weber suggested that the commitments of the social analyst are no more ultimate than the gods of the ancient religions. Weber's advice was that a student of social life must face this fact "like a man."[9] This means we must bid adieu to an understanding of social ethics that goes beyond description of various social possibilities. Normative judgments of what constitutes a genuinely good society become impossible.

Weber's description of the historical situation of intellectual inquiry has become increasingly dominant since he first presented it. There are strong currents in intellectual life today that challenge the capacity of reason to attain genuine knowledge of what actually is the case, not only in the domain of religion, but also in the humanities and even the sciences. Much postmodern thought has extended the critique of reason well beyond metaphysics and theology. The diversity of disciplinary methods and the deepening awareness of the cultural pluralism of our world discourage efforts to achieve an integration of the multiple forms of knowledge. Intellectual specialization increasingly closes disciplines to insights that arise beyond the boundaries of their field of inquiry. This situation has led a number of contemporary thinkers to conclude that all we can aspire to in intellectual life are fragments of meaning that are not really the meaning *of* anything external to those who find them meaningful. These fragments of meaning are purely human constructs rather than vistas onto what is real or true. For example, Richard Rorty maintains that a culture that is "enlightened through and through" would be "one in which no trace of divinity remained, either in the form of a divinized world or a divinized self. . . . It would drop, or drastically reinterpret, not only the idea of holiness but those of 'devotion to truth' and of 'fulfillment of the deepest needs of the spirit.' "[10] So much for normative humanism, whether Christian or secular.

This skepticism about the possibility of theoretical knowledge of the social good has practical consequences. If will is primary, action appears to be simply an expression of power. All knowledge-claims about the social good are assertions of self-interest. When a loss of confidence in the ability to know the shape of a good society is combined with the modern impulse to control, action becomes a matter of me controlling you on my terms, of us controlling them on our terms. This is a formula for battle, whether it arises in a bunker in Berlin, the offices of bond traders armed with the tools of the electronic network of today's global financial markets, or the "war rooms" of today's political campaigns. If will is normless, power expresses itself as domination of the weak by the strong.

Thus, our historical period is witnessing the return of an intellectual tendency that has appeared before, with the Sophists in ancient Greece and with the nominalists of the late Middle Ages and early modern period—a tendency that denies the capacity of the human mind to grasp the truth of reality, whether this reality be mundane or divine. As with the Sophists and nominalists in the past, this can lead to the reduction of all practical undertakings in society and the polis to matters of power and will. This undercuts the very possibility of an intellectually defensible normative vision of a good society. Thus, it challenges the very possibility of a social ethic, whether this ethic be secular or religious. In Weber's terms, words become weapons. They are "not plowshares to loosen the soil of contemplative thought; they are swords against enemies."[11] Here Weber harks back to Thrasymachus in Plato's *Republic:* justice is simply the advantage of the stronger.[12] And Rorty, in one of his more Nietzschean moods, has written that a positive assessment of personal existence is the ability to say at the end of one's days, "Thus I willed it."[13] Such a stand rejects any claim to know the human good in a way that has normative status. Thus, it casts a kind of suspicion on all metaphysical or theological approaches to social ethics that is even stronger than those suspicions based on the conviction that religion is a largely harmless illusion. But it also undercuts secular normative claims to which societies can be held accountable such as the idea of universal human rights. A successful society will be one that can say of its history and politics, "Thus we willed it."

The presence of this way of thinking in our environment can no doubt be exaggerated, but, in my judgment, it would be a mistake to underestimate its influence in both the general academic environment and the culture at large. Its presence, even *in nuce*, is a sort of virus in the body of the culture itself. It eats away at the very possibility of intellectual inquiry into what constitutes a good society or a worthy culture. The postmodern intellectual epoch in which we live, therefore, is marked by a stance of suspicion toward all schemes of meaning, all traditions, all ideologies, and all scientific and technological theories that claim total explanatory power.

And rightly so. For we recognize that explanations that lead to the kind of control sought by the impulse of modernity are partial at best and can lead to immense destruction when regarded as total. Who can deny the legitimacy of such suspicions in the face of the bloody realities of the wars of the twentieth century? Science has been put at the service of genocidal slaughter at Auschwitz and the destruction of whole cities at Dresden and Hiroshima. Psychologies that aimed at the liberation of persons from hysteria have awakened a form of self-consciousness that threatens to become routinized narcissism. An economic-political ideology that promised to unshackle workers from their chains ordered tanks into the streets against them in Budapest, Prague, and Tienanmen Square, sent them to the gulag, slaughtered them in the killing fields of Cambodia, and finally expired without a whimper in the face of velvet revolutions led by poets, shipbuilders, and priests. The retrieval of the traditions of just and limited war in the twentieth century has been accompanied by a move from forms of warfare in which fourteen percent of the victims were civilians in World War I to forms where nearly ninety percent were civilians at the century's end.[14] Religious visions of the good society have contributed to conflict and terror against the innocent in the West Bank and Gaza, Belfast, Algeria, the Sudan, and Bosnia.

Suspicion grounded in such experiences has led early twenty-first century men and women to a fork in the road. We can choose ironic detachment as a survival tactic and "change the subject" when asked what it all means. Or we can follow a path like the one that led the Buddha to affirm that the first, though not last, Noble Truth is *Dukkha*—all is suffering, pain, sorrow, misery. Those who do not resort to irony as the opium of the effete can readily say of our own century what Saint Augustine's said of the achievements of the Roman Empire: "You cannot show that men lived in happiness, as they passed their lives amid the horrors of war, amid the shedding of men's blood—whether the blood of enemies or fellow-citizens—under the shadow of fear and amid the terror of ruthless ambition. The only joy to be attained had the fragile brilliance of glass, a joy outweighed by the fear that it may be shattered in a moment."[15] When we look without flinching at the twentieth century, it is not unreasonable to draw the conclusion of both poets and mystics: the world is on fire.

This encounter with suffering and misery has shattered the modern West's hope that we can bring about progress by bringing social life under the control of enlightened rationality. It is the driving force behind the wariness and sullenness so manifest today. The question for social ethics today, then, is whether we have any ground for a hope to uncover meaning that can sustain human life and guide the vast energies of scientific, political, economic, and cultural undertakings. Or is all this work simply a way of coping with life, filling the time between young adulthood and death with activity that is perhaps interesting but ultimately pointless?

The pursuit of social ethics in the postmodern epoch, therefore, demands that we squarely face what has classically been called the "problem of evil." This is the inexorable and unavoidable issue in light of the destructiveness of the twentieth century. The early 1900s saw the rise of social ethics as a distinct intellectual endeavor. The record of the twentieth century's history raises limit questions about the viability of the undertaking as a whole. These questions touch the work of not only theologians and philosophers but every man or woman who asks Kant's questions today:

"What can I know? What ought I to do? What may I hope?"[16] Are all proposed visions of the social good so dependent on context that no normative status can be attributed to any of them? Are all such normative claims really veiled forms of self-assertion that will likely add to the domination and violence that have been so evident throughout the past century? If social life is so broken that "simply coping" is the best we can aspire to, the answer to Kant's question of what we may hope for becomes "survival—for the time being." The brokenness is undeniable. Thus, the issue is whether coping is the most intelligent approach we can adopt toward it. If so, a reprieve of temporary survival is the outcome we should seek, adopting a sort of rough "maximin" strategy that pursues outcomes that are less bad than the alternatives.

Such a strategy, I suggest, will only make matters worse. Since at least Augustine, this strategy has been diagnosed as the principal cause of violence and injustice. It represents the impulse to control run amok, for the impulse to control life, especially social life, in the face of this brokenness, leads to self-defensiveness that inevitably turns aggressive. H. Richard Niebuhr traces the destructiveness that human beings are capable of wreaking upon one another to a defensive posture toward this brokenness. In the face of it, "The color of our lives is anxiety, and self-preservation is our first law. Hence we divide our world into the good and the evil, into friends who will assist us to maintain ourselves awhile and foes intent on our reduction to beings of no significance or to nothingness."[17] But this effort to secure the self through narrow bonds of friendship or somewhat broader political alliances cannot succeed. Intensification of the effort to make it do so leads to the pursuit of more control, which only generates more hostility, leading to more injustice and more violence.

The only way to stop this downward spiral of self-defense and aggression, H. Richard Niebuhr suggests, is the discovery of an ultimate Presence that will secure our selfhood where we are unable to do so. This is a religious and theological issue not only for those with an existing loyalty to a religious tradition, but for all those who look at the last century without flinching. The possibility of humanism and of a social ethics that is more than merely coping is a question of whether there is an ultimate Presence worthy of our trust and to which we can surrender our frantic efforts to control. The issue for all critical thought in light of the twentieth century is whether the ultimate reality that surrounds, undergirds, and permeates social existence is hostile or friendly. Again, in Niebuhr's language, is the One deepest reality behind and within our fragmented, conflicted world God the Enemy or God the Friend? God the Enemy is Niebuhr's name for the final meaning of life when "we interpret everything that happens to us as issuing from animosity or as happening in the realm of destruction."[18] Such an interpretation leads to what Niebuhr calls an "ethics of death," built upon fear of death and the effort to ward it off by trying to control the world.[19] Such an ethics cannot succeed, of course. Maintaining the illusion of success requires a "denial of death" sustained by a mentality that can be called "hypermodernism," the modern impulse to control carried to extremes made possible by new technologies today.[20] If this is our only option, we are at the end not only of Christian humanism but of humanism *tout court*. And if this be the case, we also face the end of all that social ethics has sought to achieve.

The alternative is the discovery of a reality behind the conflicts and brokenness of the world that may be a source of reconciliation, indeed of redemption. But how is this possible in the face of the destructiveness of recent history? Only, I submit, through religious and theological inquiry. This challenge confronts all who seek a social ethic, not only those already seeking to relate religious belief to social existence. I am not attempting to make space for a sectarian Christian ethic or to argue that only in the church can a social ethic exist. My argument concerns the possibility of social ethics for a pluralistic, multireligious world that includes many agnostics and unbelievers. The social ethical question is fundamentally that of how we should live together in such a world. If the answer to this question is based on the conviction that the ultimate reality encompassing us all is one of hostility, our only option is to approach social life warily and on guard. Is that all that can be hoped for? If so, what we seek to achieve in society must be equally minimalist.

Historically within the Christian tradition, a positive response to this problem has often been articulated in terms of a theology of creation, with a strong stress on the human person created in the image and likeness of God. In many theological approaches to social ethics, especially Catholic ones, human reason, understanding, and freedom are seen as analogies or reflections of the wisdom and freedom of God. Hence, all reasonable social endeavors are seen in continuity with the wisdom of God. But if the analysis of this chapter is correct, this is like whistling in the dark to distract oneself from fear of what lurks dimly in the shadows, for today the reliability of human reason and the goodness of freedom are just what have been brought into question. In a world where human reason and freedom have produced the violence of the twentieth century, such a stress on the continuities of the human and the divine suggests not that God is Friend to human beings but more likely Enemy who creates only finally to destroy. Hence, a theologically grounded humanism, if it is possible today, needs a different strategy from one that simply presumes the goodness of the human and then finds a way to say that God affirms this goodness. It is here that the place of the cross in a humanistic vision and a social ethic comes fully into view.

This theology of the cross has played a central role in Christian thought, from Paul to Augustine to Luther to Reinhold Niebuhr. This strand of the tradition is strongly conscious that the goodness of the human creature is distorted by efforts to deny its creaturely status. Echoing the book of Genesis, the dignity of the person as *imago Dei* is warped by an effort to become "like God." Because of the arrogance of pride and a lust for control, human beings have a propensity for evil that leads them to destroy the good and the innocent, ultimately including the One who showed them the meaning and reality of unconditional love. The cross, in this theology, bears witness to the distortion and destruction that human beings are capable of inflicting on themselves, each other, and the whole of creation. The *theologia crucis* of these thinkers has often been used in an anti-humanistic way by cutting short the aspiration for a more humane form of life. Feminist theologians have pointed out that, in some versions, it reflects a characteristic male experience of the dangers of pride and can devalue the struggles of women to achieve independent selfhood.[21] But there is also an interpretation of the cross that can lead to a profound humanism, a humanism that has the depth needed to withstand the disenchantment of what Weber called grandiose reason and the disillusionment produced by recent historical experience. It is a humanism that stakes its hope for humanity on a conviction that compassion, not malevolence, is the ultimate attribute of the One Presence within the shards of our fractured world.

For the cross is an invitation to see that the ultimate mystery surrounding our lives embraces human finitude, including death. The source of all that is shares human suffering, including the misery inflicted by persons in pursuit of an illusory denial of death through self-defensive control. In such a vision, the cross of Jesus Christ does not point to the preeminence of a kind of self-sacrifice that acquiesces in violence or injustice. Rather, it unveils the mystery at the heart of the world as One who has utter compassion for all who suffer. The cross is the revelation of divine solidarity with every human whose experience is that of forsakenness and abandonment.

The cross, in other words, is the preeminent sign of divine friendship and mercy. Thomas Aquinas, relying on Aristotle, saw friendship as the form of love that most leads to a compassionate heart. "[S]ince one who loves another looks upon his friend as another self, he counts his friend's hurt as his own, so that he grieves for his friend's hurt as though he were hurt himself." Thomas applied this description of mercy directly to God: God enters into solidarity with broken humanity through love alone, by loving suffering human beings as friends. God's prime attribute is mercy or *misericordia*. God's heart (*cor*), so to speak, is full of the suffering (*miserum*) human beings experience, and at the cross God is joined in real union with this suffering.[22] The cross is the preeminent sign of this divine solidarity. The sign of the cross, therefore, is an invitation to interpret the ultimate mystery surrounding the fragments and pieces of human history as the reality of compassionate friendship. It opens up the possibility that we might see this encompassing mystery is one of utter solidarity with the victims of the violence of our hypermodern world.[23] Such a God could be called Friend even after the wars of the twentieth century.

The sign of the cross thus opens the possibility of an ethic of compassionate solidarity. Such an ethic has anticipations and analogies in a number of secular philosophical theories of morality. Both David Hume and Adam Smith saw sympathy as the central requisite for social morality. Rawls makes the "advantage of the least advantaged" one of the fundamental principles of justice. Rorty and Judith Shklar call for an ethic whose most basic orientation is avoidance of the infliction of pain and the alleviation of suffering. All these approaches to a social ethic echo the invitation of the sign of the cross. But Smith found a way to combine sympathy with a wholehearted embrace of a free market that far too often grinds the face of the poor. Rawls's recent work has conceded that defense of political liberalism may require not granting the least advantaged quite so central a place as they had in his *Theory of Justice*. Rorty's call for solidarity with the suffering is suffused with such a spirit of ironic detachment that one could not be blamed for asking him, Are you serious?[24]

Each of these approaches contains glimpses and hints of a social ethic under the sign of the cross. But they leave questions unaddressed and unanswered that the cross itself confronts us with. Does sympathy, or justice for the poor, or solidarity with the suffering have any meaning when, for all we can see, it fails to set the world right? Further, these ethical stances are all extrapolations from enlightened self-interest. When they call for personal behavior and social policies that challenge that self-interest, it should not be surprising that they seem dubious and unstable, for they remain silent on whether there is a larger context within which the solidarity of compassion makes ultimate sense. They hint at that context and provide glimpses of a deeper meaning for compassionate solidarity. Indeed, they may draw more inspiration from the love signified by the cross than they do from Plato's dialectic or Kant's pure reason.[24] For this reason I think they are allies of the position I am urging. But when the glimpse of meaning they contain becomes the full "shock of recognition" of what the cross signifies, social ethics under the sign of the cross comes fully into view.[25] It is an ethic that surrenders the effort to construct all moral meaning as an extension of the temporary survival of the modern self into the hands of a compassionate Friend who saves us when we cannot do so for ourselves. Such a surrender—such a faith—can empower active compassion in ways that Hume and Rawls and Rorty seek but are only partially able to attain.

This surrender is not a "sacrifice of the intellect" but a possible (though not necessary) outcome of critical reflection on human experience in light of both the lessons of history and the highest aspirations of the human spirit. In some strands of the Christian tradition, the cross has been invoked in a way that suggests one must choose between Christian belief and the full use of critical intelligence, sacrificing one or the other. For example, in light of his understanding of modern scientific rationality, Weber thought that an abandonment of critical reasoning "is the decisive characteristic of the positively religious man." For Weber, the modern, well-educated believer inevitably reaches the point where faith exists *quia absurdum est*.[26] Religious faith, understood this way, contradicts the humanistic aspiration to develop all human capacities to their fullest. Such an antihumanistic result will be the outcome if the call to carry one's cross is invoked to legitimate an ethic that cannot be supported by the reasoned reflection on human experience that is at the heart of natural law morality. Such an appeal to the cross deserves to be rejected. When we have reached such a level of suspicion toward all personal and social moral visions that irony and even cynicism threaten to become the only options, however, we need to be on guard in a different direction. We need hope in the possibility of solidarity and hope that human aspirations are not utterly futile. The cross as I have interpreted it here is an invitation to such hope. It is an invitation to hope in the possibility of the ultimate fulfillment of all that is most deeply human. This theology of the cross is, therefore, a humanism, not the negation of humanism.

A *theologia crucis* understood in this way is a source of active struggle against the conditions that produce suffering, not of passivity in the face of evil or an oppressive status quo. On this point, the work of my Jesuit colleague Ignacio Ellacuría is illuminating. Ellacuría was one of the six Jesuits murdered by the military in El Salvador on November 16, 1989. His death was a direct result of his active solidarity with the poor in their struggle for justice and his commitment to overcoming the violence of civil war.[27] All Ellacuría's thought and action sought to respond to the reality of the world today, where a vast portion of humankind "is literally and actually crucified by natural oppression and especially by historical and personal oppressions."[28] For Ellacuría, the significance both of social-historical life and of the cross of Jesus Christ is simultaneously manifest through the reality of this crucified people. Active solidarity with the suffering of the poor and oppressed is today an essential dimension of the practical enactment of the meaning of the cross of Christ. The death of Jesus was the consequence of the conflict of Jesus' active proclamation of solidarity of the reign of God in the face of an idolatrous power that is the antithesis of such solidarity.

Ellacuría was a philosopher and social thinker of considerable sophistication.[29] His humanistic commitment called him to use all the tools of reasoned reflection and social analysis at his disposal as a professor and university president. At the same time, however, his *theologia crucis* demanded that he use all these resources to enable him both to see the reality of human suffering more clearly and to respond to it effectively. In such a humanism, he wrote, "Reason and faith merge, in confronting the reality of the poor. Reason must open its eyes to the fact of suffering. Faith, which is sometimes scandal to those without it, sees in the weak of this world the triumph of God, for we see in the poor what salvation must mean and the conversion to which we are called."[30] But Ellacuría was under no illusion that these intellectual resources put him and his fellow intellectuals at the University of Central America in a position to control events in El Salvador. Indeed, he predicted that solidarity with the suffering of the world could lead to a fate like that of Jesus. Such a fate could be the outcome for anyone engaged in action that seeks to take the crucified people down from the cross.[31] This prediction was brutally fulfilled in his own bloody death and the deaths of his companions. An ethic under the sign of the cross, therefore, calls us to open our eyes to the suffering of the world today, draws us into solidarity with those who suffer, and leads to action to alleviate this suffering and overcome its causes. It is the radicalization of the social ethical stance hinted at by Hume's sympathy, Rawls's difference principle, and Jürgen Habermas's call for the inclusion of the voices of the marginalized in social discourse. It is prepared to take the risk of this kind of solidarity in action because, for those with eyes to see, the cross reveals the ultimate mystery surrounding life to be one of saving Friendship.

This appeal to the most particularistic of all Christian symbols may sound like a denial that non-Christians can have a social ethic of compassionate humanism. This need not be so if it pushes the problem of human suffering to the center of the social ethical agenda where it belongs, not only in the Christian community but in our pluralistic world as well. The sign of the cross raises a question that must be faced by every human being, by every culture, by every social ethic, whether religious or secular. As theologian Michael Buckley has argued, no humanism of any sort will be credible today unless we can broaden our understanding of humanism to include not only a celebration of the heights to which cultures can rise but also a compassion for the depths of suffering into which they can fall.[32] "Changing the subject" when the question of the ultimate significance of our bloody history is raised will simply not do. Followers of all religions and of none must engage the questions raised by this history.

This does not mean that every such humanism will be explicitly Christian. For example, Gandhi remained fully a Hindu while also acknowledging that his encounter with the cross deeply affected the way he came to understand his own religion. He believed that Jesus "belongs not solely to

Christianity, but to the entire world."[33] Gandhi took a poem about war, the *Bhagavad Gita*, and reread it as a parable of nonviolence and solidarity with outcastes, both through the influence of reform movements indigenous to Hinduism and also because he learned to read the *Gita* in a new way through his interaction with the Christian story of the cross. In the same way, all interpretations of ultimate meaning must be present in full and free discussion if we are to attain a credible humanism and a credible social ethic today. But taking the cross seriously does mean that the problem of human suffering must be directly confronted by any would-be humanism. The pursuit of universality in ethics, therefore, means that the reality of human suffering wherever it occurs must be central in the quest for some form of common morality.

But the final question remains the religious one raised by Ellacuría's death and by Jesus' death as well. Neither of these deaths has in fact overcome the injustice and suffering of the crucified people of the world. Intellectual clarity and practical realism demand that we acknowledge that our own efforts to alleviate this suffering in a society built on principles of compassion, solidarity, and justice for those at the margins will not eliminate it either. There are two options when we reach this limit point. Either we conclude that the inability to generate a scheme for the elimination of suffering means the end of humanism, or we discover a source of hope that outstrips all our ability to plan, to control, and to succeed. This is the postmodern dilemma stated in its full depth, for the postmodern dilemma, in my view, is finally religious. The answer pointed to by the sign of the cross is that there is in fact a power vastly greater than anything we can muster, and that power is in saving solidarity with all who suffer, with all who are abandoned, with all who cry out, "My God, my God, why have you forsaken me?" (Psalm 22: 1; Mark 15: 34). Simone Weil pointed to this radical form of suffering and called it affliction. When we are pierced through by such suffering, Weil said, we are "nailed to the very center of the universe. It is the true center; it is not in the middle; it is beyond space and time; it is God. . . . It is at the intersection of creation and its Creator. This point of intersection is the point of intersection of the arms of the Cross."[34] When all is said and done, it is here we can find the source of a humanism that can sustain a social ethic based on compassion. It is here we might discover a hope that is not based on the illusion that we control the world. And here, when we are faced with the choice of whether to despair or to say "into your hands I commend my spirit" (Luke 23, 46), we find the deepest source of strength to think and act in solidarity with those who suffer. This choice between despair and solidarity confronts us not only *in extremis* but daily, as we travel *in via* through history. It is, I think, the choice addressed by a social ethics under the sign of the cross. Such an ethic both responds to and reveals a God who is Friend even in the midst of the afflictions of history. It can save the threatened aspirations of humanism. It can make credible the Christian hope in resurrection and the final victory of joy.

NOTES

1. See Jacques Maritain, *Integral Humanism: Temporal and Spiritual Problems of a New Christendom*, trans. Joseph W. Owens (New York: Scribner's, 1968); Henri de Lubac, *The Drama of Atheist Humanism*, trans. Edith M. Riley (New York: New American Library, 1963).

2. René Descartes, *Discourse on Method,* in *Discourse on Method and Meditations*, trans. Laurence J. Lafleur (Indianapolis: Bobbs-Merrill, 1960), 8.

3. Charles Taylor, *Sources of the Self: The Making of the Modern Identity* (Cambridge, Mass.: Harvard University Press, 1989), 152.

4. Descartes, *Discourse on Method,* 45.

5. Albert Borgmann, *Crossing the Postmodern Divide* (Chicago: University of Chicago Press, 1992), 2.

6. Ernst Troeltsch, *The Social Teaching of the Christian Churches*, trans. Olive Wyon (New York: Harper Torchbook, 1960), vol. 2: 1012–13.

7. Max Weber, "Science as a Vocation," in *From Max Weber: Essays in Sociology*, trans. and ed. H. H. Gerth and C. Wright Mills (New York: Oxford University Press, 1958), esp. 148, 155.

8. Ibid., 152.

9. Ibid., 155–56.

10. Richard Rorty, *Contingency, Irony, and Solidarity* (New York: Cambridge University Press, 1989), 45.

11. Weber, "Science as a Vocation," 145.

12. See Plato, *Republic,* 338c. In *The Collected Dialogues of Plato*, ed. Edith Hamilton and Huntington Cairns (New York: Random House, 1961).

13. Rorty, *Contingency, Irony, and Solidarity*, 29.

14. See UNICEF, *1996 State of the World's Children Report* (Oxford: Oxford University Press, 1996), chap. 1.

15. Augustine, *The City of God*, trans. Henry Bettenson (London: Penguin, 1984), book IV, chap. 3, p. 138.

16. Immanuel Kant, *Critique of Pure Reason*, trans. Norman Kemp Smith (New York: St. Martin's, 1965), 635.

17. H. Richard Niebuhr, *The Responsible Self: An Essay in Christian Moral Philosophy* (New York: Harper & Row, 1963), 140–41.

18. Ibid., 142.

19. Ibid., 143–44, 176.

20. These phrases are borrowed from Ernest Becker, *The Denial of Death* (New York: Free Press, 1973), and Borgmann, *Crossing the Postmodern Divide*, 12–19, 78–109. H. Richard Niebuhr's discussion of the "ethics of death" has many parallels to his brother's analysis of sin. See Reinhold Niebuhr, *The Nature and Destiny of Man*, 2 vols. (New York: Scribner's, 1964), vol. 1: chaps. 7 and 8. Reinhold Niebuhr and Ernest Becker are both indebted to Søren Kierkegaard's *The Concept of Dread*.

21. See Valerie Saiving, "The Human Situation: A Feminine View," in Carol Christ and Judith Plaskow, eds., *Womanspirit Rising: A Feminist Reader in Religion* (New York: Harper & Row, 1979), 25–42, for a seminal statement of this argument. See also Judith Plaskow, *Sex, Sin, and Grace: Women's Experience and the Theologies of Reinhold Niebuhr and Paul Tillich* (Washington, D.C.: University Press of America, 1980).

22. Thomas Aquinas, *Summa Theologiae*, II-II, q. 30, art. 2. The translation used here is by the Fathers of the English Dominican Province, *Summa Theologica* (Allen, Tex.: Christian Classics, 1981), 5 vols.

23. The phrase "solidarity with victims" is Matthew Lamb's. See his *Solidarity with Victims: Toward a Theology of Social Transformation* (New York: Crossroad, 1982).

24. See Richard Rorty, "The Seer of Prague," a review of three works by the Czech philosopher Jan Patocka, *New Republic* (July 1, 1991): 40.

25. See David Tracy, *Plurality and Ambiguity: Hermeneutics, Religion, Hope* (San Francisco: Harper & Row, 1987), chap. 5, esp. 109–11, for a discussion of both partial and full recognition of the meaning of a religious symbol such as the cross.

26. Weber, "Science as a Vocation," 154.

27. For the best account of the events leading up to these murders and the subsequent efforts to insure impunity for the guilty, see Martha Doggett, *Death Foretold: The Jesuit Murders in El Salvador* (Washington, D.C.: Georgetown University Press, 1993).

28. Ignacio Ellacuría, "The Crucified People," in Ignacio Ellacuría and Jon Sobrino, eds., *Mysterium Liberationis: Fundamental Concepts of Liberation Theology* (Maryknoll, N.Y.: Orbis, 1993), 580.

29. For a fine study of Ellacuría's work, see Kevin F. Burke, *The Ground Beneath the Cross: The Theology of Ignacio Ellacuría* (Washington, D.C.: Georgetown University Press, 2000).

30. Ellacuría, "The Task of a Christian University," in Jon Sobrino, Ignacio Ellacuría, et al., eds., *Companions of Jesus: The Jesuit Martyrs of El Salvador* (Maryknoll, N.Y.: Orbis, 1992), 149–50.

31. See Jon Sobrino, *The Principle of Mercy: Taking the Crucified People from the Cross*

(Maryknoll, N.Y.: Orbis, 1994), esp. chap. 3, "The Crucified Peoples," an essay dedicated "In Memory of Ignacio Ellacuría."

32. See Michael J. Buckley, "Christian Humanism and Human Misery: A Challenge to the Jesuit University." in Francis M. Lazarus, ed., *Faith, Discovery, Service: Perspectives on Jesuit Education* (Milwaukee: Marquette University Press, 1992), 77–105.

33. Gandhi, *The Law of Love*, ed. Anand T. Hingorani (Bharatiya Vidya Bhavan: 1962), 111. Cited in James W. Douglass, *The Non-Violent Cross: A Theology of Revolution and Peace* (New York: Macmillan, 1968), 56.

34. Simone Weil, *Waiting for God* (New York: Harper & Row, 1973), 135–36.

PART TWO THE CHURCH IN AMERICAN PUBLIC LIFE

5

Religion, Morality, and Politics in the United States

Discussion of the relationship between religion and politics in the United States has been vigorous throughout the past two decades. Both the intensity of the discussion and the diverse backgrounds of the participants suggest that many thoughtful people think something important is happening in the zone where religion and politics interact today. But the agreement does not go much further than the bare fact of the significance of this heightened interaction. Some observers are cautiously hopeful that politically significant activity by religious groups can help transform American public life for the better, whereas others are fearful that this activity could shatter the fragile moral bonds that hold this pluralistic society together. This overview of some of the key issues in the United States attempts to make some contribution to the former outcome.

THE NEW CHRISTIAN RIGHT

University of Virginia sociologist Jeffrey K. Hadden's 1985 Presidential Address to the Society for the Scientific Study of Religion provides a point of entry into the topic. It is a sympathetic study of the reasons for the influence of fundamentalist Christians such as Jerry Falwell and Pat Robertson.[1] The debates about this "Christian right" have raised a number of issues that are central to the broader religion-and-politics question, so it will be useful to consider them. Hadden begins with some interesting remarks that challenge the sociological model of religion in modern society known as "secularization theory." According to this model, the modern history of religion has been a linear process in which religion has progressively lost influence in the public arena. It projects a future in which religious believers become fewer and fewer, and less and less politically potent. Hadden does not see compelling evidence for this secularization hypothesis. He thinks that it represents a hasty generalization from the decline of religious belief in the globally unrepresentative case of Western Europe. Hadden does not reject the concept of secularization entirely but instead proposes to give it a more restricted meaning: the movement from a religiously legitimated state to a secularly legitimated state. This definition of secularization does not necessarily imply a decline of religious belief or behavior. Rather, it focuses attention on "the legal and quasi-legal institutional relationships between religion and regime."[2]

Hadden believes that his definition opens up the possibility of understanding the public role of religion in a more accurate way than does the linear secularization model. It provides a way to account for the fact that countries with established or quasi-established churches, such as England and Sweden, have low rates of religious participation among their people, whereas a country with no establishment, such as the United States, has notably higher levels of belief and practice. The linear, across-the-board view of secularization cannot explain this apparent anomaly, but Hadden's approach enables him to propose the following explanatory hypothesis: "The greater the degree to which modern states legitimize their existence in secular rather than religious foundations, the greater the autonomy of religious institutions to pursue their own interests vis-à-vis the state."[3] This is another way of saying that the free exercise of religion is enhanced by the elimination of religious establishment. But Hadden's formulation has the advantage of pointing out that the free exercise of religion is not simply a private affair; it can have powerful cultural and political impact. Indeed, Hadden asserts that religions possess a unique capacity "to mobilize social movements in pursuit of reform, rebellion, or revolution" when the conditions are right.[4]

Hadden then uses this sociological framework to develop an argument that the rise of the "religious right" is not simply a temporary pause or aberration in the relentless march toward declining religious influence in public affairs. He argues that significant social movements to change the conditions of public life can be expected to emerge whenever a collectivity of persons identifies certain social conditions as intolerable and also has the resources to mobilize for change. The "religious right" possesses both of these prerequisites. It has a normative criterion of the "intolerable" and the organized resources to move people to collective action in its far-flung electronic network.

Normatively, those segments of fundamentalist and evangelical Christianity that form the constituency of "televangelists" such as Falwell and Robertson have become the principal custodians of what Hadden calls "the creation myth of America." This myth "resonates with an imagery of God's dominion, humanity's unfaithfulness to stewardship, the call for repentance, and the promise of redemption."[5] Because of the special place this myth assigns to America in the providence of God, all these images are invoked to interpret the life of the nation in religious terms. Also, this implies that special religious and moral responsibilities rest on America's shoulders, namely, those proclaimed in the Bible as interpreted in a peculiarly American way. Seen in this light, there are numerous aspects of recent American life that suggest that the nation has rebelled against the dominion of God, stands under judgment, and is in need of repentance. The assassination of public leaders, the loss of the war in Vietnam, impotence in the face of terrorism and hostage crises, Watergate, high crime rates, family breakdown, the drug culture—all of these factors seem incongruous with the image of an America under God. They are "intolerable" and point to a "deeper and fundamental cultural malady," a malady that will be cured only if we "repent and make things right with our maker . . . [so] we can resume our providential role in his divine plan."[6]

Evangelical Protestantism has traditionally exhibited two contrary kinds of response to such "crises of dominion." The first is based on a premillennial eschatology that is convinced that things are getting so bad that only the return of Christ can stem the tide. This eschatology recommends saving as many people as possible while faithfully awaiting the end. It lacks, and even delegitimates, a sense of the public/political mission of Christians. The alternative view, postmillennialism, calls for an active engagement in social and public affairs to set things back on course. The religious right is caught in a tension between these two views. Its fundamentalist reading of the Bible pulls it toward a premillenialist eschatology, which has a strong privatizing effect on its understanding of Christian faith. The fact that the religious right has also become the bearer of the myth of the special dominion of God in the life of America as a nation, however, pushes it toward much greater public engagement, even on the political level. As Hadden puts it, "Falwell is still preaching premillennialist theology, but the dominion covenant is tugging at his soul."[7] The outcome of this tug-of-war within the heart of the religious right will have a significant impact on the interaction of religion and politics in this country. Hadden's prediction of the outcome is quite rosy. He believes that there are powerful forces operating to pull the religious right much closer to the center of the nation's public life than some of its fundamentalist tenets would seem to prescribe. "If Jesus isn't coming very soon, then it behooves all who are in positions of leadership and responsibility to recognize and protect our fragile interdependence on this planet."[8]

One can question, however, whether Hadden's sociological analysis goes deep enough to ground his hope for this outcome. The question of whether premillennial apocalypticism or postmillennial engagement is the appropriate Christian stance is at root a theological question. Also, once engagement has been judged appropriate, a series of partly theological and partly political questions surfaces. Two nonfundamentalist evangelical scholars have addressed these issues in ways that shed light on the broader debate. Richard Mouw, of Fuller Theological Seminary, is a strong supporter of the effort to relate evangelical Christianity to the common life of society. He argues that this effort demands a sophisticated theological understanding of how to approach political realities that is presently lacking in the Christian right. For example, Mouw cites the widely publicized critical judgments about Bishop Desmond Tutu made by Falwell after a brief visit to South Africa. In Mouw's judgment, Falwell "was not just wrong in his judgment, he was in way over his head." And he was in over his head because fundamentalist activists "have been skilled communicators with very little to communicate by way of a carefully developed Christian perspective on the important issues of public life."[9]

Mouw maintains that Falwell and others are caught in a conflict between several theological impulses, with resulting ambivalence in their approach to political life. First, they oscillate between cultural pessimism (whose one hope is that believers will be "raptured" out of an inhospitable society before the final "tribulations") and cultural optimism (America is God's "city on a hill," a Christian nation). Second, they fluctuate between anti-intellectualism (modern rationality is both deadening to the heart and threatening to orthodoxy) and a predilection for grand classificatory schemes (the "Christian philosophy of life" versus "secular humanism"). Finally, they are caught in a conflict between "a strong individualism and an equally strong tendency toward mystical nationalism."[10] These tensions are interconnected with each other in complex ways. Common to each of them is an unresolved question about how Christian faith, rooted in the Bible, is to be related to what Hadden calls the "secular foundations" that provide legitimation for the government of this country.

If secular legitimation of government provides the conditions needed for vital public activity by religious groups, as Hadden maintains, the question that must be faced is this: are these religious groups prepared to affirm these secular warrants for the government of a pluralistic society? If they believe that all arguments about morality and politics that are not explicitly and directly biblical are a form of Godless "secular humanism," they will be unable to do so and will be logically forced to reject the legitimacy of religious freedom and perhaps democracy itself.[11] Most fundamentalists and evangelicals insist that they have no such agenda, but their lack of theological clarity about the relation between the biblical and secular warrants for political activity makes this activity somewhat confused and unpredictable.

This point has been made with considerable force by a second evangelical critic of the Christian right, Dean C. Curry, of the Department of Political Science at Messiah College, in Grantham, Pennsylvania. Curry notes that evangelical Christianity in this country is internally quite diverse in its political views, ranging from Falwell and Robertson on the right to Jim Wallis and the Sojourners community on the left. Despite their diversity, these groups are held together as a self-conscious community or subculture by the doctrine of the final authority of scripture. This conviction provides them "with their agenda for biblical living."[12] As this agenda has expanded from exclusive concern with personal salvation to concern with the public sphere, "most evangelical elites have come to accept the idea of a biblical—i.e., Christian—politics."[13] Curry traces this understanding of politics back to epistemological foundations. There is one truth, and one source of our knowledge of this truth—the Bible. "There is no truth in the realm of politics apart from special revelation."[14]

Curry has two responses to this line of reasoning, the first theological and the second practical. Theologically, he asserts that the notion that the Bible is the sole source of political wisdom "marks a break with the historic orthodox Christian understanding of biblical hermeneutics and epistemology."[15] To back up this claim, he briefly surveys the thought of Augustine, Thomas Aquinas, Luther, and Calvin to retrieve the notions of "general revelation" and "common grace," both of which imply that genuine knowledge of the ethical can be mediated through nature, human reason, and the ordering of history. In other words, Curry is attempting to convince evangelicals that they should reconsider their abandonment of the tradition of natural law, and he marshals familiar biblical and theological reasons why they should do so (e.g., the creation of all human beings in the image of God means that the basic principles of morality apply to all persons and are accessible to all persons).

Second, Curry raises practical problems for the idea of "biblical politics." Though there are clear biblical imperatives to act fairly, justly, and in a spirit of love and compassion, one may also ask, "What is the biblical approach to tax reform? What is the biblical view of aid to the Nicaraguan *contras*? What is the biblical perspective for dealing with South Africa?"[16] In order to test whether the Bible actually informs the way evangelicals answer such questions, Curry has conducted a somewhat informal experiment. He analyzed all the articles dealing with Central America that appeared in five of the major evangelical journals (*Fundamentalist Journal*, *Moody Monthly*, *Christianity Today*, *The Reformed Journal*, and *Sojourners*) between 1980 and 1985. Of the 169 articles surveyed, he found that only four contained any scriptural or theological references, and none of the four attempted to construct a systematic argument from biblical doctrine.[17] Curry admits that this does not invalidate the idea of biblical politics; the biblical texts could be operative in shaping conclusions in an implicit way. Because the ideological perspectives of the magazines differ so widely, however, if they are rooted in the scriptures it would appear that their authors and editors are reading different Bibles. Curry concludes that the central problem arises from "a failure on the part of American evangelical theology to acknowledge the limits of biblical revelation and the validity of general revelation."[18] One could add that it is also a result of some highly selective reading both of the Bible itself and of the social realities to which Christians are trying to respond.

William A. Stahl, of Luther College, in Regina, Saskatchewan, has offered an interpretation of the rise of the new Christian right in the United States that has notable implications for the larger discussion of religion and politics. Stahl argues that the movement is attractive to those who have come to perceive a moral vacuum at the center of public life. This vacuum has been created by the insistence that morality—and, even more so, religious morality—is a private matter. Politics thus becomes simply the brokering of interests. This form of politics, which Stahl refers to as "contemporary liberalism," does not possess the resources needed to respond to people's need for a sense of meaning and purpose in modern social life, which is increasingly complex, disorienting, and alienated. In his words, "Contemporary liberalism lacks the means of self-transcendence which could persuade people to put the good of the community ahead of their own selfishness. In making all moral questions purely a matter for the individual, liberals are in effect denying that there *is* a public good."[19] The simplistic understanding of the common good found among members of the new religious right, however, will not fill the void left by this withdrawal of morality into the private sphere, Stahl argues, because it is not really a vision of the *common* good at all. Rather, it is a set of moral views about how private life should be lived transposed into a political agenda. Though Stahl begs the very important question of how to distinguish private and public morality, his main point is valid. Until we develop a stronger vision of the moral content of public life, reactions such as that of the Christian right will be likely to continue.

A "CATHOLIC MOMENT"?

A second stream of writings on the religion-and-politics question deals with the contributions to American public life by the Roman Catholic community in this country. Naturally, much of this material comes from Catholic authors, to be discussed shortly. But it is noteworthy that several thinkers with Protestant backgrounds have undertaken substantive assessments of the strengths and weaknesses of the Catholic community's engagement in the public domain today. Indeed, both William Lee Miller, of the University of Virginia, and Richard John Neuhaus, formerly a Lutheran pastor and now a Catholic priest, expect a distinctively "Catholic moment" to emerge in the history of the relation between Christianity and modern American culture and politics. Toward the end of his engaging historical and constructive study, *The First Liberty: Religion and the American Republic*, Miller declares:

> In perhaps the most remarkable of all remarkable developments of this New World's system of religious liberty, the Roman Catholic Christianity against which its founding movements were rebelling has come, after two centuries, to be its single most important religious presence. It is becoming one of the most significant sources of political understanding as well. . . . [I]n the late twentieth century, now is the moment for Catholicism to have its desirable effect upon the America within which at last it is coming to be at home.[20]

Neuhaus goes further, publishing a book entitled *The Catholic Moment*. By this phrase he means,

> This . . . is the moment in which the Roman Catholic Church in the world can and should be the lead church in proclaiming the Gospel. This can and should also be the moment in which the Roman Catholic Church in the United States assumes its rightful role in the culture-forming task of constructing a religiously informed public philosophy for the American experiment in ordered liberty.[21]

Both of these statements probably have both our Protestant and Catholic forebears turning over in their graves. Despite the similarity in vocabulary, however, Miller and Neuhaus hope for very different results from what they see as this so-called Catholic moment. They significantly diverge in their judgments of the distinctive contribution Catholicism can make to American public life today. I would put the difference this way: Miller implicitly relies on the more optimistic Thomistic strand of Catholic thought about the possibilities of social existence, whereas Neuhaus stresses more pessimistic themes characteristic of the Augustinian (and Lutheran) tradition.

For Miller, the potential Catholic contribution arises from its ability to address two problems that are particularly urgent for the American republic today. The first of these is the inadequacy of an individualistic culture in a world that is daily growing more interconnected and socially dense. From the beginning, the United States has been engaged in a protracted effort to secure the freedom and rights of its citizens. Side by side with this pursuit of "liberation," the Founders were also aware of the need for a citizenry committed to the common good. But because of the vicissitudes of history, Protestant pietism and secular rationalism (especially in its utilitarian, commercial forms) have given American culture a distinctively individualistic bent. In contrast with this, the concept of the common good—the *res publica*—is a central theme running down through the centuries of Catholic social thought. Miller calls this tradition "personalist communitarianism"—"that sense of life being bound up with life . . . the awareness, as part of the fundamental religious insights and commitment, of the interweaving of human beings in community." Something like this tradition "is the necessary base for a true republic in the interdependent world of the third century of this nation's existence. And the Roman Catholic community is the most likely source of it—the largest and intellectually and spiritually most potent institution that is the bearer of such ideas."[22]

Catholicism also possesses resources needed to address a second cultural problem identified by Miller: the disparagement of moral reason. Protestant evangelicalism, with its excessive emphasis on the "heart" rather than the "head" in the moral-religious life, has combined with the skepticism of much of the secular philosophical tradition to undermine confidence in reasoned argument in public life. These historical currents were also both partly caused and partly reinforced by sustained exposure to the dynamics of a deeply pluralistic society. The result is a distinctly American form of moral relativism already observed by Tocqueville in the 1830s: a "combination of a kind of privatism with a soft, standards-destroying populist conformity."[23] This is dangerously inadequate in the face of the problems of the early twenty-first century. Miller concludes, with a little help from John Courtney Murray, that there must be "some perception of 'truths' we hold, in reason and conscience, sufficient for our common life not to be a pure power struggle of interests but a meaningful civic argument. There will need to be, for the same reason, a perception of the intrinsic goods of human life, including the common goods."[24] We need, in short, a revival of both the tradition of the common good and the tradition of reason in public life. The Catholic tradition is not the only bearer of these traditions, but it is potentially the most significant one.

Miller also argues that, if such a Catholic contribution to public life is to be realized, the Catholic Church will have to continue to appropriate the insights into the central importance of religious freedom and the self-rule of the people that have long been part of America's Protestant-Christian and secular-philosophical heritages. If mutual interaction of Catholic, Protestant, and secular philosophical traditions were to produce the creative result that Miller hopes for, it would reveal the positive potential of American pluralism at its best—"a reciprocating deep pluralism in which several communities learn from each other for the better."[25] This hopeful vision puts one in mind of the work of Aquinas, who saw Aristotle not as a threat, but as a dialogue partner, and who saw political life not simply as a restraint on human sinfulness, but as a positive expression of the social nature of human beings. In the same way, Miller regards the Catholic tradition of reasoned discourse as an avenue that opens the way to positive interaction between biblical faith and the secular philosophical warrants for U.S. political institutions, including the institutions of religious freedom. At the Second Vatican Council, this interaction helped Catholicism shed its past commitment to church establishment. It can now positively contribute to the development of a more communitarian ethos as the basis of U.S. politics at a time when this is urgently needed.

Richard John Neuhaus has another reading of what he calls "the Catholic moment." He has taken as his subject "Christian existence in the modern world and, more specifically, in American society."[26] On a worldwide scale, this was also the subject of one of the major documents of the Second Vatican Council, *Gaudium et Spes*. Neuhaus clearly intends to include himself when he refers to "anyone who wants to influence the interpretation of the Council."[27] In seeking to exert such influence, he defines the problem to be addressed by the church differently than Miller does and, not surprisingly, makes very different recommendations about how to respond to it.

The problem, simply stated, is lack of faith in Jesus Christ. The central task of the church, therefore, "is to alert the world to the true nature of its crisis. The greatest threat to the world is not political or economic or military. The greatest problem in the church is not institutional decline or disarray. *The* crisis of this time and every time is the crisis of unbelief."[28] Further, this unbelief not only exists beyond the boundaries of the church but within it as well. In fact, unbelief is wittingly or unwittingly being encouraged by several significant currents present within theology itself since the Council. This insidious form of unbelief or pseudo-faith among theologians results from collapsing the promise of the kingdom of God into the objectives of a political ideology. The terms Neuhaus uses to refer to the supposed collapse of faith and theology into politics and ideology are highly charged and occur repeatedly throughout his book: "loss of transcendence," "premature closure," "accommodation," "apostasy," "idolatry." He asserts that the leadership of the Roman Catholic church in the United States "seems hardly to be trying" to keep politics under moral-religious judgment.[29] Even more harshly, he asserts that liberation theology collapses the eschatological promise of the kingdom of God "into the 'now' of the liberation process." According to Neuhaus, this is because "the dominant liberation theologians exclude the transcendent as a matter of principle."[30]

In response to the contemporary problem so defined (in my view very unfairly), Neuhaus reaffirms that the church's principal task today is a recovery of its ability to proclaim the transcendent promise of the gospel. Christian commitment to the gospel relativizes all political objectives and activities. Thus, "it is one of the greatest obligations of the church to remind the world that it is incomplete, that reality is still awaiting something." And that which it awaits is not a new political achievement but the gift of salvation, the gift of the kingdom of God. This gift is "already" present in the life of the church itself, but it is only a partial presence, for the fulfillment of the promise has "not yet" fully occurred. Thus, in this time "between the times," the church stands in a "paradoxical" relationship with the world. In words that echo the 1975 "Hartford Appeal for Theological Affirmation," Neuhaus states that the church must stand "against the world" and all of the world's imperious delusions and tendencies to idolatry. In this very "againstness," however, the church is "for the world," bearing witness to the one and only hope for redemption, the promised kingdom of God. As a sign of its faith in this promise, the church must seek to synthesize whatever genuine truths are to be found in secular thought with the truth of the gospel. Such a synthesis, however, will never be final and complete; this side of the Parousia there will always be great tension between authentic Christian faith and the world of politics. This paradox of the church in the world "cannot be solved; it can only be superseded" by the final coming of the kingdom.[31]

This theology leads Neuhaus to conclusions about the relationship between religion and politics that some might regard as internally self-contradictory but that he would no doubt call paradoxical. The judgment that all political ideologies and achievements are incomplete in light of the promise of the kingdom of God leads him to forcefully reject liberation theology and what he regards as the moralistic and overpoliticized teachings of the National Conference of Catholic Bishops in their pastoral letters on war and peace and economic justice. At the same time, the legitimacy of seeking to synthesize Christian faith with whatever partial truths are to be found in the secular sphere leads him to affirm the liberal democracy of the American experiment on theological grounds. Precisely because American liberal democracy makes no claim to provide ultimate salvation, and because it provides a reasonable way of securing rightly ordered freedom in an imperfect world, Neuhaus concludes that there are "distinctly Roman Catholic warrants for sustaining the American experiment in republican democracy."[32] And following George Weigel, Neuhaus argues that the leadership of the Catholic community in the United States has abandoned the theology that provides these warrants and has in fact largely turned against the American experiment itself.[33]

Because I have elsewhere criticized this thesis as Weigel originally argued it, I will not repeat that evaluation here.[34] Suffice it to say that I find it odd that Neuhaus so easily adopts such an enthusiastic and uncritical stance toward the neoconservative political agenda for U.S. politics. His theology seems to lose its critical edge precisely at the point where one would expect it to be most needed, namely, in making a creative response to American political life that goes beyond the reigning ideological alternatives. Also, I think one might be forgiven for suspecting that his repeated suggestion that both U.S. Catholic leaders and Latin American liberation theologians are crypto-apostates and quasi-idolaters is related to the goals of neoconservative politics. One can ask whether the political or the theological is the controlling factor in Neuhaus's argument.

What, then, is one to make of the so-called Catholic moment? First, Neuhaus is certainly correct that Catholic and indeed all authentic Christian faith must avoid any confusion of salvation with political achievement. Second, both Neuhaus and Miller (and the Christian right as well) are convinced that something is amiss in the public moral life of modern society and that the church has a duty to help correct this. Their understandings of the nature of this duty, however, are very different. One can characterize these diverse understandings with the help of Eugene TeSelle's recent study of Augustine's theology of politics.[35] TeSelle argues that the relation between the heavenly and earthly cities is not entirely clear in Augustine's own writing and has received several different interpretations in practice through the centuries.

First, Christians can view themselves as resident aliens in the earthly city, granting the political life only provisional significance as a source of order and peace. TeSelle maintains that this is probably the most authentic interpretation of Augustine and that it may well be the required Christian response in historical circumstances where Christians see virtually no possibility of changing secular society. Though Neuhaus's analysis supports efforts to produce such change through political activity by Christians, his skepticism about whether "there is a known direction in which culture, or the world, should be moving" makes one dubious about how seriously he views the prospects.[36] It is for this reason that I think that Neuhaus is quite close to this pessimistic form of Augustinianism. And, as TeSelle observes, the earthly city is quite willing to tolerate the presence of Christians of this sort in its midst, "as long as they do not interfere with the exercise of power or the making of money."[37] I think this is where Neuhaus's analysis would finally leave us.

A second interpretation of Augustine grants the heavenly city an earthly presence, and does so by identifying the church with the city of God and giving it superiority over earthly rulers. The so-called political Augustinianism of the Middle Ages that gave the church authority over the state is an example of this. Some elements of the new Christian right seem to seek its revival. It is, however, completely contrary to the teachings of the Second Vatican Council as well as the U.S. Constitution. Third, TeSelle argues that it is not un-Augustinian to affirm that Christians should "maintain a kind of dual citizenship, living in the earthly city with the critical distance of an alien even while trying to make it the best city possible."[38] Quoting James Dougherty, TeSelle calls this view of the relation between the two cities "analogical"; it "finds Jerusalem, old and new, within the secular, historical city, and proposes there to redeem the Time Being."[39]

RETHINKING THE BOUNDARIES

This analogical view of the relation between the two cities does not conflate, much less identify, them. But it does insist that there is an element of the sacred within the temporal order. In 1987, Leslie Griffin, a law professor and moral theologian, published an informative essay examining the way the relation between the spiritual and the temporal has been understood in the official teachings of the Roman Catholic Church over the past hundred years. Griffin's central thesis is that there has been a subtle but important shift in the way the magisterium has understood this relationship, especially since John XXIII and Vatican II. This shift is not from a position that denies the importance of Christian activity in the temporal order to one that affirms it. Rather, the shift has been one in which "the spiritual and temporal aspects of human life have moved closer to one another, become more interrelated, more interdependent."[40] The *locus classicus* for the discussion of this increased interdependence is *Gaudium et Spes*, which affirms that love of God and neighbor cannot be separated, and that neglect of one's duties in the social order "jeopardizes [one's] eternal salvation."[41] Avery Dulles, who strongly stresses the transcendence of the gospel and its distinction from any political ideology, has also given a succinct summary of the Council's emphasis in *Gaudium et Spes* and *Lumen Gentium* on the intimate connection between faith and social responsibility:

> The church, rather than being a *societas perfecta* alongside the secular state, is seen as a pilgrim people, subject to the vicissitudes of history and sharing in the concerns and destiny of the whole human race (*Gaudium et Spes*, 1). The church is linked to the world as the sacrament of universal unity (*Lumen Gentium*, 1), a sign and safeguard of the transcendence of the human person (*Gaudium et Spes*, 76), a defender of authentic human rights (*Gaudium et*

Spes, 41). In a dynamically evolving world (*Gaudium et Spes*, 4) social and political liberation pertains integrally to the process of redemption and hence is not foreign to the mission of the church. . . . The church's concern for human solidarity, peace, and justice, therefore, is not confined to the sphere of supernatural salvation in a life beyond.[42]

As Griffin points out, and as the intensity of the religion-and-politics debate makes clear, the affirmation of this sort of interconnection between the spiritual and temporal leads to a host of thorny questions: the relation between biblical/theological and natural law approaches to morality; the degree to which church teachings on social matters should propose concrete solutions to pressing problems; the distinctive roles of lay persons and clergy in social or political activities; the problem of maintaining church unity in the midst of the inevitable conflicts that arise from involvement in the political domain. Griffin rather understates the situation when she observes that the developments stimulated by the Council have led to "increased difficulty in drawing clearly established boundaries between the moral and religious areas of life, or between the temporal and the spiritual."[43]

In a masterful discussion of these questions, J. Bryan Hehir gives a succinct summary of the Council's perspective that can aid in determining where the lines should be drawn. Relying on John Courtney Murray's distinction between society and the state, Hehir argues that *Gaudium et Spes* impelled the church more deeply into interaction with the modern world, rendering it "more political" in broad social terms, while at the same time *Dignitatis Humanae* (the Declaration on Religious Freedom) has made the church "less political" in its juridical relationship to the state.[44] Thus, Hehir's essay provides a theological counterpart to Hadden's sociological thesis that disestablishment and religious freedom can be conducive of greater public activity by religious communities. In this activity, the central principle is that the church's social role must always be religious in nature and finality. Nevertheless, the exercise of this role will frequently have politically significant consequences. The church's proper competence is that of addressing the moral and religious dimensions of political questions. The result will be an "indirect" engagement in the political arena. And this is where the hard questions arise. In Hehir's words, "The casuistry of keeping the Church's engagement in the political order 'indirect' involves an endless series of choices and distinctions. But the effort must be made precisely because the alternatives to an indirect engagement are equally unacceptable: either a politicized church or a church in retreat from human affairs. The first erodes the transcendence of the gospel; the second betrays the incarnational dimension of Christian faith."[45] Although this general framework does not provide ready-made answers to the question of when the church has crossed the line into illegitimately "direct" political action, it does provide a framework for serious argument about where this line is located.

A similar conclusion about the need for careful discernment of the line between legitimate and illegitimate political activity by the church has been reached on nontheological grounds by A. James Reichley, of the Brookings Institution. Reichley's study is a substantial one and cannot be dealt with adequately here, but one point is worth noting. Like William Lee Miller, Reichley has concluded from his study of the origins of American constitutional arrangements that the Founders did not intend to exclude religion from public influence. Indeed, the Founders believed that religion was an important support for the moral virtue on which the success of a democratic republic depends. Thus, Reichley states that the Founders "sought to construct a charter of fundamental law that would maintain a balance between the dual, and they believed complementary, goals of a largely secular state and a society shaped by religion."[46] Moral values and moral virtues are the mediating link between the religious and the political, and action to strengthen this link is the proper way for the churches to influence the political. In Reichley's view, the most important social role of the churches is the nurturing of virtue in their members and in the citizenry at large. This will help humanize economic life and give moral direction to our democratic society. Beyond the educational role of nurturing virtue, however, Reichley also believes that the churches can make a limited, though very important, contribution to the policy process:

> Up to a point, participation by the churches in the formation of public policy, particularly on issues with clear moral content, probably strengthens their ability to perform this nurturing function. If the churches were to remain silent on issues like civil rights or nuclear war or abortion, they would soon lose moral credibility. But if the churches become too involved in the

hurly-burly of routine politics, they will eventually appear to their members and to the general public as special pleaders for ideological causes or even as appendages to transitory political factions. Each church must decide for itself where this point of political and moral peril comes.[47]

In other words, Reichley is suggesting that there is a significant difference between church intervention on questions where the link between morality and policy is clear and those where it is tenuous. This is quite sensible.

But there remains a serious difficulty. A number of authors have pointed out that there is considerable dispute today about which public policy questions are in fact questions of morality at all. There are also serious disagreements about where to draw the line between the domain of public morality (where civil law has a legitimate role to play) and that of private morality (where civil freedom should prevail). A century and a half ago Tocqueville was confident that the different religious groups in the United States shared a common moral code, despite their differences in faith. In Richard McBrien's judgment, this is no longer the case. He maintains that debates over issues such as abortion demonstrate that there is no longer any national moral consensus.[48] This may go too far, for there are clearly areas of public life where moral consensus does in fact exist in this country today. But McBrien is surely correct about the hard cases like abortion, which would not be hard cases if consensus existed about them. McBrien proposes several guidelines for relating moral norms to the civil law in such difficult areas. In developing these guidelines, he relies on the now classic discussion of the subject by John Courtney Murray, who himself relied on Thomas Aquinas.[49]

McBrien states that the translation of moral convictions into civil law must first meet the criterion of enforceability. "Will the repressive law be obeyed? Can it be enforced against the disobedient? Is it prudent to undertake its enforcement, given the likelihood of harmful effects in other areas of social life?"[50] This enforceability argument is a part of the second criterion for the legislation of morality—namely, it must meet with the consent of the people—and the possibility of attaining such consent is obviously qualified by the reality of pluralism. In McBrien's words, "In a pluralist society like the United States of America, winning consent for a law, necessary for its enforcement, is complicated by the existence of many different moral (and religious) points of view. What are we to do?"[51]

Two easy answers to McBrien's question are clearly unacceptable. A first oversimplification would maintain that, wherever there is disagreement with the moral content of a policy or piece of legislation, the conscientious objectors should have veto power. But this really amounts to a kind of anarchy; it implies there can be no law at all when unanimity is lacking.[52] A second apparent escape from the difficulties of pluralism is strict majority rule. Those who have the votes may write their moral and religious convictions into law. But this is incompatible with the very notion of human rights against the sometimes tyrannical will of the majority. It is also contrary to the Council's rejection of an earlier Catholic position on church-state relations that would seek to establish the Catholic Church in countries where Catholics were in the majority.

Because of the inadequacy of these two simple solutions, it is apparent that a more complex approach is needed. Such an approach may be less satisfying to those who, perhaps quite rightly, are convinced of the righteousness of their cause. McBrien, adapting Murray, sketches the framework of such an approach. First, every religious community may demand conformity to its beliefs on the part of its own members. Second, no group in a pluralist society may demand that government legislate a moral conviction for which support in society at large is lacking. Third, any group, including any church, has the right to work toward a change in society's standards through persuasion and argument. Finally, no group may legitimately impose its religious or moral convictions on others through the use of force, coercion, or violence.[53] McBrien observes that these criteria are not divinely revealed norms; they are the result of an effort to discover a reasonable way of dealing with *both* the importance of religion and morality in public life *and* the reality of pluralism. Because of this, the virtue of prudence must guide their application.

I think McBrien has the matter essentially right; however, several concluding observations may be in order. There is, unfortunately, no guarantee that observation of McBrien's criteria will in fact produce morally worthy civil laws. Christopher Mooney is very much concerned about this in his book *Public Virtue*. Mooney strongly defends both U.S. constitutional institutions and criteria for church activism like those proposed by McBrien. He argues that these institutions and criteria provide the conditions that enable conflict and debate about the moral content of our laws to be creative. "Such conflicts, we have come to believe, give rise to moral judgments which are as close to the practical truth as we can get. In other words, as a free people in a pluralist society, we accept the principle that conflict among all interested parties to a decision can be creative of moral insight."[54] Here Mooney is echoing Jefferson's conviction "that truth is great and will prevail if left to herself."[55] He also places much confidence in James Madison's well-known argument in the *Federalist* that various "factions" in society will counterbalance each other, preventing tyranny and securing a basic standard of justice. This is the great hope of a liberal democratic polity, and the respect it exhibits toward the dignity and consciences of all citizens was judged to be an exigency of both Christian faith and human reason by the Second Vatican Council. Jefferson's free argument and debate and Madison's countervailing factions, however, did not prevent the institution of chattel slavery from existing under our Constitution for seventy-five years nor avert the great bloodletting of the American Civil War. Purely procedural protections of social debate and existing moral conviction, it seems from historical experience, are not sufficient to secure even minimal justice when disregard for the dignity of vulnerable and marginal persons becomes widespread in society.

Mooney is aware of this weakness in a purely procedural republic, for he notes, as does Miller, that the American experiment in democracy was premised on another conviction of the Founders and Framers. This conviction was "so obvious to them that they felt no need to incorporate it in the Constitution, namely that the pursuit of the common good was and would continue to be a major motivation of all citizens."[56] This pursuit of the common good, rooted in the sense of the way life is bound up with life, was what the Founders meant by "public virtue." Mooney sees this as significantly threatened in the United States today and suggests two crucial ways that the churches can help resist this threat. "Religion's task in this public sphere is to reverse the ever present tendency of citizens in an economically prosperous democracy to privatize their lives by immersing themselves exclusively in commercial pursuits."[57] In addition, the churches themselves (both laity and clergy) must be involved in the ongoing struggle to define and locate the common good. This is significantly different from viewing the churches as just another interest group pressing a predetermined agenda (even a religious agenda). Rather, Mooney regards the churches as having the capacity "to be the primary means by which morality and moral discourse enter politics."[58] They will have to be prepared not to see their entire moral vision enacted into law. But by seeking to transform the public debate into one about the public good rather than private or special interests, they will already have made a major contribution to the public virtue of society.

Taken together and synthesized, McBrien, Mooney, and Miller lead to several conclusions about this entire complex and controverted subject. McBrien is surely correct in his emphasis on the illegitimacy of attempting to enact a moral agenda through civil law other than through persuasion and civil argument. He is also in harmony with both the Second Vatican Council and the U.S. Constitution when he insists that government has no business granting either privileges or disabilities to any group in society simply because it is religious. Mooney takes the argument a step further with his emphasis on the need for the churches to encourage a commitment to the common good and to participate creatively in the effort to specify the substantive content of the common good through public argument. He provides a positive vision of the role of the churches that complements McBrien's emphases on the limits of the role of the churches in politics and on the difference between morality and civil law.

Finally, and with full awareness of the way the Roman Catholic Church and some of its leaders have sometimes missed the mark in their political interventions, I think Miller is right that Catholicism has something very important to contribute to American public life today. The two elements of the Catholic tradition that Miller finds to be especially needed in the late twentieth century are equally important: a moral vision of "personalistic communitarianism" and a commitment to the vigorous exercise of moral reason in addressing public issues. The vision of the common good in this personalistic communitarianism is not the same as the ultimate, eschatological good of the kingdom of God. But it is more than a modus vivendi worked out by rational egoists in a commercial, procedural republic. This vision must be nourished in numerous ways: in the life of the church itself through preaching the Word of God and the sacramental life of the community, through the church's educational efforts on all levels, and through the involvement of Christians in public affairs. It can also be communicated to the larger society beyond the church itself through manifold efforts to influence our cultural milieu. Similarly, the exercise of practical moral reason is essential to what Mooney calls the effort to locate and define the meaning of the common good. This can occur within Christian communities themselves, as members seek to understand what their response to political issues should be through dialogue and reasoned discussion. It can also occur through efforts such as the U.S. bishops' pastoral letters, which seek to provide an overarching vision that should shape our culture's attitudes toward peace and economic justice.

These letters also "get down to cases" in the policy sphere by making a number of specific recommendations for action. This was probably their most controversial aspect. In light of Miller's analysis, however, this can be seen as an additional contribution. Miller is right when he observes that "the American Protestant ethos—therefore the American ethos—resisted the concept, and even the word, *casuistry*, revealingly turning it into a pejorative."[59] But he notes appreciatively that respect for the practical intellect is the source of the Catholic tradition's reliance on "reason, argument, and conversation" rather than intuition in dealing with concrete cases in the moral life.[60] Albert Jonsen has described casuistry as "the attempt to formulate expert opinion about the existence and stringency of moral obligation in typical situations where some general precept would seem to require interpretation due to circumstances."[61] Jonsen points out that casuistry flourished in Catholic moral theology in the sixteenth and seventeenth centuries, largely because of the many new societal problems that appeared in the wake of the Reformation, the discovery of new lands, the emergence of a mercantile economy, and the development of the modern nation state.

The moral choices facing American society today as a result of new medical technologies, new dangers of massively destructive war, and new forms of global economic interdependence call for just the sort of "careful, devout effort to discover, by reflection and discussion, the right course of action" that characterizes casuistry at its best.[62] This tradition of casuistry is clearly at work in the efforts of the U.S. bishops, in both their concern to discover the fitting response to several concrete policy issues and their care to distinguish the different levels of certitude and obligation that characterize their conclusions. If it is true that American culture has lost confidence in the possibility of reasoned argument about concrete issues of public morality, this may be the single strongest reason supporting the U.S. Catholic bishops' decision not to confine their recent social teachings to the level of moral vision and general moral principles. This specificity is not simply a way of gaining public attention. Rather, it is an attempt to contribute to the recovery of the very possibility of public moral argument. And that is the single greatest need in the interaction between religion, politics, law, and morality today. It does not end the discussion of this interaction, but it does ensure that such a discussion will be an important part of the quest for the common good of this pluralistic society.

NOTES

1. Jeffrey K. Hadden, "Religious Broadcasting and the Mobilization of the New Christian Right," *Journal for the Scientific Study of Religion* 26 (1987): 1–24, at 1.

2. Ibid., 3.

3. Ibid., 4.

4. Ibid.

5. Ibid., 7.

6. Ibid., 22.

7. Ibid., 18.

8. Ibid., 22–23.

9. Richard J. Mouw, "Understanding the Fundamentalists' Retreat," *New Oxford Review* 54, no. 7 (September 1987): 11–15, at 12.

10. Ibid.,13–14.

11. For an extremely interesting and alarming discussion and critique of one school of fundamentalism that draws just these conclusions, the "reconstructionists," see Rodney Clapp, "Democracy as Heresy," *Christianity Today* 31, no. 3 (February 20, 1987): 17–23.

12. Dean C. Curry, "Evangelicals, the Bible, and Public Policy," *This World* 16 (winter 1987): 34–49, at 36.

13. Ibid., 38.

14. Ibid., 44–45.

15. Ibid., 38.

16. Ibid., 45.

17. Ibid., 48.

18. Ibid.

19. William A. Stahl, "The New Christian Right," *Ecumenist* 25 (1987): 81–87, at 86.

20. William Lee Miller, *The First Liberty: Religion and the American Republic* (New York: Alfred A. Knopf, 1986), 280, 291.

21. Richard John Neuhaus, *The Catholic Moment: The Paradox of the Church in the Postmodern World* (San Francisco: Harper & Row, 1987), 283.

22. Miller, *The First Liberty*, 288–89.

23. Ibid., 348.

24. Ibid., 345–46.

25. Ibid., 291.

26. Neuhaus, *The Catholic Moment*, 2.

27. Ibid., 54.

28. Ibid., 284.

29. Ibid., 287. For a stronger, even intemperate, argument along these lines, see Peter L. Berger, "Different Gospels: The Social Sources of Apostasy," *This World* 17 (spring 1987): 6–17.

30. Neuhaus, *The Catholic Moment*, 194–95.

31. Ibid., 23–24. This paragraph presents only the briefest sketch of Neuhaus's positive theological position. Because of the need to compress his argument here, many details have been omitted. I hope, however, that I have not done violence to the lineaments of his argument.

32. Ibid., 240. For another Lutheran argument that leads to similar conclusions, see Gilbert Meilaender, "The Limits of Politics and a Politics of Limited Expectations," *Dialog* 26 (1987): 98–103.

33. The whole of part V of *The Catholic Moment* develops this thesis.

34. See George Weigel, *Tranquillitas Ordinis: The Present Failure and Future Promise of American Catholic Thought on War and Peace* (Oxford: Oxford University Press, 1987); David Hollenbach, "War and Peace in American Catholic Thought: A Heritage Abandoned?" *Theological Studies* 48 (1987): 711–26.

35. Eugene TeSelle, "The Civic Vision in Augustine's *City of God*," *Thought* 62 (1987): 268–80.

36. Neuhaus, *The Catholic Moment*, 21.

37. TeSelle, "Civic Vision in Augustine," 278.

38. Ibid., 279.

39. James Dougherty, *The Fivesquare City: The City in Religious Imagination* (South Bend, Ind.: University of Notre Dame Press, 1980), 144, cited in TeSelle, "Civic Vision in Augustine," 279. For a approach to Luther's theology of the "two kingdoms" that moves in a similar direction, see Roy J. Enquist, "Two Kingdoms and the American Future," *Dialog* 26 (1987): 111–14.

40. Leslie Griffin, "The Integration of Spiritual and Temporal: Contemporary Roman Catholic Church-State Theory," *Theological Studies* 48 (1987): 225–57, at 249.

41. Vatican Council II, *Gaudium et Spes*, no. 26; see Griffin, "Integration," 253.

42. Avery Dulles, "The Gospel, The Church, and Politics," *Origins* 16 (1987): 637–46, at 641.

43. "Integration," 251.

44. J. Bryan Hehir, "Church-State and Church-World: The Ecclesiological Implications," *Proceedings of the Catholic Theological Society of America* 41 (1986): 54–74, at 56.

45. Ibid., 58–59.

46. A. James Reichley, *Religion and American Public Life* (Washington, D.C.: Brookings Institution, 1985), 114.

47. Ibid., 359.

48. Richard McBrien, *Caesar's Coin: Religion and Politics in America* (New York: Macmillan, 1987), 97.

49. See John Courtney Murray, *We Hold These Truths: Catholic Reflections on the American Proposition* (New York: Sheed and Ward, 1960), chap. 7.

50. McBrien, *Caesar's Coin,* 165.

51. Ibid.

52. Basil Mitchell touches on this problem in his carefully reasoned "Should Law Be Christian?" *Month* 20 (1987): 95–99, at 97.

53. McBrien, *Caesar's Coin,* 165–66

54. Christopher F. Mooney, *Public Virtue: Law and the Social Character of Religion* (Notre Dame, Ind.: University of Notre Dame Press, 1986), 58.

55. Thomas Jefferson, "A Bill for Establishing Religious Freedom," printed as appendix 1 in Miller, *The First Liberty,* 357–58.

56. Mooney, *Public Virtue,* 59.

57. Ibid., x.

58. Ibid., 19.

59. Miller, *The First Liberty,* 289.

60. Ibid., 289.

61. Albert R. Jonsen, "Casuistry," in James F. Childress and John Macquarrie, eds. *The Westminster Dictionary of Christian Ethics* (Philadelphia: Westminster, 1986), 78–81, at 78.

62. Ibid., 78–79. Following this line of reasoning, the statement of the U.S. bishops addressing the moral dimensions of the 1988 elections argues that religion has become such a visible part of the contemporary political scene precisely because of the major new moral problems that public policy must face: "From medical technology to military technology, from economic policy to foreign policy, the choices before the country are laden with moral content. . . . Precisely because the moral content of public choice is so central today, the religious communities are inevitably drawn more deeply into the public life of the nation." See United States Catholic Conference Administrative Board, "Political Responsibility: Choices for the Future," *Origins* 17 (1987): 369–75, at 371.

6

Religion and Political Life

THEORETICAL ISSUES

The debate on the proper relation of religion to politics is most intense when it touches on urgent practical issues. For example, a point of heated contention in the United States today concerns the influence of religious communities on public policy regarding abortion. The influence of religion on other practical issues such as economic justice for the poor, sex education, health services in relation to the AIDS crisis, and United States military response to terrorism have also received considerable attention. In order to illuminate the context within which practical issues are assessed, it is useful to step back from the details of specific controversies to consider the issue somewhat more theoretically. To do so, this chapter will examine the developing discussion of the place of religion in political life that has been occurring in moral theory and jurisprudence. It will consider several authors who have been exploring the theoretical grounding of the public role of religion in a democratic society.

Three general positions in the debate can be identified. The first is a liberal democratic stance with secularist implications. John Rawls's work in the 1980s and early 1990s represents this position in a moderate form, and

Richard Rorty's writings push it to radically secularist conclusions. The second position endorses the fundamental presuppositions of liberal democratic theory while seeking to provide greater public space for religion. This is the position developed by Kent Greenawalt and by Rawls in his most recent writings. The third offers both a philosophical and theological critique of standard liberal democratic theory and seeks to justify a much greater public role for religious convictions—a position defended by Michael Perry and Robin Lovin. These authors are in dialogue with each other and with other theorists, so their positions continue to evolve. Nevertheless, discussion of the positions presented here is a useful undertaking, because they continue to significantly influence both theoretical discourse and wider public opinion. It will become clear that I share the views of Perry and Lovin, but analyzing a range of theoretical approaches will shed useful light on the practical debates by making presuppositions more explicit.

LIBERAL THEORIES WITH SECULARIST IMPLICATIONS

The intellectual framework within which these authors set the problem of the relation between religion and political life is the subject of vigorous debate in moral and political philosophy about the status of liberalism. In this debate, the term "liberalism" is not used as an epithet for the views of the left wing of the Democratic Party. Rather, it refers to a political tradition that developed in the seventeenth and eighteenth century in response to the religious and moral pluralism of the emerging modern European world. It affirms human freedom and equality as the central values in public life. Because the citizens of pluralistic societies hold different convictions about God and the ultimate moral purposes in human life, if we are to treat citizens as equals we must protect the freedom of all to hold these convictions. Therefore, it is argued that theological and metaphysical beliefs may not be invoked as normative for the way society is organized. To do so would be to violate the freedom and equality of at least some citizens. This has crucial implications for the relationship of religion and politics. The basic issues can be illuminated by sketching several aspects of the contemporary defense of this liberal theory.[1]

Rawls's arguments provide a useful frame of reference. Rawls points out that institutions of liberal democracy were initially developed in the years after the Reformation in response to the wars of religion that shattered Western Europe. These wars led both Catholics and Protestants to the conclusion that their own self-interests demanded they work out a modus vivendi based on mutual toleration as the only alternative to endless civil strife. Such tolerance was initially accepted only reluctantly. At first, both Catholic and Protestant Christians continued to hold that, if their community were to become predominant in a political region, it would be the duty of the prince to uphold their faith and to repress other doctrines.[2] Religious peace is inherently unstable under such an arrangement, for it is not based on a mutual respect for freedom and equality but on achieving as much as possible for one's own community in nonideal circumstances. What Rawls calls toleration as a modus vivendi is very similar to the thesis/hypothesis approach to religious tolerance advanced in Catholic discussions of church-state questions before Vatican Council II. But Rawls maintains that, in the course of subsequent Western history, a more stable basis for ordering a pluralistic society was discovered. He calls this an "overlapping consensus" on a "reasonable political conception of justice" for a pluralistic society.[3]

A brief outline of Rawls's theoretical account of the development of this overlapping consensus goes as follows. First, it supports a conception of justice that applies to a particular subject—namely, the basic structure of a modern constitutional democracy, society's main political, social, and economic institutions. Thus, for example, it would not necessarily apply to family life, the organization of voluntary associations, or the internal governance of churches. Second, the conception of justice contained in the overlapping consensus does not claim to be the whole of morality. It is not a "comprehensive" understanding of morality that "includes conceptions of what is of value in human life, ideals of personal virtue and character, and the like, that are to inform much of our conduct (in the limit of our life as a whole)."[4] Rawls notes that religious moralities, as well as philosophies such as those of Kant, Mill, and Marx, embody just such comprehensive, even metaphysical, views of the full meaning of the good life. Because there seems to be no reasonable hope of overcoming the plurality of theological and metaphysical conceptions of the good life, a political conception of justice must avoid any claim to be comprehensive. Rather, an account of political justice demands that we deal with the historic controversies connected with religion, philosophy, and metaphysics by what

Rawls calls "the method of avoidance." "We simply apply the principle of toleration to philosophy itself."[5]

Rawls states that this form of toleration should not be construed as skepticism about or indifference to the truth of comprehensive visions of the full human good. He acknowledges that there would be no possibility that religious believers could affirm such a skeptical theory without denying their own deepest convictions. He states that disputes about religious or metaphysical questions must be avoided in politics "because we think them too important and recognize that there is no way to resolve them politically."[6] Positively, Rawls hopes that diverse religious and philosophical traditions can find reasons within their own belief systems for affirming the political conception of justice he proposes, namely, one that regards all persons as free and equal. To the extent that the diverse comprehensive moral or religious traditions of Western culture can affirm this more limited political idea of justice on the basis of their own fuller account of the good, an "overlapping consensus" will be achieved.[7]

There is much to be said in favor of this argument. It is parallel at least in intent to John Courtney Murray's insistence that the First Amendment to the United States Constitution is not a theological or ecclesiological "article of faith," but rather an "article of peace." The First Amendment is a provision that historical experience has shown to be a wise way to organize a pluralistic society, not a statement about religious truth. In Murray's words, the provisions of the First Amendment "are the work of lawyers, not of theologians or even of political theorists. They are not true dogma but only good law."[8] For Murray as for Rawls, this peace is not a mere modus vivendi to be accepted only on grounds of expediency. It has positive moral substance because it protects the dignity of the human person under conditions of pluralism. This protection is a high moral value indeed.[9] At the same time, Murray argues that this protection of human dignity is itself a theological and religious imperative for Christian believers. It is an implication of the Christian doctrine that the human person is created in the image and likeness of God. Under the influence of the historical experience of the West, Catholicism has come to appreciate that this dignity of the person can be protected adequately only where religious freedom is protected. For this reason, Vatican II declared, "The right of the human person to religious freedom is to be recognized in the constitutional law whereby society is governed. Thus it is to become a civil right."[10] Murray and Vatican II would both affirm, therefore, that Catholic doctrine can fully endorse the religious freedom that is part of Rawls's political conception of justice on the basis of the comprehensive vision of the human good that is rooted in Catholic belief.

Thus, at Vatican II, Catholicism became a participant in the overlapping consensus on religious freedom that Rawls wants to strengthen with his political conception of justice. Others, such as free-church Baptists, liberal agnostics, Kantians, or Buddhists, may all be able to participate in this overlapping consensus as well, though they will do so for their own reasons rooted in their own comprehensive visions of the deeper meaning of human life. It is Rawls's hope that historical experience will lead all these groups to discover that the institutions of liberal democracy open up a social possibility not envisioned in the premodern era: "the possibility of a reasonably harmonious and stable pluralist society."[11]

Despite the convergence between Rawls and Murray/Vatican II on the desirability and, indeed, the moral demand for these liberal institutions, there remain important differences. These differences lead to some of the most contentious aspects of the debate about the relation between religion and political life today. I do not mean the controversies about specific policy issues such as abortion and military strategy. Rather, there are major theoretical disputes in the recent literature about whether and how religious beliefs should play a role in the public life of a liberal democracy. Two issues are central: the first can be called the challenge of radical historicism, and the second the challenge of religious privatism.

First, radical historicism. On reading Rawls's major 1971 work, *A Theory of Justice*, many of his colleagues concluded that the book was an attempt to mount a defense of liberal democratic institutions based on an understanding of practical reason independent of historical traditions or cultural particularity. For example, Richard Rorty has written, "Many people, including myself, initially took Rawls's *Theory of Justice* to be such an attempt. We read it as a continuation of the Enlightenment attempt to ground our moral intuitions on a conception of human nature (and, more specifically, a neo-Kantian attempt to ground them on the notion of 'rationality'). However, Rawls's writings subsequent to *A Theory of Justice* have helped us realize that we were misinterpreting his book."[12] Rawls has acknowledged that *Theory* may have invited misunderstanding in this regard, and his more recent writings make explicit that his theory of justice, now understood as a theory of political justice only, makes no transcultural assumptions of a metaphysical or epistemological kind.[13] Rather, he wants to argue for his liberal conception of political justice by looking to "our public political culture itself, including its main institutions and the historical traditions of their interpretation, as the shared fund of implicitly recognized basic ideas and principles."[14] He puts the issue another way in a passage cited by Rorty, with approving emphasis added: "What justifies a conception of justice is not its being true to an order antecedent to and given to us, but its congruence with our deeper understanding of ourselves and our aspirations, and our realization that, *given our history and the traditions embedded in our public life*, it is the most reasonable doctrine *for us*."[15]

As noted above, Rawls is at pains to insist that his starting point is not moral or religious skepticism. He wants to keep open the possibility that persons with comprehensive, theological visions of the meaning of life and the human good can join a stable consensus on his political conception of justice. Rorty's reading of Rawls, however, raises doubt about whether this is possible when one avoids all claims about the criteria of political justice except those that are historically received and culturally mediated.

Rorty, in fact, is considerably more radical than Rawls in affirming that the *only* criteria of morality, whether political or comprehensive, are culturally embedded. For Rorty, there are no transcultural norms of morality for there is no transcultural knowledge at all. The difference between acceptable and unacceptable behavior is not determined by appealing to some universal rational norm. Instead, the distinction between the moral and the immoral is a "relatively local and ethnocentric" matter. Morality is simply what *we do*, and immorality is what *we do not do*. "According to this view, what counts as rational . . . is relative to the group to which we think it necessary to justify ourselves—to the body of shared belief that determines the reference of the word 'we.'"[16] The appeal to morality, therefore, is an appeal to a sense of identity that is "overlapping and shared" with other persons who make up the "we" of a particular community.[17] It has no other basis.

For this reason, Rorty maintains that notions such as transcendent human dignity and human rights cannot be invoked to stand in judgment of particular historical traditions from outside these traditions. Such transcultural norms simply do not exist. Rather, ideas such as religious freedom and tolerance are affirmed by those of us who are heirs of the Western tradition of constitutional democracy simply because this tradition has made us the kind of people who in fact affirm such things. The tradition of democracy is more important to us than are theological and philosophical disputes about "human nature, the nature of selfhood, the motive of moral behavior, and the meaning of human life."[18] So we tailor our philosophies and theologies to fit the requirements of liberal democracy, not the other way around. Rorty calls this the priority of democracy to philosophy.

For Rorty, those who refuse to accept the priority of democracy to philosophy cannot be compelled to do so by apodictic arguments, for that would imply the existence of a kind of rationality that Rorty denies. Rather, he says that those who refuse to accept the democratic way of life he supports should simply be regarded as fanatics—people who are "mad" or "crazy." In a bizarre linkage, Rorty cites Ignatius Loyola and Friedrich Nietzsche as examples of this fanaticism. He says they are to be judged crazy "because the limits of sanity are set by what *we* can take seriously. This, in turn, is determined by our upbringing, our historical situation."[19] And what Rorty cannot take seriously is any value or truth more important than the freedom of liberal democracy.

This historicism leads directly to Rorty's privatization of religious and philosophical matters. Theological and philosophical questions may well be of interest to certain people who have a particular, idiosyncratic vocation to explore them, but they need not be addressed at all in expounding a liberal theory of political justice. Rather, Rorty suggests that the whole point of liberal democracy is to avoid having to address such matters in public life. Opinions on these questions will be exempt from legal coercion in a liberal society, under one condition: that such opinions "be reserved for private life." Liberal democracy aims at "disengaging discussions of such questions from discussions of public policy."[20] Rorty acknowledges that this conclusion can be characterized as philosophical "light-mindedness," but he says it serves the same purpose as liberal "light-mindedness about traditional theological topics." It "helps along the disenchantment of the world. . . . It helps make the world's inhabitants more pragmatic, more liberal, more receptive to the appeal of instrumental rationality."[21]

The theoretical issues underlying Rorty's position touch on a central debate in contemporary philosophy and political theory: the issue of relativism. This is not the place to grapple with all the complexities of the current formulations of this perennial question, but Rorty's reading of Rawls raises two crucial questions for an understanding of the relation of religion and political life.[22] First, can Rawls's effort to deal with the problem of pluralism by applying the principle of tolerance to philosophy itself avoid the skepticism that Rawls himself wants to avoid? If Rorty is right, the answer is no. Second, does Rawls's theory imply the privatization of religion and the triumph of instrumental reason in all of public life? Rawls is open to several interpretations on this point. The differences in these interpretations can be traced back to what Rawls has said about the kind of reasoning that should govern public life.

Rawls insists that matters of public morality—those that fall within the domain of the overlapping consensus of a democratic society—must be adjudicated by what he calls "public reason." He has not, however, always been fully clear about the religious implications of this appeal to public reason and his understanding of what public reason means has been developing. In the mid-1980s, he appeared to adopt the position he has since called the "exclusive" interpretation of the implications of public reason for the role of religion in political life.[23] In this interpretation, public reason is seen as a form of argument that appeals "only to presently accepted general beliefs and forms of reasoning found in common sense, and the methods and conclusions of science when these are not controversial." In this view, reasoned arguments appeal to "the plain truths now widely accepted, or available, to citizens generally."[24] Public reason, on this reading, means a form of rationality based on premises about which citizens already have a working consensus. Because a religiously pluralistic society does not have a consensus about religious convictions, such convictions cannot be appealed to in public arguments about the shape of public life.[25] Rawls acknowledges that persons who hold religious conceptions of the good life—for example, deeply faithful Christians—will regard these understandings of the good life as formative of their very identity. They will find it difficult to imagine what their lives would be like without these particular convictions and attachments, but these convictions and attachments should be formative only of persons' "nonpublic (or nonpolitical) identity."[26] Thus, in the exclusive view of public reason, religious conceptions of the full human good "are not to be introduced into political discussion" and are not to be allowed to have any influence in the formulation of public policy.[27]

LIBERAL THEORIES SUPPORTIVE OF RELIGION

In *Political Liberalism*, however, Rawls has abandoned this exclusive position and taken up what he calls there the "inclusive view" of the relation between public reason and religious beliefs. In this inclusive interpretation, believers may publicly introduce religious reasons for adopting political values, provided they do so in a way that strengthens the ideal of public reason itself.[28] As examples of this, Rawls cites both the movement to abolish slavery on the eve of the American Civil War and the civil rights movement of the 1960s in the United States. In these cases, public advocacy of fundamental political principles was based on religious beliefs and also led to the strengthening of public reason. On both occasions, there was profound division in the country about the fundamental demands of justice. In the case of the abolition movement, this division went to the roots of constitutional democracy—the values of freedom and equality for all.[29] In the civil rights movement, the deeply disputed issue was how the values of freedom and equality for all ought to be made effective in practice.

Rawls acknowledges that in both the abolitionist and civil rights cases the ideal of a rightly ordered society had not been achieved and the requirements of public reason were not governing the most important institutions of social life. In such circumstances, he is willing to concede that "the nonpublic reason of certain Christian churches" was legitimately introduced into the public debates about slavery and civil rights. He says that the abolitionists and Martin Luther King "would not have been unreasonable" in appealing to their religious convictions "if the political forces they led were among the necessary historical conditions to establish political justice, as does indeed seem plausible in their situation." Despite this concession, in *Political Liberalism* he continues to hold that, ideally, such direct appeal to religious convictions would not be necessary. It was legitimate for the abolitionists and King only because their religious arguments helped bring about the kind of society in which the "ideal of public reason could eventually be honored" or because they could have recognized on reflection that in acting on their religious beliefs they were in fact acting "for the sake of public reason itself." Because of the historical conditions faced by the abolitionists and King, bringing their religious convictions about racial equality into the public domain was a way of supporting "the ideal of public reason itself."[30] Conceptually (as opposed to historically), there was no conflict between the appeal to the "nonpublic reason of certain Christian churches" and the requirements of public reason. The abolitionists and King could appeal to the former because in doing so they were implicitly supporting the latter.

This "inclusive" view, which grants religion a possibly remedial role in reforming and correcting public reason, was further broadened in Rawls's last writings. He adopted what he called a "wide view" of public political culture that granted considerable public space to religion.[31] This wide view derives from the conviction that being reasonable in public life means being civil. Civility is the commitment of citizens to cooperate with each other with genuine reciprocity and mutual respect. It affirms that all are entitled to participate in determining what the cooperative arrangements of social life will be, especially the most important institutions of government. All are entitled to set forth the reasons for their proposals. But whether these reasons be religious or nonreligious, they must be proposed in ways that respect the freedom and equality of all who will be affected. One should be able to argue that it would at least be reasonable for others to accept what is being proposed. Politics will become a form of manipulation or a pursuit of domination if one advocates important political institutions or policies that one knows cannot be reasonably affirmed by one's fellow citizens.[32] The reciprocity and mutual respect of genuine political deliberation thus have important consequences for the way citizens enter the political process, for the kind of policy proposals they support or advocate, and for the overall institutional framework that governs the activities of political life. In this broad framework, religious grounds for political values may be proposed in public, provided one argues that it is at least reasonable for others to accept the grounds proposed. This is a consequence of a commitment to reciprocity. The reciprocity and mutual respect of genuine political deliberation thus have important consequences for the role of religion in politics. Rawls's "wide view" of this question does not lead to the privatization of religion his earlier arguments had implied.

Both John Courtney Murray and Vatican II would support the direction in which Rawls's thought moved, just as they would strongly resist his earlier suggestions that "private" conceptions of the full human good should not be introduced into political discussion or allowed to have any influence in the formulation of public policy. If assent to such a privatized understanding of the full human good is a precondition for participation in Rawls's overlapping consensus, it is clear that contemporary Catholicism (and many other religious communities as well) could not sign on. As Vatican II's *Declaration on Religious Freedom* put the matter, "It comes within the meaning of religious freedom that religious bodies should not be prohibited from freely undertaking to show the special value of their doctrine in what concerns the organization of society and the inspiration of the whole of human activity."[33]

It will, therefore, be useful to examine several other writers who have recently addressed this problem in a way that points toward and develops a position like Rawls's final one. Kent Greenawalt, a professor at Columbia University Law School, states that his concern is "with the extent to which citizens and officials in this liberal democracy properly rely on their religious convictions when they decide what political actions to take."[34] Greenawalt prefaces his study with some brief autobiographical remarks that indicate the source of his interest in the subject. As a young man, his comfortable acceptance of the idea that religious convictions may affect one's political judgment was supported by his liberal Protestant background, his undergraduate studies of both political science and religion, and the fact that several family members and close friends were ministers concerned with questions of social justice. Later, as a young legal scholar, when he read and admired Rawls's *Theory of Justice*, he "did not realize the extent to which acceptance of its basic premises would exclude religious perceptions from the political sphere." But the debate about abortion and the claim often heard in this debate that some were trying to impose their religious beliefs on others stimulated his focused intellectual interest in the topic. In this context, Yale law professor Bruce Ackerman published a book arguing "for the exclusion of religious premises [from political life] with a novel starkness and clarity."[35] These challenges convinced Greenawalt that the political role of religious convictions was a subject that deserved most careful attention.

Greenawalt is reflecting on a deep tension in the liberal democratic stance toward the role of religion in political life. He characterizes the tension this way. First, government is legitimated by the consent of the governed and by its protection of basic rights. These rights are natural rights (i.e., they can be understood in nonreligious terms). Thus, government has a secular warrant, which does not exclude the idea that it may *also* be warranted theologically as "ordained by God."[36] Second, this secular foundation for government implies that government should neither seek to promote religious truth nor sponsor any religious organization. Rather, "laws adopted by the government should rest on some secular objective. By this I mean that laws should seek to promote some good that is comprehensible in nonreligious terms."[37] Third, for many people, religious convictions do in fact have important bearing on ethical choices, including ethical choices about laws and public policies. These religious convictions can influence the political views of citizens in several ways: by supplying direct ethical prescriptions; by recommending attitudes of heart and mind; by providing a vision of the ultimate meaning of human life and the kind of God who governs the universe; by providing a sense that God can guide choices directly in prayer.[38] Fourth, it is a central tenet of liberal democracy that "people are free to develop their own values and, at least within limits, styles of life; they are free to express their views not only about political questions but about other human concerns."[39]

The tension Greenawalt addresses is that between the principle that government has a secular purpose and a secular warrant and the principle that citizens are free to seek to influence public policy in light of their own values. When these values are religious, the potential for a conflict of principles is real. This conflict has been evident in the abortion debate and in numerous other areas of public life where the "nonestablishment" and free-exercise clauses of the First Amendment compete for primacy.

Greenawalt recognizes that the relationship between secular and religious warrants for moral stances on political issues is not univocal. For some believers—Roman Catholics and liberal Protestants, for example—religious convictions are often understood as confirming what can be known about political morality from natural law or reflection on human experience. For others, such as Jonathan Edwards, Karl Barth, and Evangelical Protestants generally, religious conviction "critically affects the resolution of every moral question." Intermediate between these two views are those that maintain that religion provides a supplement to secular moral reflection or adds greater depth and motivation to the effort to live morally. Further, in some cases, it may be virtually impossible to disentangle the threads of religious conviction and secular moral reflection.[40]

How, then, is one to deal with the tension between the competing liberal-democratic assertions that government and law should have secular purposes and that citizens should be free to seek to influence public life in accordance with their freely held convictions even when these are religious? Greenawalt partially but not completely agrees with Rawls on this question. Like Rawls, he maintains that the justification of law and public policy must rest on public reason, or, in Greenawalt's terminology, on "the shared premises and publicly accessible reasons" that prevail in society. Greenawalt, like Rawls, is not maintaining that justification must rest on transcultural rationality as such. Justification must reflect those canons of rationality that are in fact widely shared within the society in question. In our society, they include logical deduction and scientific or ordinary empirical enquiry.[41] Because Greenawalt is convinced that religious judgments are not based on such publicly accessible reasons, he concludes that religious reasons should not be invoked either to advocate or to justify a public policy or law.

Greenawalt is also convinced that "publicly accessible reasons" do not settle a number of important moral questions relevant to public policy that are hotly debated today. He presents extensive analyses of the abortion issue and of our ethical responsibilities for the environment to show this. In both issues, we confront "borderlines of status." These concern the crucial question of "how much living human beings owe to fetuses, nonhuman animals, plants, and ecosystems."[42] In order to answer these questions, some vision of what it means to be a human person and of what value is to be attributed to nonhuman beings must be invoked. Such a vision will at least implicitly contain the sort of metaphysical or religious elements that Rawls wants to exclude from his concept of political justice. The publicly accessible reasons of logic, science, and ordinary empirical inquiry have been unable to resolve these questions de facto. Greenawalt argues that this state of affairs reveals the inherent limits of these forms of reasoning. Therefore citizens and public officials who must make decisions about issues such as abortion or environmental policy cannot be faulted on liberal grounds if they turn to religious convictions for guidance in these areas. Sometimes they may have no other choice.

Greenawalt maintains that citizens who rely on religious convictions to reach their own conclusions on such matters should not appeal to these religious convictions in advocating these conclusions in the public forum. They may rightly discuss policy questions in religious terms with those who share their faith, but they should not do so when engaged in political advocacy in a pluralistic society. So, even though Greenawalt wants to provide space for religion in shaping the stance of believers toward public affairs, he remains committed to keeping religious talk out of the public square. "The common currency of political discourse is nonreligious argument about human welfare. Public discourse about political issues with those who do not share religious premises should be cast in other than religious terms."[43] Thus, Greenawalt continues to support a central tenet of liberal theory.

RELIGION AND THE LIMITS OF LIBERAL THEORY

Robin Lovin has written a very useful analysis of the strengths and weaknesses of Greenawalt's argument. Although Lovin appreciates Greenawalt's challenge to the secularist idea that "it is undemocratic, or even irrational, to apply religious ideas to public problems" and his effort to provide a "more careful and nuanced integration of an individual's identity as a member of a religious community with his or her role as citizen,"[44] he is dissatisfied by the degree to which Greenawalt retains a characteristic liberal presupposition about the nature of public discourse. According to this presupposition, "The political forum is simply the place where individuals come together to register their conclusions. Aspirations, values, and preferences of whatever sort are formed in some other realm of human experience—religion, emotion, or economic interests, to name a few. They are commitments that people bring to politics for implementation, not for transformation or evaluation. For the most part, politics must take these commitments as given."[45]

In other words, Lovin is saying that Greenawalt grants religion a role in the political process by treating it just like any other individual choice or "interest." This interest plays a legitimate role in shaping how a citizen votes, but there can be no real argument about it. Particular religious convictions about specific public policies may be rational, in light of the deeper premises shared by a particular religious community. But because the adequacy of such premises cannot be assessed in any public way, when policy conclusions that depend on these premises enter the public square they are "as remote from rational persuasion as are the most arbitrary preferences. There is no alternative but to treat these convictions as simply choices and to deal with them in politics with the same mixture of prudent limitation and tolerant respect that liberal democracy accords to any other choice. Thus, in the end, Greenawalt's argument is not a case for the public relevance of religious reasons, but for the public acceptance of individual choices that rest on religious reasons."[46] Religion, therefore, remains a private affair.

To sketch the elements of an alternative approach, Lovin appeals to the work of Michael J. Perry. Perry is a specialist in jurisprudence and the philosophy of law whose writings indicate that he has theological interests as well. His 1988 book, *Morality, Politics, and Law,* and subsequent books are important contributions to the theoretical debate we are considering.[47] It is impossible to encapsulate Perry's arguments here, for they touch on matters ranging from fundamental issues in epistemology regarding the question of relativism to highly disputed questions about how the courts should interpret the United States Constitution. It will be enough for present purposes to note several of the philosophical points made by Perry that Lovin employs in his own theological contribution to the argument.

Perry is a Roman Catholic, and his basic stance in this debate reflects a characteristic Catholic hope that faith and reason are allies, not adversaries. His views, however, are far from those of Catholics who think that moral principles governing public life are both eternally valid and easily known by all who are of good will (especially by those who hold the true faith). Perry takes the historicity and exploratory nature of all human knowledge with deep seriousness. But it is precisely because he does so that he grants much more importance than does Greenawalt to the public role of particular traditions, including religious traditions.

For Perry, people—including religious believers—do not enter the public square simply to negotiate how best to secure their own privately chosen interests. Perry shares Benjamin Barber's aspiration that democratic politics ought not to be an exchange among a throng of individuals asserting "I want *X*" in a market of ideas governed by instrumental rationality. Rather, democratic citizens ought to approach the public square with proposals in this form: "*X* would be good for the community to which I belong."[48] They should be fully prepared for conversation and argument about all such proposals. Perry thinks that much liberal theory encourages the former rather than the latter approach to public discourse. He wants to encourage and open up public space for people to propose visions of what would be good for the larger community. And they should be able to do so not only when these proposals are part of a current overlapping consensus backed by publicly accessible reasons, but also when they are premised on religious convictions that are particularist and distinctive.

So Perry challenges the predominant liberal view that conversation and argument about a comprehensive vision of the good life must be fruitless in a pluralistic society. He has greater confidence than do Rawls or Greenawalt that public debate about the comprehensive meaning of the good life can get us somewhere. Rather than proposing that fundamental religious and philosophical differences be dealt with by Rawls's "method of avoidance," Perry advocates an approach to these questions that is "ecumenical" rather than "neutral."[49] This means that politics is not about instrumental adjustment to competing private interests, but conversation and argument about "competing conceptions of human good . . . questions of how human beings, individually *and collectively*, should live their lives."[50]

Rawls says such questions are "too important" to be subjected to the heat of politics and holds out little hope that they can be resolved in the public debate. Perry agrees on their importance, but draws the opposite conclusion about their place in public discourse. "Questions of human good—and in particular deep questions of what it means to be authentically human—are too fundamental, and the answers to them too determinative of one's politics, to be marginalized or privatized."[51] In this way, Perry challenges a fundamental presupposition of most versions of liberal politics today: the idea that this politics can be neutral about competing conceptions of what authentic human existence is all about. Such neutrality cuts off liberal thought from some of the richest resources for thinking about the human: "the resources of the great religious traditions."[52]

Lovin relies on Perry's basic argument while advancing it a step further in a theological direction. Lovin, like Perry, is fully supportive of the institutions of a free society. He has no desire to reinstitute the authoritarianism of the ancien régime or to support the spirit of "restoration" that currently seems to be animating some in the Catholic community. His purpose is quite the opposite: to enable religious believers to both inform and be informed by the diverse knowledge-claims in our pluralistic world.

Where Lovin differs most from Greenawalt is in the description of what really motivates religious believers in their public, political action.

Greenawalt starts with the presupposition that the norms of liberal democracy set the terms for legitimate employment of religious convictions in politics. He concludes that the indeterminacy of arguments based on publicly accessible reasons leaves space for believers to rely on their religion in reaching their own personal political decisions as "private citizens" (to employ an oxymoron that has become common in our culture today). Lovin, on the other hand, points out that many religious believers will not find that Greenawalt's argument "authorizes them to do something that they would have otherwise refrained from doing."[53] They do not perceive themselves as needing permission to appeal to their faith when taking political stances. Greenawalt's analysis does not explain why religious believers often seek to shape the public debate about what our social projects, goals, and ideals ought to be, not simply to register what their personal choices or interests might be.

Lovin identifies three reasons why people bring the language of faith to bear on public choices. He calls these reasons "proclamation," "conversion," and "articulation." Proclamation proposes a religious way of life that stands as an alternative to the taken-for-granted expectations of the wider society. Lovin's example of this way of relating religious convictions to public life is the Mennonite theology of John Howard Yoder. It does not expect public life to be radically transformed in accord with its conviction that the gospel demands and makes possible a nonviolent way of living. But neither does it regard its Christian witness as entirely irrelevant to public life. Rather, it "reminds the world of a higher will and another order" that undergirds the life of nonviolent love. Secularist liberals might be prepared to respect the religious convictions that lead members of such a community to become conscientious objectors on the ground of religious freedom, but respect for religious freedom hardly accounts for the reasons these men and women seek to live a life of nonviolence. As Lovin puts it, "The deed itself is incomplete without the proclamation."[54] The proclamation, therefore, could not be true to itself were it to remain a purely private affair. To say it should remain private deprives public society of a resource for thinking about its own well-being and simultaneously denies such Christians the freedom to say what they mean.

The second reason for bringing faith to bear on public choices is an effort to resolve public disagreement by conversion. When believers and their fellow citizens disagree about public policy because they do not share the same premises, "one solution is conversion of the secular citizens to the religious premises."[55] For this to be ruled out in principle by the requirements of liberal democracy would be an odd way to interpret religious liberty. Greenawalt acknowledges that efforts at conversion are legitimate on liberal grounds, but he suggests that such efforts ought to be pursued by showing how the moral implications of religious convictions are congruent with the present moral beliefs of nonbelievers. Although this may be strategically and psychologically sound advice, Lovin points out that "conversion to a new religious belief . . . is quite different from being persuaded that some of the convictions of that belief are attractive on the basis of values one already holds."[56] Also, believers are often convinced that shared moral values need stronger and deeper grounds than de facto agreement on these values can provide. Again, the importance of religious reasons and public conversation about religion will be central for one who seeks to influence public life in this conversionist way. Though abuses (usually called proselytism or propaganda) are surely a danger here, does it make sense to eliminate these abuses by cutting off the possibility of this sort of discourse altogether? Lovin and Perry say no. So do I.

Third, religious arguments can be used "in the articulation of an idea of the human good."[57] This approach will build on the possible congruence between a religious vision of the good life and the aspirations of secular persons. The appeal to a religious vision, however, is not simply endorsement of prevailing cultural standards. Rather, the believer explicitly appeals to religious convictions because of their capacity to "enrich our sense of the possibilities life offers, extend our concerns to people and places we have heretofore ignored, and transform our sense of what would make us happy by showing us ways of life that our own limited experience could not devise."[58] Such an appeal to religion in public is not simply a ratification of secular values for reasons that are different than those proposed in secular discourse. It seeks to enrich and transform the vision of the human good that shapes our common life in a pluralistic society, without necessarily expecting a full-fledged religious conversion of members of that society.

For Lovin, therefore, all three ways of invoking religious beliefs in public discourse aim at transforming the terms of debate. There is of course a considerable danger in any one of these sorts of appeal to religion in political life. Greenawalt is especially sensitive to the way religious beliefs can become rigid and cause significant discord in public.[59] Lovin argues, however, that the fear that public religion will become a source of conflict and even violence is presented in a one-sided way in much liberal discussion of the matter. For the active participation of religious believers in political discourse can be an important occasion for the development and transformation of religious convictions themselves.[60] The fear of what will happen if religion appears in public rests largely on the presupposition that there is something inherently uncivil or fanatical about all religion.

To counteract this fear, Lovin, following Perry, argues that the nature of human language and thought is such that our convictions about how we ought to live are embedded in a complex web of ideas, including ideas drawn from "scientific studies in biology and psychology, personal experience of what is and is not satisfying over the long run, social experience of what does and does not work in dealing with other persons, and religious or philosophical beliefs about what is of lasting value in human life and human achievements."[61] All ideas—whether scientific, moral, or religious—take their meaning from their relationship to the other parts of this complex web. It is therefore impossible to reach judgments about the truth or falsity of any of our ideas without relying on other ideas that form part of the web. There are no first principles that have no presuppositions. Lovin and Perry share this "antifoundationalist" conviction with Rorty, but they draw a different conclusion, for they reject the notion that historical consciousness implies a historicist abandonment of the quest for truth.[62] The debates of public life are not just interesting but finally inconclusive talk. They take us somewhere: toward an increasingly adequate but always revisable understanding of the good life.

Thus, it is simultaneously the case that the meaning of one's political convictions will be shaped by one's religious convictions and that the meaning of one's religious convictions will be shaped by scientific, social, and political ideas. There are no airtight compartments in human consciousness, but rather a rich interweaving of its diverse elements. This implies that religious convictions can be transformed by social experience and the emergence of new political ideas, just as politics can be transformed by moral and religious belief. The interaction is reciprocal, a two-way street. The effort to isolate religion from politics is impossible in this view of human understanding. And it will be just as impossible to develop a religious approach to public life without taking one's best understandings of history, psychology, and social experience into account.[63] Because the proposal to keep religious reasons private abstracts from these interconnections, it risks undermining the dynamic that can sometimes lead religious believers to develop or change their religious convictions. In doing so, it risks precipitating the sort of fundamentalism, intolerance, and conflict that it seeks to prevent.

Religious convictions are potentially explosive when confined to small spaces. And rightly so. They are, after all, about God. And beliefs about God entail convictions about the whole of human life, not simply a small compartment of it. Whether one professes the *shema* of Israel ("Hear, O Israel: the Lord our God is one God"), the Christian *credo* ("We believe in one God, the Father Almighty, creator of heaven and earth), or the Muslim *shahadah* ("There is no God but God"), private religion is theologically self-contradictory. Because religion is about the ultimate good of the whole of human life, it will be untrue to itself if it accepts the private niche to which liberal theory would assign it. And from a sociological point of view, liberals by now ought to have recognized that the alternatives are a *civil* role for religion in public or full-fledged secularism. Rorty sees this choice accurately and opts for secularism. Rawls, and to a lesser extent Greenawalt, seem to be searching for a way to avoid the choice. This effort is understandable, in light of their presuppositions, but historical and present-day experience suggest it is not likely to succeed.

A PUBLIC ROLE FOR RELIGION

Thus, for both theological and political reasons, religious discourse deserves to be a free participant in the public exchange of a pluralistic society. Abuses of this public space by believers have and will continue to occur, but, as Lovin concludes, "We will have a better understanding of both faith and politics if we try to describe their relationship and construct their norms in terms that fit the discourse to which we aspire, rather than the distortions that we fear."[64] What would such a discourse look like? Four brief conclusions can be drawn from this survey of the theoretical issues that lie just below the surface of the popular debate today.

First, Christians should fully endorse what Rawls calls an overlapping consensus on the moral principles shaping the fundamental institutions of constitutional democracy. Rawls is right that a simple modus vivendi among diverse groups who share no common moral commitments about how to conduct public life is bound to be unstable. He is also right that most religious communities in the West have discovered grounds within their own belief systems for the affirmation of these constitutional institutions. This happened in Catholicism at Vatican II through the influence of Murray, Maritain, and others, under the pressure of their historical experience. There is no going back on this fundamental institutional insight.

Second, I think secular and quasi-secular liberals are wrong about the purely private role of religious reason and religious imagination. Religious traditions are the bearers of many of humanity's deepest convictions about the human good. This is not to say these traditions are simply human constructs. To exclude the insights of these communities from public discourse in the name of common sense or the procedures and conclusions of uncontroversial science would impoverish our common life in a self-destructive way. Martha Nussbaum has observed that we will need considerably more imagination about what it is to be human than common sense and uncontroversial science can provide if we are to negotiate the rapids of contemporary social existence. We need a vision of the good life. Such a vision arises from "myths and stories from many times and places, stories explaining to both friends and strangers what it is to be human rather than something else. The account is the outcome of a process of self-interpretation and self-clarification that makes use of the story-telling imagination far more than the scientific intellect."[65] Our imaginations need to be engaged by these stories not only in private enclaves, but also in civil society. And to the degree that they are present in civil discourse, they will have political impact. Though Nussbaum's writing is noncommittal on religious truth-claims, she is right that religious and metaphysical beliefs can make important contributions to a social understanding of the genuine human good.

Third, religion should be part of public discourse precisely because not all religious communities now participate in the overlapping consensus on the moral values that support the liberal democratic institutions Rawls advocates. Some communities do not so participate in this consensus for religious and theological reasons. Serious religious and theological discourse is the only noncoercive route by which their stance can be changed. It took Murray a lifetime of conversation and argument to develop his theological rationale for an official Catholic endorsement of religious freedom. He was helped to develop this rationale by his ecumenical engagement with other Christian communities and by his full participation in public discourse. Had Murray been less ready for public dialogue about both theology and politics, his contribution would never have been achieved. Rawls's "method of avoidance" for dealing with religious diversity would never have produced this outcome in Murray's life. It will not produce it today.

Finally, it must be acknowledged that these reflections are not likely to provide a quick settlement for contentious practical questions such as abortion, military policy, or economic justice. But perhaps these practical questions are debated so interminably because the reigning categories of public discourse are inadequate to deal with them.[66] The literature discussed here suggests as much. The question of the relation between religion and politics has a long history in the United States and the entire Western democratic tradition. It continues to be vigorously alive today. The fundamental issues are more important for the long-term health of this tradition than are the concrete controversies. Controversies about specific policies shape more fundamental convictions, but the opposite is also true. It is hoped that this analysis of some of the theoretical dimensions of the current argument can contribute to a wiser, truer, and more faithful response in the fog that threatens these arguments today.

NOTES

1. For further clarification of this multileveled debate, see R. Bruce Douglass, Gerald R. Mara, and Henry S. Richardson, eds., *Liberalism and the Good* (New York: Routledge, 1990); Nancy Rosenblum, ed., *Liberalism and the Moral Life* (Cambridge, Mass.: Harvard University Press, 1989). On the relation of the debate to some aspects of Christian ethics, see David Hollenbach, "Liberalism, Communitarianism, and the Bishops' Pastoral Letter on the Economy," *Annual of the Society of Christian Ethics* (1987): 19–40 and "The Common Good Revisited," *Theological Studies* 50 (1989): 70–94.

2. John Rawls, "The Idea of an Overlapping Consensus," *Oxford Journal of Legal Studies* 7 (1987): 1–25, at 4.

3. Ibid., 2.

4. Ibid., 3, n. 4.

5. Ibid., 12–13.

6. Rawls, "Justice as Fairness: Political not Metaphysical," *Philosophy and Public Affairs* 14 (1985): 223–51, at 230.

7. Rawls, "Overlapping Consensus," 6–7.

8. John Courtney Murray, *We Hold These Truths: Catholic Reflections on the American Proposition* (New York: Sheed and Ward, 1960), 56.

9. Compare Rawls's statement that the virtues of cooperation that are associated with his political conception of justice are *"very great* virtues" with Murray's assertion that the peace of a pluralistic society secured by the First Amendment "is altogether a moral norm, . . . One may not, without moral fault, act against these articles of peace." Rawls, "Overlapping Consensus," 17; Murray, *We Hold These Truths*, 62–63.

10. *Dignitatis Humanae*, in Walter M. Abbott and Joseph Gallagher, eds., *The Documents of Vatican II* (New York: America, 1966), no. 2.

11. Rawls, "Overlapping Consensus," 23.

12. Richard Rorty, "The Priority of Democracy to Philosophy," in Merrill D. Peterson and Robert C. Vaughan, eds., *The Virginia Statute for Religious Freedom: Its Evolution and Consequences in American History* (Cambridge: Cambridge University Press, 1988), 257–82, at 264–65.

13. Rawls, "Political not Metaphysical," 224.

14. Ibid., 228.

15. Rawls, "Kantian Constructivism in Moral Theory," *Journal of Philosophy* 77 (1980), 519, italics added by Rorty, "Priority of Democracy," 259.

16. Rorty, "Priority of Democracy," 259.

17. Rorty, "Postmodernist Bourgeois Liberalism," in Robert Hollinger, ed., *Hermeneutics and Praxis* (Notre Dame, Ind.: University of Notre Dame Press, 1985), 214–21, at 218.

18. Rorty, "Priority of Democracy," 261.

19. Ibid., 266–67.

20. Ibid., 263.

21. Ibid., 271–72. For fuller exposition of Rorty's views, see *Contingency, Irony, and Solidarity* (Cambridge: Cambridge University Press, 1989).

22. The shape of the debate is presented in Michael Krausz, ed., *Relativism: Interpretation and Confrontation* (Notre Dame, Ind.: University of Notre Dame Press, 1989).

23. Rawls, *Political Liberalism* (New York: Columbia University Press, 1993), 247.

24. Ibid., 224–25; see also Rawls, "Overlapping Consensus," 8.

25. Rawls, "Overlapping Consensus," 15.

26. Rawls, "Political not Metaphysical," 240, n. 23.

27. Ibid., 231. Rawls states that appeals to comprehensive doctrines of the good must be avoided both in arguments about the basic structure of society and also in the formulation of more specific social policies. See "Overlapping Consensus," 20.

28. Rawls, *Political Liberalism*, 247.

29. Ibid., 251.

30. Ibid., 249–51.

31. Rawls, "The Idea of Public Reason Revisited," in *The Law of Peoples with "The Idea of Public Reason Revisited"* (Cambridge, Mass.: Harvard University Press, 1999), 152–56.

32. Ibid., 136–40.

33. *Dignitatis Humanae*, no. 5. Murray's footnote to this passage in the Abbot-Gallagher edition of the Council documents comments: "Implicitly rejected here is the outmoded notion that 'religion is a purely private affair' or that 'the Church belongs in the sacristy.' Religion is relevant to the life and action of society. Therefore religious freedom includes the right to point out this social relevance of religious belief" (*The Documents of Vatican II* 683, note 11).

34. Kent Greenawalt, *Religious Convictions and Political Choice* (New York: Oxford University Press, 1988), vii.

35. See Bruce Ackerman, *Social Justice and the Liberal State* (New Haven, Conn.: Yale University Press, 1980).

36. Greenawalt, *Religious Convictions*, 16–17.

37. Ibid., 20–21.

38. Ibid., 31–32.

39. Ibid., 16.

40. Ibid., 39–40.

41. Ibid., 57.

42. Ibid., 98.

43. Ibid., 217.

44. Robin W. Lovin, "Perry, Naturalism, and Religion in Public," *Tulane Law Review* 63 (1989): 1517–39, at 1521.

45. Ibid., 1521–22.

46. Ibid., 1522.

47. Michael J. Perry, *Morality, Politics, and Law: A Bicentennial Essay* (New York: Oxford University Press, 1988). This book is the subject of extensive discussion in "Symposium: Michael J. Perry's *Morality, Politics, and Law*," *Tulane Law Review* 63 (1989): 1283–1679. Lovin's essay on Greenawalt and Perry is part of this symposium, and Perry commends Lovin for clarifying the basic issue in the debate. Perry's explicit response to Greenawalt is in "Neutral Politics?" *Review of Politics* (fall 1989): 479–509, and in *Love and Power: The Role of Religion and Morality in American Politics* (New York: Oxford University Press, 1991). See also his *Religion in Politics: Constitutional and Moral Perspectives* (New York: Oxford University Press, 1997).

48. Benjamin Barber, *Strong Democracy: Participatory Politics for a New Age* (Berkeley: University of California Press, 1984), 171.

49. Perry, "Neutral Politics?" 499.

50. Perry, *Morality, Politics, and Law*, 182.

51. Ibid.

52. Ibid., 183.

53. Lovin, "Religion in Public," 1523.

54. Ibid., 1528.

55. Ibid.

56. Ibid., 1529.

57. Ibid., 1530.

58. Ibid., 1531–32.

59. Greenawalt, *Religious Convictions*, 158–62. Robert Audi has concluded that even Greenawalt's defense of a limited place for religious convictions in political life goes too far and risks encouraging religious conflict. See his "Religion and the Ethics of Political Participation," *Ethics* 100 (1990): 386–97, at 395–96. Audi critiques Greenawalt from a more secularist perspective, while Lovin and Perry want more public space for religion than does Greenawalt.

60. Lovin, "Religion in Public," 1526.

61. Ibid., 1532. Perry develops this in chapter 2 of *Morality, Politics, and Law*.

62. Rorty's ideal liberal culture would be one that was "enlightened through and through. It would be one in which no trace of divinity remained, either in the form of a divinized world or a divinized self. Such a culture would have no room for the notion that there are nonhuman forces to which human beings should be responsible. It would drop, or drastically reinterpret, not only the idea of holiness but those of 'devotion to truth' and of 'fulfillment of the deepest needs of the spirit.' . . . [D]oubts about whether the aims of liberal society were 'objective moral values' would seem merely quaint." *Contingency, Irony, and Solidarity*, 45.

63. Lovin, "Religion in Public," 1535.

64. Ibid., 1539.

65. Martha C. Nussbaum, "Aristotelian Social Democracy," in Douglass, Mara, and Richardson, eds., *Liberalism and the Good*, 203–52, at 217.

66. Lovin, "Religion in Public," 1521.

7

Freedom and Truth

In April 1966, but a few months after the close of Vatican Council II, John Courtney Murray wrote that the fundamental intention of the Council "was to bring the Church into courageous confrontation with the new moment of history" it faced.[1] He said that it would be a "disastrous error" if the post-Conciliar task of studying and appropriating the teaching of the Council documents were to "turn the Church in upon itself—to make it the complacent auditor of its own voice." This chapter will argue that a major outcome of the Council has in fact been to turn the church outward in a new and positive relation to secular society. In particular, it will try to show that the Council has led to a growing awareness that the right to religious freedom empowers Christians to exercise positive and active responsibility for the shape of the wider societies in which they live. It is true that Murray's writings on the Council's *Declaration on Religious Freedom* repeatedly pointed out that the right to religious liberty affirmed there "is understood to be an immunity, a freedom from coercion, whether legal or extralegal."[2] Nevertheless I argue that understanding religious liberty simply as the freedom from external coercion in matters religious fails to do justice to the active engagement of the Christian community in public life that the Council urged and in some measure successfully stimulated.

The discussion proceeds in several steps. First, evidence for a new and positive relationship between the Catholic Church and democracy is sketched. Second, two possible objections to a close linkage between the church and democratic politics are presented, both rooted in a fear that commitment to the truth of religious belief may be in tension or even conflict with a genuine commitment to democracy. Third, the way early arguments about religious freedom at Vatican II manifested similar fears are recalled. Fourth and fifth, the two arguments by which Murray successfully resolved these debates will be outlined. The conclusion will present the schematic case for interpreting Murray and the Council as empowering the Catholic community for a vigorously active role in public life, a role that must be exercised in a way that is fully congruent with the principles of a free and democratic society.

CATHOLICISM AND DEMOCRACY: A NEW PARADIGM

Before turning to the task of clarifying the conceptual issues in the argument about the right to religious freedom as immunity or empowerment, it may be useful to consider briefly how the Catholic Church's involvement in public life has developed in the years since the Council. A recent essay by Harvard political scientist Samuel P. Huntington paints a vivid picture of this evolution.[3] I will simply note some of his main points.

Huntington observes that there have been three waves of democratization in modern world history. The first, from the 1820s to the 1920s was rooted in the American and French revolutions. Protestant and Enlightenment thought inspired it. The second, from the end of World War II to the mid-1960s, was promoted by the Allied victors, who encouraged the creation of democratic institutions in the Axis powers. Western decolonization also launched democracy in a few Asian countries during this period, and some Latin American countries became democratic. Both of these waves were partially reversed in the years that followed them. For example, by one estimate one-third of the countries that had been democratic in 1958 were under authoritarian rule by the early 1970s.

Huntington's discussion of the third wave of democratization is especially relevant for our purposes. He sees this beginning in 1974 with the end of dictatorship in Portugal and continuing into the present in a way that is not yet complete. From 1974 to 1989, more than thirty countries in Europe, Asia, and Latin America have moved from authoritarianism to democracy. In most of these countries, the majority of the population is Catholic, and Catholicism has shaped their cultures in important ways. "In its first fifteen years, the third wave was overwhelmingly Catholic." From Portugal and Spain in the mid-1970s, to South America in the late 1970s and early 1980s, to the Philippines in the mid-1980s, to Poland and Hungary in the late 1980s, "Catholic societies were in the lead, and roughly three-quarters of the countries that transited to democracy between 1974 and 1989 were Catholic."[4]

This is an extraordinary development that goes against the received sociological wisdom that Catholicism is in large measure antithetical to democracy, in contrast to Protestantism, which played such an important role in the Puritan democratic revolution in England and in the birth of democracy in the United States. In Huntington's analysis, a partial explanation of this reversal of the relationship between Catholicism and democracy is the fact that in the 1950s some Catholic countries began to have higher economic growth rates than formerly and that such growth is often associated with democracy. He maintains, however, that a more fundamental cause was the change in the church itself initiated by Pope John XXIII, deepened by the Second Vatican Council, and expanded by both clergy and laity in the years since the Council. Further, Pope John Paul II moved the church to center stage in the struggle against authoritarianism. "Papal visits came to play a central role. John Paul II seemed to have a way of showing up in full pontifical majesty at critical points in democratization processes. . . . The purpose of these visits . . . was always said to be pastoral. Their effects were almost invariably political."[5] This judgment has been reinforced by Mikhail Gorbachev's straightforward statement that "everything that took place in Eastern Europe in recent years would have been impossible without the Pope's efforts and the enormous role, including the political role, he played in the world arena."[6] Similarly, the emergence of grass-roots movements such as the ecclesial base communities in Brazil and other parts of Latin America and the mobilization of "people power" strongly linked with the Philippine church have had strong political impact.

In Huntington's view, therefore, the Roman Catholic Church has become a major actor in the public life of many countries. It has exerted pressure toward democracy through its papal, episcopal, and clerical leadership. In countries such as Chile, the Philippines, Korea, and Poland, it has provided legitimacy, support, protection, and leadership for popular opposition movements challenging dictatorial and authoritarian regimes. This represents a major shift in the identity and self-understanding of the Catholic Church throughout the world. The church has turned almost 180 degrees from its traditional alliance with forces of reaction and authoritarianism to a new and vigorous commitment to the democratic freedom of citizens as responsible, self-governing agents. The free expression of religious conviction by post-Conciliar Catholics has been an important cause of the democratic empowerment of large numbers of people formerly reduced to passivity by authoritarian regimes of both the left and the right.

In my judgment, Huntington's argument that the Catholic community has played a very important role in the recent spread of democracy is unquestionable. He fails to mention, however, several internal currents in the present-day church that suggest the transformation of the Catholic ethos from affinity with authoritarian regimes to commitment to democratic values may be less than total. For example, there are strong signs that recent episcopal appointments may carry church leadership back to its more traditional style of action in the public sphere. It is also clear that the Holy See under John Paul II is strongly opposed to the growth of a more democratic style of internal church governance.[7] If one is convinced that the new link between the Catholic Church and democracy has been a very good thing, it will be important to understand the intellectual roots of this recent transformation and the possible sources of objection that might threaten its continuance.

THE RELATION OF TRUTH AND FREEDOM

Two kinds of objection to this new linkage between the church and democracy have actually surfaced in recent days. The first has arisen within the church itself. It suggests that a commitment to democracy must in no way be confused with moral relativism. It rejects any defense of democracy based on the notion that all ideas deserve respect in the political forum because there is really no way to determine which ideas are true and therefore deserve greater respect on their merits. John Paul II is clearly worried that such an interpretation of democracy is present in the West today and that it must be resisted. As he put it in his encyclical letter *Centesimus Annus*,

> Nowadays there is a tendency to claim that agnosticism and skeptical relativism are the philosophy and the basic attitude that correspond to democratic forms of political life. Those who are convinced that they know the truth and firmly adhere to it are considered unreliable from a democratic point of view, since they do not accept that the truth is determined by the majority, or that it is subject to variation according to different political trends.[8]

The pope rejects this interpretation in no uncertain terms. He affirms that "obedience to the truth about God and man is the first condition of freedom."[9] He states that authoritarian and totalitarian regimes have violated people's consciences by imposing a vision of reality upon them coercively. In rejecting this coercion, the pope states that conscience can be "bound only to the truth, both natural and revealed."[10] He further maintains that "no authentic progress is possible without respect for the natural and fundamental right to know the truth and live according to that truth. The exercise and development of this right includes the right to discover and freely accept Jesus Christ, who is man's true good" and that "freedom attains its full development only by accepting the truth."[11]

Claims of this sort lead to the second objection to recent increased involvement of the church in public life. Secularist thinkers and non-Catholic believers alike have become concerned that an intensified presence of the Catholic Church in the political sphere could presage a new effort to achieve a form of religious hegemony, despite the church's democratic protestations. For example, the economist Milton Friedman has found much to praise and agree with in John Paul's *Centesimus Annus*, but he avers that the pope's statement that obedience to truth is the first condition of freedom "sent shivers down my back. . . . Whose 'truth'? Decided by whom? Echoes of the Spanish Inquisition?"[12] These are not surprising questions coming from the best-known libertarian economist on the American scene today. It is perhaps inevitable that they should be raised, for the Catholic Church's embracing of democracy has certainly not been based on libertarian principles. They do, however, highlight a question that goes to the heart of the meaning of the right to religious liberty, namely, the relation of freedom and truth.

In practical terms, the question can be put this way: has the Catholic participation in the third wave of democratization been a pragmatic strategy adopted as a means by which the church sought to open social space in closed societies within which it might advance its own religious and ethical agenda? Is there a danger that the church might use its new freedoms in formerly authoritarian polities to impose its own authority whenever doing so might be politically feasible? John Paul's statements that obedience to the truth about God and the human person is the precondition of freedom has led some to suspect this.

John Paul's statements about truth as the foundation of freedom, however, are more careful than the fears voiced by Friedman might suggest. He says that, in proclaiming its vision of the truth about God and humanity, "the Church's method is always that of respect for freedom." This method is one of dialogue with those who share other visions rather than coercion, and the church must be willing to learn from these others as well as teach them:

> While paying heed to every fragment of truth that he encounters in the life experience and in the culture of individuals and of nations, [the Christian] will not fail to affirm in dialogue with others all that his faith and the correct use of reason have enabled him to understand.[13]

In addition, John Paul voices the hope that not only Christians, but also nonbelievers and adherents of the other world religions, can make important contributions to establishing a more just and peaceful social existence:

> There is a reasonable hope that the many people who profess no religion will also contribute to providing the social question with the necessary ethical foundation. . . . I am convinced that the various religions, now and in the future, will have a preeminent role in preserving peace and building a society worthy of man.[14]

These statements suggest that fears of a new quest for hegemony by the church are unfounded.

Nevertheless there remains an ambiguity in the way the relation between truth and freedom is discussed in recent papal statements. At times it appears that adherence to the truth is a precondition of freedom. At others it is suggested that freedom is a prerequisite for the discovery of truth. The genre of the papal encyclical is not suited to the exploration of such theoretical issues, despite the fact that John Paul II is probably more philosophically oriented than any of the previous occupants of the chair of Peter. But it is a fortunate fact that the theoretical question of the relation of truth and freedom received considerable theoretical attention in the debates on religious freedom at Vatican II, and in Murray's writings during and after the Council. It will therefore be useful to take a retrospective look at these earlier discussions to determine what light they might shed on the future interaction of Catholicism and democracy.

EARLY CONCILIAR ARGUMENTS FOR RELIGIOUS FREEDOM

At least three different arguments about religious freedom were proposed during the debates at the Second Vatican Council. The first supported the form of religious tolerance that had become the practical stance of "confessional" states, both Protestant and Catholic, since the Peace of Westphalia in 1648 and which Pope Leo XIII endorsed in his condemnation of nineteenth-century efforts to confine religion exclusively to the private sphere.[15] This theory of tolerance maintained that, in ideal circumstances, Catholicism should be the established religion of the nation and that the public expression of other religious faiths should be forbidden and repressed. It argued for this conclusion by maintaining that any genuine human right must be based on the dignity of the human person. It further affirmed that, as rational and moral beings, human beings are constituted in their proper dignity by their adherence to what is true and good. All human beings, therefore, must be free to profess and act upon what is true and good. The objective referents of such truth and goodness are the faith and morality revealed by God, contained in natural law, and taught by the church. The defense of religious freedom, therefore, is the defense of Christian faith and morality against any form of persecution.[16] No right exists to profess publicly a religion other than Catholicism, for all rights must be founded on the objective truth about the human person. People who in good conscience hold religious and moral convictions other than those of the Catholic Church have a right to reverence and respect—they have a right not to be forced to abandon their religious convictions or to accept those of the Catholic church. But this right is limited to respect for interior personal freedom. It is not a right to the free exercise of these religious convictions in public. As Murray explained this view, "the reason is that error has no public rights; only the truth has public rights, scil., rights to be exercised within society."[17]

The ideal relationship between religion and society in this view, therefore, is a Catholic state, a regime where Catholicism is granted unique and privileged status in public life and where other creeds may exist only privately. The proponents of this view recognized, of course, that the achievement of the ideal was impossible in many nations because of the presence of large numbers of non-Catholics. Enforcement of the ideal in such circumstances could be achieved only at the cost of great social conflict, and this conflict could do considerable harm to the Catholic Church itself. In such circumstances, the public profession and practice of non-Catholic belief should be tolerated as a lesser evil than the evils that would result from efforts to institutionalize the ideal. Such tolerance, however, is not good or desirable in itself. It is a concession to unfortunate circumstances. Murray stated the basic thrust of this view succinctly. It "established a rule of jurisprudence with regard to tolerance and intolerance. This rule prescribes intolerance whenever possible; it permits tolerance whenever necessary."[18]

This theory of religious tolerance was fortunately and definitively abandoned by Vatican II. The church's move from a theory of concessionary tolerance to a full embrace of the right to religious liberty as it is understood today did not, however, occur without serious debate and argument. There are echoes of this argument in the recent writings of John Paul II, so it will be useful to take note of several points in the Conciliar discussion as these have been analyzed by Murray.

The first and second schemata (drafts) of what became the Council's *Declaration on Religious Freedom* argued for the right to religious freedom on the basis of a theory of freedom of conscience. Respect for freedom of conscience had been affirmed in a very limited way by the theory of concessionary toleration, for this theory held that the interior, personal freedom of all persons demanded respect even in the case of persons holding erroneous convictions. The first two drafts on religious freedom at the Council challenged the theory of tolerance by challenging its contention that conscience would receive genuine respect by avoiding interior coercion of religious convictions while restricting its external exercise in public. Rather, it was argued that the ethical obligation to respect conscience not only required that the inner heart and mind of each person be free from coercion but that freedom to act in accord with conscientious convictions be guaranteed in the external, public forum of society as well. As Murray explained the *Relatio* to the first draft (the presentation of the draft to the bishops at the Council), "This personal freedom (of conscience) is not really or effectively recognized, if it cannot express itself in external and public activity. For this reason, no one is to be deprived of the external exercise of his freedom (of conscience) in the human community and in civil society."[19]

There are several objections to this line of argument. The traditional concessionary tolerance theory had argued that error has no public rights. Some of those who opposed revision of this traditional teaching believed that the affirmation of the right to religious freedom would entail an abandonment of the claim that the Roman Catholic faith is in fact the true religion. They saw the right to religious freedom as rooted in religious indifferentism, a conviction that truth in the sphere of religion is not only beyond our grasp, but that it is an unimportant matter anyway. This had clearly been the case when the *lumières* of the French Revolution hurled the cry of *écrasez l'infâme* against the church and when the Law of Separation was enacted in 1905 by the Third Republic in France. Murray argued that the American tradition of religious liberty, when rightly understood, entailed no such indifferentism. He was worried, however, that this interpretation was being displaced by a growing relativism regarding moral and religious questions in the United States of his own day.[20] The evidence that his worries were not unfounded has continued to grow.

In Murray's view, the effort in the first two drafts to base the *right* to religious freedom on the *ethical* and *theological* principle that persons have a duty to follow the dictates of their consciences introduced an unfortunate confusion into the Conciliar debate. This was a confusion of the juridical order, in which the right to religious liberty is properly located, with the order of ethics and theology, where the obligation to seek the truth and live in accord with it is the operative norm. This confusion opened the way for supporters of the concessionary tolerance theory to object that "no one may ever urge rights against the truth."[21] Murray agreed that this objection was valid: "all rights must be founded on what is objectively true."[22] Further, on the juridical level, the existence of a right implies the duty of others to respect it. If one bases the right to religious freedom on freedom of conscience, therefore, one is asserting all persons have a duty to respect a person's moral and religious convictions even when those convictions are in error. In Murray's judgment, the arguments of those who reject this conclusion "are not negligible. . . . Another's error of conscience can create no duties in me, nor can it guarantee for me the rightness of his action."[23] Such a line of reasoning, of course, will hardly be persuasive to someone convinced that truth is unknowable in the religious and moral domains, but it has real force if one is convinced that such knowledge is available and in fact already in possession.

This might be illustrated by an example that Murray did not use, but that shows the force of the objection to a juridical right to religious freedom based directly on freedom of conscience. In South Africa, a considerable number of white Afrikaners have in the past believed that the Bible teaches that the separation of the races is the will of God. Some still hold this view today and do so sincerely. For these people, the system of apartheid is the natural result of the free exercise of their religious convictions in the public domain. Most people outside South Africa, and many within that country today, are convinced that apartheid is an immoral system and that it should be thoroughly abolished. In the face of this conviction, does the fact that some Afrikaners are convinced that apartheid is the will of God create a duty to allow them to express this conviction publicly by excluding blacks from their towns and from the businesses they conduct, or from seeking to create a new white "homeland" based on racial exclusion? Those who are convinced that the Afrikaners' beliefs about the races are simply false, no matter how sincerely held, cannot coherently argue that the Afrikaners possess a true *right* to act on these beliefs in public and that this right should be juridically protected. At most, it might be conceded that the apartheid system created on the basis of Afrikaner beliefs should be tolerated only so long as there is no way to dismantle it without creating evils worse than apartheid itself, such as a bloody race war. When apartheid can be abolished without disproportionate conflict, the truth of the moral (and religious) principle of racial equality implies that there is an obligation to do so. And when this occurs, those Afrikaners who continue to be convinced that apartheid is the will of God can legitimately be constrained from acting on their beliefs in public, though their inner convictions should remain immune from coercion.

This example may lend enough plausibility to the objections against a right to religious liberty based on freedom of conscience to show why the argument cast in these terms proved inadequate in the Conciliar debates. The affirmation of the right would have to be made on different grounds if it were to succeed in displacing the concessionary tolerance theory that the Conciliar traditionalists continued to support. Through Murray's influence, other grounds were indeed found. These can be called the arguments from the *nature of the juridical and political relationship* among persons in civil society and from the *historical nature of all claims about religious and ethical truth* (which Murray, following Bernard Lonergan, called "historical consciousness"). The two arguments are closely related, and I will argue that their interconnection provides important insights into the developing relationship between Catholicism and democracy.

THE JURIDICAL-POLITICAL ARGUMENT

Murray maintained that the problem with the first two drafts of the religious freedom declaration was linked with the fact that they were a part of the draft document on ecumenism. To be sure, the issue of religious freedom was a crucial question on the ecumenical agenda that the Council was seeking to address. The concessionary tolerance theory was perhaps the single greatest source of Protestant suspicion toward the Catholic Church's intentions in the political sphere, as Murray well knew from his interaction with Protestant Christians in the United States. But the linkage of the issue of religious freedom with the ecumenical question created a conceptual confusion in the argument. It meant that questions of theological and ethical *truth* became inappropriately entangled with the juridical and political question of the right to free exercise of religion. Murray maintained that the ecumenical/dialogic question should be separated from the political/legal question. Ecumenical dialogue is properly conducted as a mutual quest by different Christian groups and by Christians with non-Christians in search of mutual understanding. In this domain, no one can claim "freedom from" the claims that truth has on conscience. Indeed, that truth is precisely what ecumenical dialogue is pursuing. In ecumenical dialogue, no one has rights against the truth—in this context, invoking the idea of "rights" rests on what some philosophers have called a "category mistake." It transfers the juridical notion of a right as a freedom from external coercion into a sphere that ought to be governed by the duty to understand the other and to seek truth with the other in mutual conversation and argument. The freedom characteristic of ecumenical dialogue is a "freedom for" the discovery of this mutual understanding and ultimately of the religious and ethical truth about human existence. In the pursuit of this understanding, respect for freedom of the others engaged in the dialogue is of course essential. One must listen to the other, and a precondition for such listening is the other's freedom to speak. Respect for the other's freedom is thus a precondition for ecumenical dialogue.

But Murray went on to distinguish the issue of "religious freedom as a formally juridical concept" from the ecumenical question.[24] By doing so, he sought to break the impasse that had developed in the Conciliar debate. In Murray's view, the question of the existence of a juridical right to religious freedom should be separated from the issue of the question of the truth or falsehood of the beliefs of those who exercise this freedom. He was only partially successful in having this distinction written into the final text of the *Declaration*. In his most careful analysis, Murray identifies three arguments in *Dignitatis Humanae* for the juridical right to religious freedom, only the third of which he regards as fully successful. The first argument grounds the right to religious freedom in the fact that "all persons should be at once impelled by nature and also bound by a moral obligation to seek the truth, especially religious truth. They are also bound to adhere to the truth, once it is known, and to order their whole lives in accord with the demands of truth."[25] Because this seeking and embracing of truth can occur only through free deliberation and personal assent, the *Declaration* affirms persons have a right to immunity from coercion in fulfilling this obligation.

Murray observed that this argument was included because some bishops feared that without it the Council would appear to endorse a kind of separation between truth and freedom or, more precisely, a separation between the order of truth and the juridical order that equips man with rights against others. In Murray's view, this was a legitimate concern. Nevertheless he maintained that "the speculative question remains: Is it correct to place the ontological ground of religious freedom in man's natural and moral relationships to truth? On this point doubt may be allowed."[26]

These doubts arise for the same reason that the argument based on freedom of conscience was unsuccessful. The first Conciliar argument begs the question of whether government rightly possesses the juridical power to limit the public expression and enactment of erroneous convictions. The same problem arises for the Council's second argument. It affirms that, though religious belief is an "internal, voluntary, and free" act, the social nature of human beings requires that religious beliefs be externally expressed in community. Thus, there exists a right to the free exercise of religion in the public forum. But this is what needs to be established, and neither of these arguments has successfully shown that government may not restrict the external expression of conscientiously held convictions when these convictions are false and when action based on them would be harmful to the common good of society.

Murray finds the third argument for the right to religious freedom in the Conciliar document to be the decisive one. This is not surprising, for it is the one that Murray had strongly urged during the drafting of the document. It is not based on the theological claim that the act of Christian faith must necessarily be free or the ethical principle that human beings have a duty to follow the dictates of their consciences. These principles are certainly true, but neither of them is sufficient to answer the question about the rightful power of government to restrict external behavior based on conviction of conscience. To say that government possesses no such power is effectively to adopt an anarchist political theory. To say that the government has this power whenever the convictions acted upon are false is to adopt the presuppositions of the concessionary tolerance theory. The central question, therefore, is not primarily theological or ethical. It is political and juridical: what are the scope and limits of the power of government and law to regulate external human activity, both activity that is religious in nature and all other forms of activity as well? In Murray's words, "The political aspect becomes decisive. It is necessary to confront the question, whether and under what conditions government has the right to restrain citizens from action according to their own beliefs. . . . Or in more general terms, what are the functions and the limits of the powers of government in what concerns religion?"[27]

As Leon Hooper has shown in his very close reading of the Murray corpus, there was a considerable evolution in the way Murray addressed the theoretical question of the scope and limits of governmental power.[28] His final formulation of the issue is particularly important to the present relation of Catholicism and democracy and the future development of this relation. This version of his argument begins from an ontological first principle: "every human person is endowed with a dignity that surpasses the rest of creatures because the human person is independent [in charge of himself, autonomous]. The primordial demand of dignity, then, is that man acts by his own counsel and purpose, using and enjoying his freedom, moved, not by external coercion, but internally by the risk of his whole existence."[29] This last phrase is crucial: human beings risk not only making right or wrong choices when they act in freedom. They risk themselves; they are responsible for who they become and for whether they become truly human and realize their destiny as human beings or fail to do so. No one can exercise this responsibility for another. "So great is this dignity that not even God can take it away—by taking upon himself or unto himself the responsibility for man's life and his fate."[30] For this reason, any hint of an effort to coerce internal convictions or beliefs is excluded as fundamentally contrary to the dignity of the human person.

The second principle in Murray's final argument he calls "the social principle." It states that "the human person is the subject, foundation, and end of the entire social life." This means that the purpose of all social institutions, including but not limited to government, is the service and support of human dignity. Such institutions cannot undertake to exercise the personal responsibility through which human beings achieve their destiny. In light of the first principle of human dignity, the idea that any social power or institution could substitute itself for a person's freedom and responsibility for his or her own fate is an ontological impossibility. This affirmation should not be interpreted in an individualistic manner, for the exercise of personal responsibility is always in interaction and association with others. But what might be called the "service character" of social institutions means that these institutions must respect, support, and embody the fact that persons are responsible for themselves. Murray concludes from this that there is an "indissoluble connection between the moral and juridical orders." Thus, it is impossible to speak of having respect for the inner moral and religious freedom of persons while simultaneously prohibiting the exercise of that freedom in public. "The juridical order cannot be sundered from the moral order, any more than the human person can be halved."[31] The social principle, in other words, is not separate from the ontological principle of human dignity, but a further expression of it. The two principles, taken together, provide the central insight that leads to the affirmation to the right to religious freedom as an immunity from both coercion of interior belief and restriction on the free exercise of belief.

From the ontological and social principles, taken together, follow three further steps in Murray's argument. The so-called principle of the free society affirms that human beings are to be accorded as much freedom as possible in social life and that freedom is to be restricted only where such restriction is necessary for the preservation of the conditions that make social life possible at all. These are the conditions of public peace, justice, and that level of public morality on which consensus exists in the society. The juridical principle that all persons are equal before the law "rests upon the truth that all are peers in dignity of nature and that every human being is equally the subject, foundation, and end of human society." Finally, the political principle states that the paramount duty of government is "to protect the inviolable rights proper to human beings and ensure that everyone may discharge his duties with greater facility."[32]

All five of these principles, taken together, specify the scope and limits of the power of government. They therefore specify the proper role of government with regard to religion. The principle of the free society applies to religious freedom, just as to all other freedoms that are essential expressions of human dignity. The rule is this: as much religious freedom as possible; only as much restriction as necessary to protect the basic conditions of public order (i.e., peace, justice, and minimal conditions of public morality). Government has no responsibility to advance or even to protect religious truth. Rather, the truth to which government is accountable is the truth of human dignity, the truth that in matters religious, as in all other matters in which human beings' very selves are determined, "man should act by his own deliberation and purpose, enjoying immunity from all external coercion so that in the presence of God he takes responsibility on himself alone for his religious decisions and acts. This demand of both freedom and responsibility is the ontological ground of religious freedom as it likewise is the ground of the other human freedoms."[33]

Murray's argument for religious freedom thus rests on the basic principles of democratic self-government. It affirms that, in political life, the person "is fully citizen, that is, not merely subject to, but also participant in, the processes of government."[34] The virtue of society is built from the bottom up, not mandated from the top down, and it is built by citizens who take responsibility for their lives and for the well-being of society through active participation in public life. A fundamental element of this social well-being is a robust commitment to the freedom of one's fellow citizens. In such a society, there is no way the church could legitimately claim freedom for itself and in turn use this freedom to impose its vision on others in society. Just as the affirmation of the right to religious freedom is a self-denying ordinance by which government acknowledges the limits of its power in the religious sphere, so too the affirmation of this right is a self-denying ordinance on the part of the church. It is a renunciation of any appeal by the church for assistance from governmental power to advance its religious purposes. This represents an abandonment of the church's historical claim that it had a right to aid from the secular arm (*auxilium brachii saecularis*). Affirmation of the right to religious freedom thus entails a fundamental shift in the church's understanding of the nature of governmental power and also of the church's relation to that power.

THE ARGUMENT FROM HISTORICAL CONSCIOUSNESS

Murray repeatedly stated that the fundamental issue that confronted the church at the Council was the question of the development of doctrine. This question was most pointed in the debate on religious freedom because the explicit ecclesial statements on this matter in the nineteenth century were so clearly on the side of those opposing affirmation of the right to religious liberty. As Murray put it, *Dignitatis Humanae* was "the most controversial document of the whole Council, largely because it raised with sharp emphasis the issue that lay continually below the surface of all Conciliar debates—the issue of development of doctrine. The notion of development, not the notion of religious freedom, was the real sticking point for many of those who opposed the Declaration to the end. . . . But the Council formally sanctioned the validity of development itself; and this was a doctrinal event of high importance for theological thought in many other areas."[35] This sanction was stated explicitly when the Council declared, "In taking up the matter of religious freedom this sacred Synod *intends* to develop the doctrine of recent Popes on the inviolable rights of the human person and on the constitutional order of society."[36]

The acceptance of the possibility and indeed the necessity of such development was the result of a fundamental shift in mentality, from what Lonergan called classical consciousness to historical consciousness. To tell the full story of this shift is too large a task to be undertaken here, but several aspects of it that are important to Murray's mature understanding of religious freedom can be highlighted. First, for classical consciousness, truths grasped by the human mind exist apart from history. "Classicism designates a view of truth which holds objective truth, precisely because it is objective, to exist 'already out there now' (to use Bernard Lonergan's descriptive phrase). Therefore, it also exists apart from its possession by anyone."[37] It can be formulated in verbally immutable propositions that are timeless. In the realm of religion, the entire ensemble of propositions formulating Catholic doctrine contains the religious truth. Any development in the understanding of Christian life that might be legitimate is limited to a new application of these religious truths to changing historical circumstances. Thus, for example, the concessionary tolerance theory applies the truth of the Catholic religion to the political sphere in circumstances where the establishment of Catholicism as the religion of the state is impossible.

Historical consciousness was shaped by recognition in the nineteenth and early twentieth centuries that knowledge has a history. Murray argued that the church resisted this recognition because it was interpreted in a way that undermined the notion of truth itself, leading to relativism in religion and morality. This continues to be a major concern of Pope John Paul II, as was noted above. Following the lead of Lonergan, however, Murray maintained that the historicity of knowledge does not imply the abandonment of the notion of objective truth. Rather, it demands much greater attention to the dynamics and structure of *knowing*, the personal reality of the subjects of knowledge. As he put it, "historical consciousness, while holding fast to the nature of truth as objective, is concerned with the possession of truth, with man's affirmations of truth, with the understand-

ings contained in these affirmations, with the conditions—both circum-
stantial and subjective—of understanding and affirmation, and therefore
with the historicity of truth and with progress in the grasp and penetration
of what is true."[38]

As Leon Hooper has persuasively argued, this turn to the historicity of
the human subject of knowledge brought Murray to stress that coming to
knowledge of the truth is a profoundly personal responsibility. No one else
can know for me. No one else is responsible for my convictions about the
meaning of human life or about the way life is to be lived. In forming such
convictions the human person "is subject only to the laws that rule the order of truth—truth is so accepted only on pertinent evidence, the assent
to truth is to be personal and free, and the search is to be pursued in free
communion with others."[39] That all knowledge is knowledge by a personal
subject and that all knowing persons are historical beings are the core insights of historical consciousness. They explain why personal knowledge is
of necessity a developing reality. At the same time, such knowledge is
essentially social; it is attained, as Murray says, "in free communion with
others." As a social attainment, knowledge is also subject to growth and development. Knowledge of the truth by an individual person is not simply
the appropriation of the accumulated understandings of an already existing culture. Though it is this in part, it is also a process that involves ques-
tioning such traditional understandings and, where evidence warrants,
changing them.

This understanding of historical consciousness, therefore, leads *simultaneously* to the insight that the Catholic Church's understanding of the
role of government with regard to religion *can* legitimately be changed
and that it *ought* to be changed. It can be changed because knowledge of
the truth is not timeless, but developing because of the historicity of human knowers. It ought to be changed because the historicity of knowledge
means that the truth about God, the human person, and the cosmos can
be attained only by people living in a "zone of freedom." Thus, Murray's
argument for religious liberty on the basis of historical consciousness con-
verges with his argument based on the nature of the political-juridical relationship. The argument for the possibility of a development in the
church's self-understanding has the same root as the argument for the validity of the institutions of a free society: the dignity of the human person
can be realized only through a free, socially embodied, quest for meaning.

CONCLUSION: BOTH IMMUNITY AND EMPOWERMENT

Hooper has argued that, at the very end of his life, Murray was led by this line of thinking to regard the right to religious freedom as a positive social empowerment rather than simply a negative civil immunity from coercion.[40] By this he means that religious freedom enables religious believers and nonbelievers alike to enter into a community of discourse that seeks to discover the truth about how they should live together. I think Hooper is exactly right. Historical consciousness leads not only to the insight that the grasp of truth by individual persons is a dynamic and developing reality, but also that persons come to understanding and knowledge only through a social process of active engagement with others. For such a process to occur, persons must be willing to both listen and speak. When they do so with authenticity, freedom becomes not only an individual possession, but also a social reality. A *community of freedom* comes into being, a community whose members are neither atomistic monads nor passive subjects, but active participants in a shared quest.[41]

Murray observed that the Council's affirmation of religious freedom was no breakthrough to new insight into the requirements of human dignity by the church. The Council's "achievement was to bring the Church, at long last, abreast of the consciousness of civilized mankind, which had already accepted religious freedom as a principle and as a legal institution."[42] The development of doctrine that occurred at the Council, in other words, was a result of the church's willingness to learn from secular society as well as its willingness to retrieve dimensions of the Catholic tradition that had been obscured in the context of nineteenth-century polemics. The Council's achievement thus shows how active participation in intellectual and cultural dialogue is essential to the discovery of truth in a historically conscious world. Thus, in Murray's late writings, the Council's argument for religious freedom is implicitly reconnected with the ecumenical question from which he had earlier thought it should be separated. But now ecumenism is interpreted in the broad sense of active conversation not only with other Christians, but also with the full array of intellectual currents present in culture. Religious freedom empowers Christians for such participation while simultaneously demanding that they exercise the intellectual humility that enables them to listen as well as speak.

It should be noted, however, that this does not mean that religious liberty is a positive empowerment *rather* than a civil immunity. The right to immunity from coercion remains as an essential precondition for the existence of the empowerment. A community of discourse can be such only when it is immune from coercion. The relation between truth and freedom is a mutual and reciprocal one. Religious truth claims should not be excluded from public discourse. Religious freedom means believers have as much right to make their case regarding public affairs as do those who make political claims based on nonreligious grounds. At the same time, religiously based claims about the truth on which public life should be constructed must be subject to the same criteria of the free exchange of ideas as are all other proposals about laws and policies in a democratic society.

Murray noted that the *Declaration on Religious Freedom* in no way accepted the secularist view that religion is simply a private affair. It did, however, accept the idea that secular society has a rightful autonomy as a sphere distinct from the church. He regarded this differentiation of the secular and the sacred as genuine progress in human self-understanding. The nonestablishment of religion and the freedom of individuals from coercion in matters religious are the principal institutional and juridical expressions of this differentiation. But Murray also observed that nonestablishment and immunity from coercion are not the end of the argument about religious liberty. "A work of differentiation between the sacral and the secular has been effected within history. But differentiation is not the highest stage in human growth. The movement toward it, now that it has come to term, must be followed by a further movement toward a new synthesis, within which the differentiation will at once subsist, integral and unconfused, and also be transcended in a higher unity."[43]

I take it that the positive empowerment and participation of those motivated by religious conviction in public life is what Murray means by this higher synthesis. But his insistence that the sacral-secular differentiation must remain integral and unconfused within this synthesis means that religious freedom from coercion remains central when believers seek to shape the public life of society.

Murray observed that the task of pursuing this higher synthesis is "manifold, complicated and delicate," and that Catholic universities are principle venues where it ought to be pursued.[44] He made this suggestion, I think, because the synthesis of religious convictions with understandings of the goods of public life is a long-term project involving fundamental questions in theology, philosophy, the arts and the sciences, including the social sciences. It may be the case in some circumstances that debates about specific policies or laws are appropriate occasions for seeking such a synthesis. The U.S. Catholic bishops' pastoral letters on nuclear strategic policy and on economic justice were in my judgment examples where this was the case. But more often the effort at synthesis will occur in the cultural sphere rather than the political or judicial. Where no consensus exists in the cultural domain on what values should shape public life and policy, it will frequently be difficult to move directly from religious convictions to policy or legislation without endangering or infringing the right to freedom from coercion in religious matters. That is why the U.S. bishops' pastoral letters in the 1980s were so carefully cast as documents that sought to persuade rather than coerce. The existence of such documents suggests that the pursuit of a higher synthesis of sacral and secular need not be confined to the Catholic university. It should be taking place wherever the intellectual quest for the truth about how we should live our public life together is underway. And it should always take place in the fullness of freedom. Freedom and truth are mutually and reciprocally linked. This is the case in the lives of individuals, in the public life of societies, and in the life of the church itself. Failure of commitment to one of these surpassing values inevitably leads to the destruction of the other.

NOTES

1. John Courtney Murray, "The Declaration on Religious Freedom: Its Deeper Significance," *America* 114 (April 23, 1966): 592.

2. Murray, "Religious Freedom," in Murray, ed., *Freedom and Man* (New York: P. J. Kenedy & Sons, 1965), 135.

3. Samuel P. Huntington, "Religion and the Third Wave," *National Interest* 24 (summer 1991): 29–42. Huntington's argument about the sources of democratization is more fully developed in his *The Third Wave: Democratization in the Late Twentieth Century* (Norman: University of Oklahoma Press, 1991).

4. Ibid., 30.

5. Ibid., 34.

6. Mikhail S. Gorbachev, "My Partner, the Pope," *New York Times*, March 9, 1992: A17.

7. See, for example, Sean O'Riordan, "Toward a Decisional Model of Church," *Furrow* (November 1991): 607–15.

8. John Paul II, *Centesimus Annus,* no. 46.

9. Ibid., no. 41.

10. Ibid., no. 29.

11. Ibid., nos. 29 and 48.

12. Milton Friedman , comments in the symposium "The Pope, Liberty, and Capitalism," *National Review*, Special Supplement, 1991: p. S-4.

13. *Centesimus Annus,* no. 46.

14. Ibid., no. 60.

15. See Murray, "Religious Freedom," in Murray, ed., *Freedom and Man*, 133–34.

16. Murray, *The Problem of Religious Freedom* (Westminster, Md.: Newman Press, 1965), 7.

17. Ibid., 9.

18. Ibid., 12.

19. Cited in Murray, "The Declaration on Religious Freedom: A Moment in Its Legislative History," in Murray, ed., *Religious Liberty: An End and a Beginning* (New York: Macmillan, 1966), 19.

20. See, for example, *We Hold These Truths: Catholic Reflections on the American Proposition* (New York: Sheed and Ward, 1960), chap. 3.

21. Murray, "The Declaration on Religious Freedom: A Moment in Its Legislative History," 24.

22. Ibid., 23.

23. Ibid., 25.

24. Ibid., 27.

25. Vatican Council II, *Dignitatis Humanae* (Declaration on Religious Freedom), in Walter M. Abbott and Joseph Gallagher, eds., *The Documents of Vatican II* (New York: America Press, 1966), no. 2.

26. Murray, "The Arguments for the Human Right to Religious Freedom," originally published as "De argumentis pro iure hominis ad libertatem religiosam," in A. Schönmetzer, ed., *Acta Congressus Internationalis de Theologia Concilii Vaticani II* (Vatican City: Typis Polyglottis Vaticanis, 1968). The translation used here is from Murray, *Religious Liberty: Catholic Struggles with Pluralism,* ed. J. Leon Hooper (Louisville, Ky.: Westminster/John Knox Press, 1993), 236.

27. Murray, "The Declaration on Religious Freedom: A Moment in Its Legislative History," 31–32.

28. J. Leon Hooper, *The Ethics of Discourse: The Social Philosophy of John Courtney Murray* (Washington, D.C.: Georgetown University Press, 1986). I am much indebted to Hooper's interpretation of Murray's post-Conciliar writings, which I regard as most accurate and perceptive.

29. Murray, "The Arguments for the Human Right to Religious Freedom," 238.

30. Ibid.

31. Ibid.

32. Ibid., 239. Here Murray is quoting John XXIII, who in turn is quoting Pius XII.

33. Ibid., 240.

34. Murray, "The Declaration on Religious Freedom," in *War, Poverty, Freedom: The Christian Response*, Concilium, no. 15 (New York: Paulist Press, 1966), 13.

35. Murray, "Religious Freedom," introduction to the *Declaration on Religious Freedom,* in Abbott and Gallagher, eds., *The Documents of Vatican II*, 673.

36. *Dignitatis Humanae,* no. 1, emphasis added.

37. Murray, "The Declaration on Religious Freedom," 11.

38. Ibid.

39. Murray, "The Declaration on Religious Freedom: A Moment in Its Legislative History," 39.

40. See *The Ethics of Discourse*, 154–56 and all of chap. 6.

41. I have developed this further in "Afterword: A Community of Freedom," in R. Bruce Douglass and David Hollenbach, eds., *Catholicism and Liberalism: Contributions to American Public Philosophy* (Cambridge: Cambridge University Press, 1994), 323–43; and in my *The Common Good and Christian Ethics* (Cambridge: Cambridge University Press, 2002), chaps. 5 and 6.

42. Murray, "The Declaration on Religious Freedom: Its Deeper Significance," 592.

43. Ibid., 593.

44. Ibid.

8

The Context of Civil Society and Culture

This chapter will suggest that recent discussions of the role of religious arguments in debates about public policy sometimes rest on oversimplified presuppositions. The discussion often seems polarized between two opposing camps. On one side are those who hold that it is appropriate for citizens to appeal directly to their religious convictions in advocating positions on policy issues. On the other side are those who hold that appeal to religious beliefs is always inappropriate in a liberal democratic society. Though many of the participants in this discussion hold views that are considerably more complex than either of these two positions, I think that stating the alternatives this way can help illuminate certain aspects of the debate that I want to call into question. Formulating the matter this way points to a tendency to assume that the relation of religion and politics is governed by just two variables—religious convictions, on the one hand, and recommendations about policy or law, on the other. It further suggests that the question of whether religion should have a public role in society is identical to the question of whether either the advocacy or the justification of public policies should be based directly on religious convictions.

I will argue that the debate needs to be framed in a different way. Religion is not simply a set of convictions that one should or should not invoke in political debate. It is a considerably more dynamic and multidimensional reality than the term "convictions" might suggest. Likewise, political debate is not simply argument about whether to adopt or reject certain policies. There are, of course, many ways to demarcate the sphere to which the term "political" can be applied, but if we agree that the political sphere encompasses all human activities that occur in the public life of society, it is surely a mistake to limit it to the policy decisions reached in legislative, executive, or judicial fora. The *res publica* is much larger than the sphere of government. It includes all those communities and institutions that form the rich fabric of civil society. It also includes all those public forms of discourse, conversation, and argument that constitute a culture.

So this chapter will argue that we need to frame the question of the relation of religion to public life in a way that goes beyond discussion of the direct impact of religious convictions on policy choices. Religious faiths and traditions have perhaps their most important influence on government, law, and policy formation in an indirect way. The impact of religion on politics understood as the sphere of governmental activity is mediated through its influence on the multiple communities and institutions of civil society and on the public self-understanding of a society called culture. The first two sections of the chapter will consider these public influences of religion. The third section will then address the more specific question of how religious beliefs ought to be related to public policy in light of the discussion in the first two.

CIVIL SOCIETY AND THE MEANING OF "PUBLIC"

One prominent version of the argument for insulating the political process from the influence of religious convictions harkens back to the dismaying historical record of the Catholic and Protestant communities during the sixteenth- and seventeenth-century wars of religion. This history is seen as a precedent for what is likely to happen today if religious communities decide to press their beliefs as guides for governmental decision making or public policy. Sometimes this historical appeal is augmented by references to "moral majorities" insisting on prayer in public schools, the teaching of "creation science" in these schools, and the imposition of religious convictions about abortion on those who do not share these convictions. Occasionally, such arguments are reinforced by references to the contemporary Islamic world and to nations where attempts have been made to base both constitutional and penal law on the Shari'ah. These historical and contemporary examples lead to considerable fear of what are seen as the likely results of public, political activity by religious communities.

At the root of these fears of a public role for religion is what John Rawls calls "the fact of pluralism." The regimes of modern democratic societies evolved historically as a way of responding to the diversity of conceptions of the meaning and purpose of life. This diversity is most evident in religious disagreement, but there is also a deep pluralism in philosophical conceptions of how to live a good life. Rawls says that this religious and philosophical pluralism "is not a mere historical condition that will soon pass away; it is, I believe, a permanent feature of the public culture of modern democracies. Under the political and social conditions secured by the basic rights and liberties historically associated with these regimes, the diversity of views will persist and may increase."[1] Under these conditions, the "common sense political sociology of democratic societies" tell us that agreement on a single conception of the good life among all citizens is unattainable. Such agreement could be maintained "only by the oppressive use of state power."[2]

Rawls accurately points to the deep disputes that exist about the meaning of the good life in our society. For him, there is no way to resolve these disputes. Therefore, he argues that the fact of pluralism demands that in politics we must deal with disagreements about the comprehensive good of human life by what he calls "the method of avoidance." This method demands that in political life "we try, so far as we can, neither to assert nor to deny any religious, philosophical or moral views, or their associated philosophical accounts of truth and the status of values."[3] Avoidance of such basic questions is necessary in politics, Rawls thinks, if we are to have a chance of achieving consensus. "We apply the principle of toleration to philosophy itself" when debating the basic political and economic institutions that will structure social life.[4] Each man or woman must be free to hold his or her view of what the full good really is, but these comprehensive views of the good life must remain the private convictions of individuals. "In applying the principle of toleration to philosophy itself it is left to citizens individually to resolve the questions of religion, philosophy and morals in accordance with the views they freely affirm."[5] Or, as Richard Rorty puts it, religious and philosophical convictions should be exempt from coercion in a liberal society under one condition: that such convictions "be reserved for private life." Argument about the common good is also to be avoided in debates about more specific public policies. Liberal democracy aims at "disengaging discussions of such questions from discussions of public policy."[6] This privatization of "thick" visions of the good is not only a sociologically given fact; it is a moral constraint on political activity.

This analysis assumes that the presence of religious or comprehensive philosophical views of the good in public life inevitably leads to conflict. It further presupposes that the public sphere is identical with the domain governed by the coercive power of the state. From these presuppositions taken together, it follows that religious influence in public is identified with the coercive enforcement of the religious or philosophical convictions of whatever group is strong enough to gain control of government. Because this is clearly an unacceptable outcome, the alternative proposed is the privatization of religion.

I fully agree that the coercive imposition of religious beliefs is morally unacceptable, as does the vast majority of religious believers in the West today. The privatization of religion is not, however, the only alternative to such a coercive outcome if religion appears in public. Another approach to the question is founded on a more capacious understanding of what public life is, or at least could be. Drawing on my own Roman Catholic tradition, I want to outline such an approach. Reflection on the role played by a broader vision of the meaning of public life outside the United States may reinforce its plausibility.

For liberal thinkers like Rawls, the discussion of the role of religion in public life is framed by certain presuppositions about the institutions that structure social interaction. Their emphasis is on the state and the market as the principal domains in which social existence unfolds. At the same time, different forms of liberalism embody diverse attitudes of suspicion toward the institutions of government and the market. Libertarians regard the state as the principal threat to human freedom and dignity. Consequently, their aim is to minimize governmental intervention. Those with a more social democratic orientation fear that the market is the principal threat and seek to limit its impact on individuals through governmental regulation and the institutions of the modern welfare state. In both of these ways of thinking, the paradigm that shapes analysis envisions individual persons confronting the "megastructures" of either government or the market economy.[7] The relation of the private and public spheres is pictured as the relation of isolated individuals to large, anonymous, and impersonal institutional structures. Public activities are those conducted within the spheres of government or the market. The public sphere thus becomes the area of human life ruled either by the power of government or by the constraints of the marketplace. The defense of freedom, therefore, is viewed as the effort to secure a zone of action that is protected from governmental power or market determinism. This zone is private. To use Rawls's terms, it is the domain in which individuals can live "in accordance with the views they freely affirm."

A number of recent analyses of the contemporary social problematic have raised worrisome questions about the adequacy of this bipolar disjunction of human activity into public and private spheres. For example, Alan Wolfe's important book, *Whose Keeper? Social Science and Moral Obligation*, has argued that the increasingly dense and interdependent spheres of politics and the marketplace threaten to overwhelm whatever remnants of private freedom still exist in advanced modern societies. The sphere of freedom is "increasingly squeezed from two directions"—from the one side by the bureaucracy of the administrative state and from the other by powerful determinisms of markets linked in an increasingly global network.[8] Wolfe argues that, if the freedom promised by modernity is to survive under the conditions that prevail in advanced societies in the twenty-first century, we need a counterweight to this pressure from the state and the market. Solitary, private individuals cannot provide this counterweight. "We need civil society—families, communities, friendship networks, solidaristic workplace ties, voluntarism, spontaneous groups and movements—not to reject, but to complete the project of modernity." He further maintains that the solidarity associated with closer and more intimate relations in the realm regarded as private by liberal theory "requires that we extend the 'inward' moral rules of civil society 'outward' to the realm of nonintimate and distant social relations."[9] Wolfe does not mean to suggest that the moral framework that guides political or economic life can be based directly on the values of family life, close friendships, or the solidarity of groups that share common religious or philosophical convictions, but he does argue that these bonds of community need to be given much greater *public* space than the sharp split of the political from the private advocated by Rawls or Rorty. The strong communal links found in the diverse groups of civil society must have greater public presence. Otherwise individuals will experience further diminishment of their freedom and power in the face of the growing complexity of distant governmental and economic megastructures. The image of human life as divided between a public sector of governments and markets and a private sector of individual autonomous freedom is unrealistic. Freedom will not flourish, or perhaps even survive, unless it enjoys greater presence and support in public. We need a more complex and differentiated picture of the world we really live in.

This is not the place to rehearse the sociological arguments on which Wolfe bases his conclusions. For the purposes of this chapter, I will presume that Wolfe's analysis has revealed a significant problem in the prevailing conception of the relation of the public and private realms, and ask readers to assess my argument about the role of religion in political life in light of this presupposition.

To be even clearer about presuppositions, it will be obvious why Wolfe's analysis is congenial to one who, like myself, has been shaped by the tradition of Roman Catholic social thought. Especially since the birth of modernity, the Roman Catholic tradition has been suspicious both of social theories extolling the primacy of the state and of theories granting primacy to the market. At the same time, this tradition has rejected individualistic understandings of freedom. In fact, its rejection of an individualistic understanding of the self is the source of its suspicion of both liberal contract theories of politics and laissez-faire models of economic life. Its view of the public-private relationship is not bipolar, with the "megastructures" of the state or the market defining the public sphere and the autonomous freedom of the individual defining the private sphere. Rather, it proposes a model of social life that is richer and institutionally more pluralistic than that of standard liberal theory.

Modern Catholic teaching, to be sure, is strongly concerned with the fate of individuals. For example, Pope John XXIII stated, "The cardinal point of this teaching [of the Catholic Church] is that individual persons are necessarily the foundation, cause, and end of all social institutions."

But, the pope immediately added, "We are referring to human beings, insofar as they are social by nature."[10] Human dignity and worth is never achieved in solitude, nor is the protection of this dignity simply a matter of insulating individuals from the costs (and denying them the opportunities) that attend interaction with others. Rather, the task of protecting human dignity and freedom is a task of protecting the quality of the relationships among persons in such a way that freedom and dignity can be realized. In this sense, there is no strictly private sphere. Because humans are relational beings whose identity, worth, and dignity are attained in interaction with others, human flourishing is always public or social. Thus, Catholic social thought emphasizes the multiple forms of human relationship and community in which persons are formed and nurtured. Social space is not occupied only by the large institutions of government and market, on the one hand, and individuals, on the other. This is evident in the tradition's stress on the importance of securing the well-being of "intermediary" institutions such as families and voluntary associations, and it is a key to understanding how we can envision a form of political life that is communal without being statist. It also suggests a way of envisioning the public role of religion that avoids the charge that, whenever religion becomes public, religious coercion will be the result.

The distinction between the public sphere and the domain of governmental power was central to the discussion of the relation of the Catholic Church to democracy that took place in the middle decades of the twentieth century and that bore fruit at the Second Vatican Council. In the 1950s, Jacques Maritain and John Courtney Murray argued for the compatibility of a public role for religion with the institutions of democracy by reaffirming the distinction between society and the state. Society is composed of a rich and overlapping set of human communities such as families, neighborhoods, churches, labor unions, corporations, professional associations, credit unions, cooperatives, universities, and a host of other associations. These communities are not private, but public. Especially when they are small or of intermediate size, they enable persons to come together in ways that can be vividly experienced. The bonds of communal solidarity formed in them enable persons to act together, empowering them to shape some of the contours of public life and its larger social institutions such as the state and the economy. In a democratic society, government does not rule, but rather serves the social "body" animated by the activity of these intermediate communities. Pope Pius XI formulated the matter in what came to be known as the principle of subsidiarity: government "should, by its very nature, provide help [*subsidium*] to members of the body social, it should never destroy or absorb them."[11] Or, in Maritain's words, "the state is inferior to the body politic as a whole and is at the service of the body politic as a whole."[12] The body politic or civil society is the primary locus in which human solidarity is realized.

In the writings of Maritain and Murray, the society-state distinction is at the root of their affirmation of both religious freedom and constitutional democracy. It is the basis for their firm opposition to all forms of totalitarianism, state absolutism, or religious coercion. The writ of government does not reach as far as the full scope of the public life of society. The defense of the free exercise of religion and the defense of the existence and freedom of the communities that make up civil society are directly linked to each other. Thus, the right to religious freedom and the rights to public association and public expression are inseparable. As Murray concluded, "The personal or corporate free exercise of religion, as a human and civil right, is evidently cognate with other more general human and civil rights—with the freedom of corporate bodies and institutions within society, based on the principle of subsidiary function; with the general freedom of association for peaceful purposes, based on the social nature of man; with the general freedom of speech and of the press based on the nature of political society."[13]

This argument reveals one way that a Catholic understanding of the institutions of democracy and the human rights that undergird them presents a challenge to those forms of liberalism concerned exclusively or primarily with the defense of the freedom of individuals to act as they please in a zone of privacy. The presupposition about the basis of democracy is not the sovereign autonomy of the individual. Participation in public life and the exercise of freedom in society depend on the strength of the communal institutions that give persons a measure of real power to shape their environment, including their political environment. As John Coleman has argued, this kind of commitment to democracy rests on "a presumptive rule about where real vitality exists in society"—in the diverse and overlapping communities that make up civil society.[14] The public and the social, therefore, are not to be identified with the sphere of government. Social practices and institutions can be truly public, even though not under governmental control. Thus, churches, just like all the other associations that make up civil society, must be both free from domination by the state and free to act and express themselves in public.

The importance of civil society as a public sphere that is not dominated by the state was powerfully illustrated by the way the collapse of communism was so rapidly brought about in Central and Eastern Europe. The power of the dissident workers and intellectuals of the "velvet revolutions" of 1989 grew out of their success in creating the solidarity of a genuine civil society, not out of direct seizure of state power or out of the barrel of a gun. What were initially extragovernmental bonds of community at Gdansk's shipyards and Prague's Magic Lantern Theater empowered men and women to effect a stunning transformation of supposedly untransformable totalitarian regimes. In the words of Bronislaw Geremek, speaker of the parliament in Poland, the emergence of civil society from under the dominant apparatus of the state became possible when "dissidents engaged in their own peculiar type of mental resistance, which typically began with a refusal to participate in falsehood, grew into a desire to bear loud witness to one's own views and conscience, and then finally drove one to political action. . . . The idea of civil society—even one that avoids overtly political activities in favor of education, the exchange of information and opinion, or the protection of the basic interests of particular groups—has enormous antitotalitarian potential."[15]

The public role of religion in the revolutions of 1989 varied from one country to another, and the churches were surely not the sole agents of this transformation.[16] But there is no question that the commitment of the churches was crucial in sustaining the many overlapping communities that make up civil society—communities that refused to submit to state domination. Adam Michnik, a Jewish intellectual and Solidarity activist, described the Catholic Church's role in Poland this way several years before the revolution occurred: "The problem faced by Polish society is that civil society doesn't exist. Society is not recognized as capable of organizing itself to defend its particular interests and points of view. . . . [T]he present totalitarian system insists that every person is State property. The Church's view is that every person is a child of God, to whom God has granted natural liberty. . . . It follows from this that in Poland and other communist countries religion is the natural antidote to the totalitarian claims of the State authorities."[17] In East Germany, Czechoslovakia, and Hungary, as well as in Poland, the recovery of freedom, the revival of civil society, and the public presence of the churches (Catholic, Orthodox, and Protestant) were closely connected phenomena.

These recent events in Central and Eastern Europe may seem irrelevant to an effort to clarify the proper public role for religion in the United States. There is an analogy, however, between the destruction of civil society under Communist rule in the Eastern bloc and the weakening of civil society in the West that Alan Wolfe fears is occurring. To be sure, if the alternatives to present patterns of American society are communist totalitarianism, the authoritarian oligopolies that have been dominant in much of Latin American history, or the one-party states common in Africa, there can be no doubt of the superiority of the democratic institutions of the North Atlantic. But the choice we face in the politics of the United States today is not one between democracy and authoritarianism. Rather, it is at least a plausible hypothesis that here the more immediate threat to a civil society capable of nurturing freedom is not an authoritarian state, but the dominance of the market and its instrumental rationality over increasingly large domains of social and cultural life.

If this hypothesis is correct, the liberal instinct to treat all activities that are not directly governmental as private is not only sociologically inaccurate but also politically dangerous. Among the many "nongovernmental organizations" that have a crucial role to play in sustaining the vision of public life that is crucial to democracy are the churches. This is so for two reasons.

First, the assertion of the right to religious freedom was a key factor in the movement that brought about modern constitutional democracy. This right was not only "cognate" with the full range of the human rights of a democratic society, as John Courtney Murray maintained in the passage cited above. It was one of the principal causal forces, socially embodied in religious communities, which led to the rise of modern democracy. For this reason, the freedom of the many diverse communities of solidarity in civil society and the freedom of the churches rise or fall together. An effort to privatize religion, whether in practice or in theory, therefore, is "cognate" with an effort to privatize every human activity that is not properly part of the exercise of state power. A successful move in this direction will leave the individual human being alone and defenseless in the face of the encroaching power of the market. It will also leave the individual unable to form those bonds of solidarity that are essential if government is to be made to function in a way that keeps the market in its place. An active, public role for religion, therefore, would seem to be one of the preconditions of a vibrant democratic life.

Second, the churches possess unique resources that can contribute to the strengthening of other communities of solidarity in civil society. Ideas about love of neighbor—about commitment to the well-being of other persons—are present in all religious traditions. The meaning of this love and commitment, of course, is interpreted in different ways in different religious traditions, but all these traditions possess resources that can serve as an antidote to the idea that a democratic society can be successfully constructed on self-interest or, as Rawls would have it, mutual disinterest. More than this is needed if any public realm is to thrive, or even survive, in the face of market pressures and the logic of instrumental market rationality.

Further, sociologist Robert Wuthnow's empirical survey research has shown that people's spiritual concerns translate into active efforts to respond to the needs of their neighbors only when these concerns are lived out in the context of a publicly visible and active religious community. Wuthnow's data suggest that understanding religion or spirituality as a purely private affair between an individual and his or her god, without the mediation of a religious community with a public presence in society, has little effect on believers' responses to their neighbors: "I interpret these results to mean that religious inclinations make very little difference unless one becomes involved in some kind of organized religious community. Once you are involved in such a community, then a higher level of piety may be associated with putting yourself out to help the needy. But if you are not involved in some kind of religious organization, then a higher level of piety seems unlikely to generate charitable efforts toward the poor or disadvantaged."[18] The increasing privatization of religion as not only separated from the sphere of government but also as a purely personal affair independent of any organized religious community thus seems to threaten to undermine any positive effects religion can have in society. Wuthnow concludes that, "If religious values have been an inducement for people to care for their neighbors historically, then the spread of individualism within modern religion is likely to have a dampening effect on charitable behavior."[19]

Wuthnow's conclusion on the link between religious convictions and charitable behavior is echoed in the findings of a study of political activism in the United States conducted by my colleague Kay Schlozman in cooperation with Sidney Verba and Henry Brady.[20] One of the conclusions of this study is that participation in church activities sows seeds of political activism. "Churches are 'incubators' for tomorrow's political activists." Engagement in church-related activity teaches organizational skills that are readily transferable to politics. In addition, the study found that, "contrary to political scientists' assumptions, personal gain played a minimal role in causing people to become active. The responses [of those surveyed in the study] indicate that psychological rewards, such as commitment to community and 'doing one's civic duty,' are primary motivators."[21] This suggests that an active presence of religious communities in the public life of the country can strengthen, rather than threaten, democracy. If one fears that public life is becoming increasingly fragile, the prescription would appear to be more church involvement in public life, not less.

CULTURE, PUBLIC DISCOURSE, AND THE COMMON GOOD

Such a proposal for strengthening the bonds of communal solidarity in society, of course, can be expected to be greeted with suspicion by those who fear that it will lead to coerced cohesion. This is particularly so when the proposal includes the suggestion that religious communities should play a more public role in shaping the bonds that link persons together in public. There is apprehension that this will lead churches to act simply as special interest groups, seeking power to press their own agendas through the political process. Thus, the position being advocated here must respond to the legitimate question of whether any strong vision of solidarity can be pursued beyond the boundaries of small and intermediate-sized communities without sacrificing intellectual freedom and social pluralism. Scholars such as Rawls are very skeptical that this is possible. Because he thinks the effort to achieve some consensus about the common good of the larger society is necessarily futile, he concludes that we will have to get along with a politics that is neutral on competing conceptions of the good life.

Thus, all talk about the "comprehensive" human good should be restricted to the private sphere.

The experience of history shows that these fears are not products of fantasy. Societies characterized by strong bonds of solidarity have sometimes been oppressive of freedom. Religious groups have sometimes used state power to stifle pluralism. These dangers have not gone away, and our recognition that they are present is growing. Nevertheless, if the argument in the first part of this chapter is correct, paying exclusive attention to the dangers of closed communities and the difficulty of establishing dialogue among the subgroups in a pluralistic society also poses a serious threat to the quality of social life. So we would do better, as Robin Lovin has suggested, to try to pursue our hopes for a positive relationship of religion to politics than simply to avoid the dangers we fear in their interaction.[22]

Lovin points out that theories that support efforts to insulate the political domain from any religious influence are "curiously abstract" and do not well describe the role religious beliefs actually play in the lives of many people.[23] In fact, people's conceptions of how life ought to be lived—including religious conceptions—are routinely introduced into public discourse. Even those who profess to support public neutrality on the meaning of the good life find it difficult to live up to their ideal in practice. The interconnection of our lives and the common institutions we share make the demand that we remain silent on the deeper issues of how we should live together itself seem like a form of repression. Is it even possible to maintain that fundamental convictions about the meaning of the good life can be regarded as private preferences rather than matters of high public importance in a society like ours? At a historical moment when persons are increasingly interdependent and in which their fates are so obviously worked out in a shared natural environment, a negative answer to this question seems almost obvious.

We also need to question whether the method proposed for securing justice in public life by those who argue for political neutrality on the full human good can actually succeed. According to Rawls and others who follow his lead, we can publicly debate the means that will satisfy the maximum number of private preferences about the good, but they maintain that the terms of this debate must be set by "public reason." This is defined as "the shared methods of, and the public knowledge available to, common sense, and the conclusions of science when these are not controversial."[24] Rawls adopts this criterion for public morality because he thinks that no other standards of judgment are available in the face of contemporary philosophical and religious pluralism. Rorty goes further. For him, the exclusion of religious and philosophical understandings of the good life from the public domain is desirable in itself, not just a necessary consequence of the fact of pluralism. It "helps along the disenchantment of the world. . . . It helps make the world's inhabitants more pragmatic, more liberal, more receptive to the appeal of instrumental rationality."[25]

Common sense, uncontroversial science, and instrumental rationality are very shaky foundations for the civic unity of the nation. In fact, there is considerable evidence that the lack of more substantive discourse about the common good is a source of the alienation of many citizens from participation in political activity today. In an insightful book titled *Why Americans Hate Politics*, E. J. Dionne argues that this alienation can be attributed to the fact that current political discourse fails to address the real needs of communities. This failure is itself partly the result of the fact that interest-group politics is frequently incapable of even naming the social bonds that increasingly destine us to sharing either a common good or a "common bad."[26] Politics is perceived as a contest among interest groups with little or no concern for the wider society and its problems. Thus, the "common sense" that shapes American public life today becomes increasingly governed by a cynical "I'll get mine" attitude. In this way, neutrality about the good on the level of theory becomes a self-fulfilling prophecy on the level of practice. A principled commitment to avoiding sustained discourse about the human good produces a downward spiral in which shared meaning, understanding, and community become even harder to achieve. It can lead to a politics that is little more than a quasi-market in preferences and power.

Are there alternatives to political neutrality about the meaning of the good life that could generate greater social solidarity without stifling freedom and suppressing pluralism? A closer look at the historical record shows that memories of the role religion has played in generating political conflict and even violence, though accurate, are not the whole story. Other memories suggest ways of responding to Lovin's call to develop our thinking in ways that fit the discourse to which we aspire rather than the distortions we fear.

For example, the Catholic tradition provides some noteworthy evidence that discourse across the boundaries of diverse communities is both possible and potentially fruitful when it is pursued seriously. This tradition, in its better moments, has experienced considerable success in efforts to bridge the divisions that have separated it from other communities with other understandings of the good life. In the first and second centuries, the early Christian community moved from being a small Palestinian sect to active encounter with the Hellenistic and Roman worlds. In the fourth century, Augustine brought biblical faith into dialogue with Stoic and Neo-Platonic thought. His efforts profoundly transformed both Christian and Greco-Roman thought and practice. In the thirteenth century, Thomas Aquinas once again transformed Western Christianity by appropriating ideas from Aristotle he had learned from Arab Muslims and from Jews. In the process, he also transformed in fundamental ways Aristotelian ways of thinking. Not the least important of these transformations was his insistence that the political life of a people is not the highest realization of the good of which they are capable—an insight that lies at the root of constitutional theories of limited government.[27] And, though the church resisted the liberal discovery of modern freedoms through much of the modern period, liberalism has been transforming Catholicism once again through the last half of our own century. The memory of these events in social and intellectual history as well as the experience of the Catholic Church since the Second Vatican Council leads me to the hope that communities holding different visions of the good life can get somewhere if they are willing to risk conversation and argument about these visions. Injecting such hope back into the public life of the United States would be a signal achievement. It appears to be not only desirable but also necessary today.

The spirit that is required for such discourse about the public good can be called intellectual solidarity—a willingness to take other persons seriously enough to engage them in conversation and debate about what they think makes life worth living, including what they think will make for the good of the polis. Such a spirit is partially the same but entirely different from an appeal to tolerance as the appropriate response to pluralism. Tolerance is a strategy of noninterference with the beliefs and ways of life of those who are different. It leads to what Rawls calls the "method of avoidance" as the appropriate way to deal with persons or traditions that are "other." The spirit of intellectual solidarity is similar to tolerance in that it recognizes and respects these differences. It does not seek to eliminate pluralism through coercion, but it differs radically from pure tolerance by seeking not avoidance but positive engagement with the other through both listening and speaking. It is rooted in a hope that understanding might replace incomprehension and that perhaps even agreement could result. And, because it seeks an exchange that is a *mutual* listening and speaking, it can develop only in an atmosphere of genuine freedom. Furthermore, because this exchange is mutual, the freedom in which it takes place is not the private freedom of an atomistic self. Where such conversation about the good life begins and develops, a *community* of freedom begins to exist, and this is itself a major part of the common good. Indeed, it is this freedom in reciprocal dialogue that is one of the characteristics that distinguishes a community of solidarity from one marked by domination and repression.[28]

What might such public discourse look like? First, it will concern visions of those human goods that are neither strictly political nor strictly economic. Broadly speaking, this is conversation and argument about the shape of the culture the participants either share because of their common traditions or could share in the future through the understanding of each other they seek to achieve. The forum for such discussion is not, in the first instance, the legislative chamber or the court of law. It is the university and all the other venues where thoughtful men and women undertake the tasks of retrieving, criticizing, and reconstructing understandings of the human good from the historical past and transmitting them to the future through education. It occurs as well wherever people bring their received historical traditions on the meaning of the good life into intelligent and critical encounter with understandings of this good held by other peoples with other traditions. It occurs, in short, wherever education about and serious inquiry into the meaning of the good life take place.[29]

This education and inquiry is at the heart of intellectual solidarity and the public life of society, and its presence (or absence) will have crucial political implications. As John Courtney Murray once noted, "The great 'affair' of the commonwealth is, of course, education."[30] He was referring to education in the broadest sense: the organization of schools and their curricula, but even more to the level of critical cultural self-understanding among both the populace at large and among its elites. In both theory and practice today, this entire cultural and educational project of understanding, criticizing, and reconstructing visions of what it is to be authentically human (Rawls's "comprehensive understandings of the good") is often treated as a private affair. Murray's insistence that this project is not only *an* affair but also *the* great affair of the commonwealth challenges this presupposition frontally. To the extent that moral and political theories seek to exclude the task of education and inquiry from the public forum by privatizing all full visions of the human good, they undermine the very foundations of public life.

David Tracy fears that this process of undermining is already far advanced. He has argued that the privatization of these cultural concerns so threatens to instrumentalize and technicize public life as to destroy it altogether.[31] In much contemporary liberal thought, both theoretical and popular, tolerance of diversity has become the premier cultural lesson to be learned, but, if a community that prizes both solidarity and freedom is to be realized, engagement with the other, and not just tolerance, is required. In such engagement, a person's own deeper convictions are set forward as potential contributions to public understanding and simultaneously placed at risk of revision.

Seen in this light, it is no accident that the arts, the theater, and philosophy played a central role in breaking the grip of totalitarianism in Czechoslovakia.[32] Although the task of sustaining and strengthening public life in the United States today is without doubt very different than in Central Europe, the importance of genuinely public conversation and argument about what forms of human living are truly good is equally important here. As will be considered below, such discussion occurs partly in our discourse about the institutions of political and economic life and also in discussion of more particular policies in both spheres. The quality of these political and economic debates, however, will be dependent on the depth of the larger cultural exchange. The achievement of solidarity in the political and economic domains is dependent on the strengthening of free discourse in the cultural sphere—intellectual solidarity in a cultural community of freedom.

Second, the possibility and necessity of such a truly free cultural exchange has direct implications for the role of religion in public life. We must begin to entertain the possibility of conversation about the visions of the human good held by diverse religious communities and of intellectual engagement with them. Such a suggestion will be beyond the pale if one views all religious convictions as a rigid set of beliefs held on nonrational grounds. In this view, religion is very likely to be a source of division, conflict, and even violence when it appears in public. It is inherently uncivil.

The Catholic tradition and many Protestant traditions as well, however, reject the notion that religious faith must be irrational and, therefore, uncivil. Faith and understanding go hand in hand in both the Catholic and Calvinist views of the matter. They are not adversarial but reciprocally illuminating. As Tracy puts it, Catholic social thought seeks to correlate arguments drawn from the distinctive religious symbols of Christianity with arguments based on shared public experience.[33] This effort at correlation moves back and forth on a two-way street. It rests on a conviction that the classical symbols and doctrines of Christianity can uncover meaning in personal and social existence that common sense and uncontroversial science fail to see. So it invites those outside the church to place their self-understanding at risk by what Tracy calls conversation with such "classics." At the same time, the believer's self-understanding is also placed at risk because it can be challenged to development or even fundamental change by dialogue with the other—whether this be a secular agnostic, a Christian from another tradition, a Jew, a Muslim, or a Buddhist.

Intellectual solidarity has religious implications. It means that, in a community of freedom, religion should be represented in the discourse about the goods of public life. It equally means that religious believers must enter this discourse prepared to listen as well as to speak, to learn from what they hear, and, if necessary, to change as a result of what they have learned. The experience of the Catholic Church over the last half-century has been a vivid example of such listening, learning, and changing through its encounter with liberalism. This process must and will continue as Catholics develop their self-understanding into the future. Is it too much to expect that the experience of transformation through engagement rather than tolerance could strengthen America's public philosophy in an analogous way?[34]

Serious dialogue is risky business. At least some religious believers have been willing to take it. The future of public life in our society could be considerably enhanced by the willingness of a considerably larger number of people to take this risk of cultural dialogue, whether they begin as fundamentalists convinced of their certitudes or agnostics convinced of their doubts. Our society needs more imagination about how to deal creatively with the problems it faces than instrumental rationality can provide. In Martha Nussbaum's words, a vision of the full human good arises from "myths and stories from many times and places, stories explaining to both friends and strangers what it is to be human rather than something else. The account is the outcome of a process of self-interpretation and self-clarification that makes use of the story-telling imagination far more than the scientific intellect."[35]

Religious traditions and communities are among the principal bearers of these imaginative sources for our understanding of the human. They can evoke not only private self-understanding, but also public vision. Believers and nonbelievers alike have reason to risk considering what contribution religious traditions might make to our understanding of the public good. For a society to try to exclude religious narratives and symbols from public simply because they are identified with religion would be to impoverish itself intellectually and culturally. This would deprive society of one of its most important resources for a more publicly shared cultural self-understanding. Religious communities make perhaps their most important contribution to public life through their involvement in the formation of culture. If they seek to make this contribution through a dialogue of mutual listening and speaking with others, it will be fully congruent with the life of a free society.

RELIGION AND PUBLIC POLICY, MORE NARROWLY CONSIDERED

These perspectives on the role of religion in sustaining civil society and forming culture provide a context for considering the more pointed question of the relation of religious belief to the political sphere more narrowly conceived. What role should belief play in the decisions of those who draft legislation, reach judicial decisions, administer the domestic and foreign affairs of the nation, or exercise the responsibilities of citizenship (minimally through the vote)? This is the question that has been central in the recent debate about the political role of religion among legal scholars and political philosophers, and it is an important and entirely legitimate one. But the perspectives outlined in this chapter may shed some new light on how to go about addressing this issue.

The presupposition of those who would place stringent limits on appealing to religious belief in the formulation of law and public policy is that there is a sharp discontinuity between a community of religious believers and the larger body of public society. They see a similar discontinuity between religious reasons for particular policy choices and publicly accessible reasons for such choices. In Kent Greenawalt's analysis, religious belief is not accessible to public reason because it is deeply rooted in the personal experience of the believer. It is the experience of the believer that confirms religious truth for him or her. Thus, other persons who do not share the same experiences have no way to assess the truth of the beliefs involved. Because there is "no interpersonal way in which the weight of personal experience is to be assessed," there is no interpersonal way to assess the truth of the religious beliefs grounded in such experience.[36] Though Greenawalt rejects the idea that religion is a purely private or idiosyncratic affair, the presence of subjective experience in religious belief means that, in the end, its truth cannot be publicly assessed. This chapter has argued that these presuppositions ought to be questioned. Though religious belief is doubtless confirmed and supported by personal experience, so is the insight into the beauty of a great work of literature, music, or sculpture. In the domain of the aesthetic, judgments of value are not publicly assessable by the criteria of common sense and uncontroversial science, but that does not make them purely subjective. We can and do make judgments about the relative merits of novels, poems, and paintings. The loss of the ability to make such judgments in a particular society is a sign of decadence and decline in its culture. Religious understandings of the human good play an important role in shaping the culture of civil society. To regard religious convictions as beyond the reach of any public assessment is to deny the possibility of the kind of dialogue within a pluralistic society advocated here. Similarly, religious communities are constituent parts of civil society, and efforts to confine their activities to a zone of privacy will weaken civil society in dangerous ways.

The framework for considering the place of religious belief in the formulation of public policy thus shifts from a discussion of the role of private communities and convictions in shaping political life to a discussion of the proper role of the many public communities of civil society and the diverse public traditions within a culture in reaching decisions about policy in a pluralistic society. Framed this way, the proper role of religious convictions in the advocacy of particular political choices is the same as the role of convictions that are not religious. Persons or groups should not face political disability or disenfranchisement simply because their political views are rooted in religious traditions and beliefs.

At the same time, it has been argued here that it would be a serious mistake for religious communities to operate in public simply as interest groups seeking to enforce their views through state power. How is it possible to affirm that religious communities can legitimately operate in the political sphere just like nonreligious communities do and yet to reject the idea that they can rightly function like interest groups playing the game of majoritarian politics? The answer to this question depends on clarifying the *manner in which* believers or churches move from their faith convictions to their conclusions about policy.

The issue of how churches should make this move is itself partly a religious and theological one. Certain religious traditions hold that the Bible, other normative scriptures, or some form of church authority can provide direct guidance for decisions about public policy. In this view, for at least some areas of public life, conclusions about public policy or law are directly entailed by religious convictions with no intermediary steps in the argument. For example, some conservative evangelical or fundamentalist Christians draw policy conclusions about the rights of homosexuals or about prayer in public schools directly from the Bible, while Mennonites conclude that a pacifist rejection of all war is an immediate consequence of the teachings of Jesus. Some more conservative Catholics regard the legal banning of abortion as similarly entailed by the moral teachings of the pope and the Catholic bishops. From what has been said above about the need for believers to enter into dialogue with others in society as they develop their vision of the larger meaning of the social good and its consequences for policy, it is evident that I do not accept this understanding of the relation between religious belief and policy conclusions as immediate and direct. Roman Catholic thought, like much of Protestant thought, maintains that religious belief must be complemented by the careful use of human reasoning, both philosophical and social scientific, in the effort to reach decisions about policy that are both religiously and humanly adequate. In David Tracy's terms, when Christians advocate public policies, convictions rooted in the Bible and Christian tradition must be brought into mutually critical correlation with understandings based on human experience and reasoned reflection on this experience. Such a stance reflects a religious and theological perspective that views faith and reason as complementary, not as opposed or fundamentally bifurcated.

Not all Christians share this theological stance. For example, some Christians hold that human reason is so corrupted by the fall that it is an unreliable guide for both religion and morality and that culture is so distorted by sin that it should be simply opposed, not regarded as a dialogue partner. Therefore it can be asked whether the dialogic framework for the relation of religious convictions and public policy is really compatible with full participation by all religious groups in the shaping of public life. David Smolin has raised such an objection to Michael Perry's argument that religious convictions are properly admitted to the debate about policy if these convictions are open to revision through dialogue with those who do not share them but that convictions that are taken as fixed and unreformable should be excluded from this debate. Smolin concludes that "Perry has used his own vision of good religion as the standard for admission to political and legal debate."[37] Perry's standard excludes "theologically conservative theists, including various Protestant Christians (evangelicals, fundamentalists, and pentecostals) and traditionalists (Roman Catholics, Anglicans, and Lutherans). Those excluded, moreover, include the religious groups most active in trying to displace the cultural hegemony of America's highly secularized elites."[38]

Perry has acknowledged the force of Smolin's complaint. He agrees that his former argument for the inclusion of some religious convictions in the public debate and for the exclusion of others rests on theological/epistemological views that are widely contested in American society. Perry's most recent position is that because these views are contested, they ought not to be excluded from the actual public debate where this contest takes place. He proposes that his disagreement with conservative Protestants and traditionalist Catholics ought to be part of the public debate, not excluded from it. He would conduct this argument in public on properly religious and theological grounds, not exclude it from the public sphere. In an ironic way, Perry now wants to admit *all* religious-moral convictions to the public square for the same reason that Rawls et al. want to exclude them: because they are controverted. Perry thus proposes that engagement with religious and philosophical difference be carried to its full conclusion—public debate should include debate that is properly theological. Perry would argue with Smolin and in this argument try to show that Smolin's views rest on bad theology and bad epistemology. "It is one thing to say to a David Smolin: 'Although your arguments, no less than mine, may serve as a (sole) basis for political choice, this is why I reject your arguments and think others should too.' It is another thing to say: 'I don't even have to try to meet your arguments on the merits, because, unlike mine, they may not serve as a basis for political choice.' "[39]

I am in fundamental agreement with the thrust of Perry's response to Smolin's critique. There should be no religious tests for entry into public debate in a democratic society, but it can be questioned whether the real differences between Perry and Smolin, which are religious and theological, are best dealt with in arguments about quite precise issues that are up for decision in the spheres of law and public policy. As Greenawalt has observed, there is reason for skepticism about "the promise of religious perspectives being transformed in what is primarily political debate."[40] For example, I do not think it would be helpful for two judges, one a liberal Catholic and the other a conservative Protestant, to launch into epistemological and theological reasoning to explain why their responses to a piece of legislation regarding abortion are different. These theological and epistemological differences are better dealt with in the discussions that take place in the sphere I have called cultural, not that of the political sphere conceived narrowly as the judiciary or legislature. This cultural domain is fully public, and participation in it should be open to all comers. The work of the legislature and the courts, however, depends on the preexistence of some consensus in civil society and culture, and lawmakers must rely on this consensus if their activity is to be in any sense democratic. For the legislature or the courts to undertake the settlement of controverted religious or philosophical differences would border dangerously close to a form of political absolutism, even totalitarianism.

The arguments that Perry wants to have with Smolin about theology and religious epistemology should be vigorous and public. Similarly, serious contributions by the churches to public conversation and argument about our cultural understanding of the meaning of human life should be encouraged, not discouraged. It will be precisely through the development and refinement of such understanding in our culture that a stronger consensus about the goods to be pursued in politics will be generated. To the extent that this larger cultural dialogue is in some measure successful, the reasons offered by believers for their more specific decisions about policy will become more publicly accessible in society at large.

Although the domains of government and policy formation are not generally the appropriate ones in which to argue controverted theological and philosophical issues, it is neither possible nor desirable to construct an airtight barrier between politics and culture. In general, public policy should reflect the cultural consensus about the social good that is present among the people. But at times, urgent questions of law and politics raise new questions about the cultural consensus that already exists. This was clearly the case during the civil rights movement of the 1960s. Discriminatory laws and policies were themselves the problem that had to be addressed, and religious leaders such as Martin Luther King, Jr., did not hesitate to seek to overcome the racist history of American culture by advocating political and legal change directly. In the civil rights movement, argument about the larger cultural vision of the human good was stimulated by debate about specific policies. This seems to me a fully legitimate example of religious engagement in the sphere of policy. Similar examples, in my view, are the United States Catholic bishops' recent pastoral letters on war and peace and on economic justice. They raised fundamental questions about the values of American society and culture in the context of addressing the more detailed questions of policy regarding nuclear strategy, unemployment, and poverty.

Thus, religious contributions to policy debates need not always wait until a larger cultural consensus is achieved. Rather, public discourse between religious communities and the larger society will move back and forth between larger cultural questions of value and meaning on the one hand and more specific policy questions on the other. The more general understandings of the human good present in the culture and the more specific questions to be addressed in policy and law will mutually illuminate each other, both for religious communities and for the larger society as well. In this way, a genuine public conversation about the social good might be generated. An attempt to keep religious communities and convictions entirely separated from matters of policy will silence this conversation, especially at moments when it is most urgently needed.

Only when such conversation occurs does a free society or a community of freedom really exist. Religious arguments have a proper place in this conversation. And their presence should be governed by the conditions necessary for all genuine conversation and mutual inquiry: pursuit of the truth and respect for the other in an atmosphere of freedom. Such conditions, rather than neatly drawn lines or high walls of separation, should determine the proper role of religious belief in a pluralistic and democratic society.

NOTES

1. John Rawls, "The Idea of an Overlapping Consensus," *Oxford Journal of Legal Studies* 7 (1987): 4.

2. Ibid. See note 7 of Rawls's essay for a sketch of the presuppositions of this "common sense sociology."

3. Ibid., 12–13.

4. Ibid., 13.

5. Ibid., 15.

6. Richard Rorty, "The Priority of Democracy to Philosophy," in Merrill D. Peterson and Robert Vaughan, eds., *The Virginia Statute for Religious Freedom: Its Evolution and Consequences in American History* (Cambridge/New York: Cambridge University Press, 1988), 263.

7. The term "megastructures" is taken from Peter L. Berger and Richard John Neuhaus, *To Empower People: The Role of Mediating Structures in Public Policy* (Washington, D.C.: American Enterprise Institute for Public Policy Research, 1977), 2.

8. Alan Wolfe, *Whose Keeper? Social Science and Moral Obligation* (Berkeley: University of California Press, 1989), 20 and passim.

9. Ibid., 20.

10. Pope John XXIII, *Mater et Magistra*, in David J. O'Brien and Thomas A. Shannon, eds., *Catholic Social Thought: The Documentary Heritage* (Maryknoll, N.Y.: Orbis, 1976), no. 219.

11. Pope Pius XI, *Quadragesimo Anno*, in O'Brien and Shannon, eds., no. 79.

12. Jacques Maritain, *Man and the State* (Chicago: University of Chicago Press, 1951), 13.

13. John Courtney Murray, *The Problem of Religious Freedom* (Westminster, Md.: Newman Press, 1965), 26–27.

14. John A. Coleman, "Religious Liberty in America and Mediating Structures," in his *An American Strategic Theology* (New York: Paulist Press, 1982), 226.

15. Bronislaw Geremek, "Civil Society and the Present Age," in *The Idea of Civil Society* (Research Triangle Park, N.C.: The National Humanities Center, 1992), 11–12.

16. Neils Neilsen, *Revolutions in Eastern Europe: The Religious Roots* (Maryknoll, N.Y.: Orbis Books, 1991).

17. Erica Blair, "Towards a Civil Society: Hopes for Polish Democracy," interview with Adam Michnik, *Times Literary Supplement* (February 19–25, 1988): 199.

18. Robert Wuthnow, *Acts of Compassion: Caring for Others and Helping Ourselves* (Princeton, N.J.: Princeton University Press, 1991), 156.

19. Ibid.

20. Sidney Verba, Kay Lehman Schlozman, and Henry E. Brady, *Voice and Equality: Civic Voluntarism in American Politics* (Cambridge, Mass.: Harvard University Press, 1995).

21. See the interview with Schlozman in John Ombletts, "Activists Get Their Training at Church," *Boston College Biweekly*, March 26, 1992: 5.

22. Robin W. Lovin, "Perry, Naturalism, and Religion in Public," *Tulane Law Review* 63 (1989): 1539.

23. Ibid., 1518–19.

24. Rawls, "The Idea of an Overlapping Consensus," 8.

25. Rorty, "The Priority of Democracy to Philosophy," 271–72.

26. E. J. Dionne, Jr., *Why Americans Hate Politics* (New York: Simon & Schuster, 1991).

27. For documentation and analysis of the medieval roots of constitutionalism and theories of limited government, see Brian Tierney, *The Crisis of Church & State, 1050–1300* (Englewood Cliffs, N.J.: Prentice Hall, 1964).

28. I initially developed these ideas in my "Afterward: A Community of Freedom," in R. Bruce Douglass and David Hollenbach, eds., *Catholicism and Liberalism: Contributions to American Public Philosophy*, Cambridge Studies in Religion and American Public Life (Cambridge: Cambridge University Press, 1994), 323–43. I have elaborated on them further in *The Common Good and Christian Ethics* (Cambridge: Cambridge University Press, 2002).

29. The similarity of this cultural endeavor with what Michael Perry calls "ecumenical politics" is evident. See Perry, *Love and Power: The Role of Religion and Morality in American Politics* (New York: Oxford University Press, 1991). I am not fully clear, however, about the degree to which Perry sees this dialogue about the good life (what he calls "the question of the truly, fully human") as occurring principally in the sphere of politics conceived as the domain of government and law, or whether he has a broader understanding of politics in mind (i.e., the political as all that occurs in the public life of society). If the latter, his understanding of ecumenical politics is very similar to what I am here calling cultural conversation and argument. There is also a similarity between what I am proposing and Alasdair MacIntyre's understanding of a "tradition of enquiry," though MacIntyre is virtually silent

about how this understanding is related to the domain of government, law, and the political sphere narrowly conceived. See MacIntyre, *Whose Justice? Which Rationality?* (Notre Dame, Ind.: University of Notre Dame Press, 1988), esp. chaps. 18–20.

30. John Courtney Murray, *We Hold These Truths: Catholic Reflections on the American Proposition* (New York: Sheed and Ward, 1960), 9.

31. See David Tracy, "Catholic Classics in American Liberal Culture," in *Catholicism and Liberalism*, Douglass and Hollenbach, eds., 200–202.

32. See Václav Havel, *Disturbing the Peace: A Conversation with Karel Hvizdala*, trans. Paul Wilson (New York: Vintage Books, 1991). Richard Rorty has taken a dim view of the role of philosophy in the Czechoslovakian revolution, or at least of the idea that Havel and other Charter 77 leaders could take "metaphysical" claims for the basis of public morality at face value. See Rorty's review of several books by Jan Patocka, the philosopher who was the symbolic leader of Charter 77, "The Seer of Prague," *New Republic* (July 1, 1991): 35–40.

33. See Tracy, "Catholic Classics in American Liberal Culture," 205–8.

34. See Perry, *Love and Power*. See also Lovin, "Perry, Naturalism, and Religion in Public," 1517–39. Both Perry's earlier work and Lovin's theological reflection on it are discussed in my "Religion and Political Life: Theoretical Issues," chapter 6 in this volume.

35. Martha Nussbaum, "Aristotelian Social Democracy," in R. Bruce Douglass, Gerald R. Mara, and Henry S. Richardson, eds., *Liberalism and the Good* (New York: Routledge, 1990), 217.

36. Kent Greenawalt, "Religious Convictions and Political Choice: Some Further Reflections," *DePaul Law Review* 39 (1990): 1031.

37. David M. Smolin, "Regulating Religious and Cultural Conflict in a Postmodern America: A Response to Professor Perry," *Iowa Law Review* 76 (1991): 1076–77.

38. Ibid., 1077–78.

39. Michael Perry, "Religious Morality and Political Choice: Further Thoughts—and Second Thoughts—On *Love and Power*," *San Diego Law Review* 30, no. 4 (fall 1993): 717–18.

40. Greenawalt, "Religious Convictions and Political Choice: Some Further Reflections," 1034.

9

Politically Active Churches and Democratic Life

The activity of religious communities in the political sphere has been the subject of much apprehension and debate in recent years. In the United States, the visibility of the so-called religious right has been of particular interest. This political involvement by conservative Christians leads to fears that public activism by religious communities inevitably tends to support right-wing politics. But several journals of opinion noted for their progressive orientations have harked back to religious involvement in the abolitionist, labor, and civil rights movements to propose a different scenario. They suggest that more public activity by religious communities, if it is of the kind they favor, can contribute to a politics more to their liking. For example, the *Washington Monthly* featured an article titled "Why We Need a Religious Left." *The Nation* offered an essay by a theologian on the relevance of "The Transcendent Dimension." Its subheading declared: "To Purge the Public Square of Religion Is to Cut the Values that Nourish Us."[1]

Such ambivalence toward political involvement by religious communities is also evident in discussions of the global picture. In his much-noted article in *Foreign Affairs*, Samuel Huntington conjectured that the conflicts in the world politics of the emerging post–cold war era would be driven by a clash of civilizations and cultures rather than of ideology or economics. Huntington noted that civilizations are communities distinguished from each other by "history, language, culture, tradition, and, most important, religion."[2] Huntington's diagnosis raises the specter of religious war on a global scale. But Huntington also noted that one of the most visible religious forces in the domain of world politics, the Roman Catholic Church, has been the most effective source for the global advancement of democracy over the past several decades.[3]

These are confusing developments to those observers who have identified the modern and the secular. The so-called theory of secularization hypothesized that in modern societies religious belief would exert declining influence in the public sphere. The church-state issue would be more or less automatically solved by the withering away of the church, or at least the elimination of the church's presence in the public square. It has become apparent that this interpretation of the direction of the trends is at least questionable today. Gilles Kepel, of the *Centre d'études et de recherches internationales*, in Paris, wrote a book on the reemergence of religion as an important political factor that became a best seller in France. Kepel is not entirely happy with these developments, as is evident from the book's title: *La Revanche de Dieu*, provocatively rendered in English as *The Revenge of God*.[4] Its best-seller status is a sign that the descendants of Voltaire are a bit worried that the "infamous thing" is not entirely *écrassé*. Kepel examines movements such as the Ayatollah Khomeini's revolution in Iran, the militant Zionism of the Gush Emunim in Israel, the highly politicized Catholic lay movement *Communione e Liberazione* in Italy, and the Moral Majority inspired by Protestant fundamentalism in the United States. I will suggest below that Kepel is mistaken in taking such movements as adequate representations of the public role of religion today. Nevertheless he points to the fact that the disappearance of religion from the political domain seems not to be working out the way the secularization hypothesis had predicted.

One of the results of these developments is that the proper role of religion in politics has become a much-discussed topic among moral philosophers and political theorists. The strength of these fields is their careful analysis of important theoretical issues raised by the religion and politics issue. The discussion of the role of reason in adjudicating religious-political issues has in turn stimulated a discussion of the meaning of rationality and of moral epistemology. Important as these discussions surely are, they are several steps removed from the conflicts and possibilities that arise when religious communities actually enter the public square.

This chapter, therefore, will approach the question of the political activism of religious communities from an angle that is somewhat different from that adopted in recent moral and political theory. These theoretical discussions need to be linked to the historical situation we face today if they are to provide practical guidance. Thus, I will take note of several empirical studies that have raised questions about the state of civic life in the United States today and that have made suggestions about the de facto contributions of religious communities to that civic life. Once some descriptive approaches to the religion/politics dynamic have been laid out perhaps we will be in a position to make more helpful prescriptive or normative judgments. Though the focus will be primarily on the United States, broader international aspects will occasionally be noted.

THE DECLINE OF CIVIC PARTICIPATION

In a series of articles and a book noted widely outside the academy, Robert Putnam has argued that the United States has been undergoing a notable decline in overall civic participation in recent decades. The United States has been experiencing a depletion of the "social capital" that is requisite for effective democracy. Putnam describes social capital as the "networks, norms, and trust . . . that enable participants [in social life] to act together more effectively to pursue shared objectives."[5] It includes a rich associational life in groups like the Elks Club, the League of Woman Voters, labor unions, churches, and even bowling leagues. In more classical terms, a high level of social capital is another way of speaking about the strength of civil society. Civil society is a complex web of human communities including families, neighborhoods, churches, labor unions, corporations, professional associations, credit unions, cooperatives, universities, and a host of other associations. Calling this network of associations "civic" implies that the domain of public life is broader than that directly under the control of state power, as noted in the previous chapter.

Politically Active Churches and Democratic Life

Putnam cites extensive data to argue that the associational life of civil society in the United States is weakening. For example: participation by Americans in religious services and church-related groups has declined by about a sixth since the 1960s; membership in labor unions in the nonagricultural sector has dropped by more than half; participation in parent-teacher associations declined from 12 million in 1964 to 5 million in 1982 before recovering to 7 million in 1993; volunteer activity declined by about a sixth between 1974 and 1989 (by 26 percent in the Boy Scouts, 61 percent in the Red Cross). Putnam illustrates the trend with an example that has caught the imagination of commentators: between 1980 and 1993 the number of Americans who went bowling increased by 10 percent, while league bowling declined by 40 percent. This means that the social interaction and even occasional political conversations that occur among those who regularly bowl together have dropped. Thus, Putnam has used bowling alone as a whimsical symbol of a serious reality: the decline of the associational life needed to undergird and support democratic politics.[6]

Putnam's argument that strong associational life in civil society is essential to democracy is in harmony with the civic-republican tradition in political theory. It also coheres with the Roman Catholic tradition's stress on the principle of subsidiarity as one of the key normative bases of politics. According to this principle, civil society is the soil in which the seeds of human sociality grow. When communities are small or of intermediate size, they enable persons to come together in ways that can be vividly experienced. The bonds of communal solidarity formed in them enable persons to act together, empowering them to shape some of the contours of public life and its larger social institutions such as the state and the economy. Thus, in a democratic society, government does not rule but rather serves the social "body" animated by the activity of these intermediate communities. Pope Pius XI formulated the principle of subsidiarity this way: government "should, by its very nature, provide help [*subsidium*] to members of the body social, it should never destroy or absorb them."[7] Civil society is the primary locus in which human solidarity is realized. Its strength is essential to the success of participatory government. In Putnam's words, it is a prerequisite to "making democracy work."

Putnam's studies add a particularly helpful element to the ideas drawn from the civic-republican and Catholic traditions in setting the context for discussions of the public role of religion. His argument is based on extensive empirical data and analysis. Before launching his recent work on American civic participation, Putnam conducted long-term empirical research in Italy to determine the factors influencing the success or failure of new institutions of decentralized regional governance that were launched there in 1970. Very briefly put, Putnam concluded that the new institutions of regional government were successful in encouraging strong democracy in those regions of Italy that possessed a richly developed life in civil society and did not succeed where the communities of civil society were weak. In Italy's northern regions the "horizontal civic bonds" that build social capital had long been "embodied in tower societies, guilds, mutual aid societies, cooperatives, unions, and even soccer clubs and literary societies."[8] Putnam found that both the state and the market worked to serve the needs of the people better in the north because of the presence of strong bonds of civic life resulting from the extragovernmental social solidarities he identified as present in northern regions. In the south of Italy, on the other hand, the new regional governmental institutions were considerably less effective and citizen satisfaction with them notably lower because the mutual bonds of civil society were less developed there. Analyzing the data on Italy's regions, Putnam observed that the stronger the civic context, the better the government and the more successful the economy. Appealing to a congenial example of northern Italian civic life, he observed that

> The harmonies of a choral society illustrate how voluntary collaboration can create value that no individual, no matter how wealthy, no matter how wily, could produce alone. In the civic community associations proliferate, memberships overlap, and participation spills into multiple arenas of community life. The social contract that sustains such collaboration in the civic community is not legal but moral. The sanction for violating it is not penal, but exclusion from the network of solidarity and cooperation.[9]

Thus, by induction from empirical study rather than deduction from moral or political theory, Putnam concluded that Tocqueville was right: effective democratic government depends on civic virtue and the vigorous bonds of civil society that promote it.

Politically Active Churches and Democratic Life

Putnam's study of the regions of Italy is relevant to many other parts of the world. His own subsequent work has pursued its relevance to the civic and political life of the United States; others are pursuing analogous lines of inquiry on the conditions needed to make democracy work in the nations of the former Soviet bloc. The major study by Sidney Verba, Kay Lehman Schlozman, and Henry Brady, *Voice and Equality: Civic Voluntarism in American Politics* (noted above, in chapter 8) is most illuminating on the question of the public role of religion in the United States today. Verba, Schlozman, and Brady present the most comprehensive and detailed study of participation in political activity in the United States yet produced. It is based on a large-scale, two-stage survey of the way Americans are involved in politics and in various forms of voluntary activity, including church life. They define political activity broadly as "activity that is intended to or has the consequence of affecting, either directly or indirectly, government action."[10] This activity takes a number of forms: voting, working in election campaigns, contributing money to candidates and political causes, becoming active in local communities, contacting public officials, joining political parties or other political organizations, attending rallies, protests, or demonstrations, serving on governing bodies like school or zoning boards. Verba et al. go beyond the compilation and interpretation of data on who becomes involved in such political activities; they seek to explain why and how people do so. This leads them to detailed empirical investigation of the relation between political activity and the dynamics and structures of association in American civil society. They state the overall import of the study this way:

> We show that both the motivation and the capacity to take part in politics have their roots in the fundamental non-political institutions with which individuals are associated during the course of their lives. The foundations of political involvement are laid early in life—in the family and in school. Later on, the institutional affiliations of adults—on the job, in non-political organizations, and in religious institutions—provide additional opportunities for the acquisition of politically relevant resources and a sense of psychological engagement with politics.[11]

Voice and Equality thus strongly supports Putnam's argument.

Verba, Schlozman, and Brady have also made interesting discoveries about the role actually played by churches in American politics. One of the major findings of *Voice and Equality*, somewhat to the surprise of its authors,[12] is that religious institutions make a major contribution to political participation in the United States. In their analysis, three factors are at the basis of political involvement: the *motivation* to become politically active, the *capacity* to do so, and involvement with *networks of recruitment* through which requests for political activity are mediated.[13] The data lead them to the conclusion that all three of these factors are enhanced in the life of individual citizens who are actively involved in a church or other institutional religious community. That the factors of motivation and recruitment for political activity are present in religious communities is perhaps intuitively evident. Pastors preach about matters that touch the well-being of the polis; religious values orient those who hold them to pursue the realization of these values in the public domain. Churches can provide an institutional base for political mobilization, as has been evident across the ideological spectrum from the civil rights movement to antiabortion campaigns. *Voice and Equality* provides a wealth of data that backs up such intuitions and that clarifies their import with illuminating analysis.[14]

But Verba, Schlozman, and Brady have reached an important finding that goes beyond what many would have suspected without benefit of this study. Active involvement in church life not only provides *motivation* and a context for *recruitment* for political activity; it also has a significant, measurable impact on the *capacity* of Americans to become politically involved. This capacity is dependent on the possession of certain resources, chiefly money, time, and civic skills. Verba, Schlozman, and Brady measured who has the civic skills needed for political activism by asking those surveyed whether during the past six months, in any setting whether political or otherwise, they had written a letter, gone to a meeting where they took part in making decisions, planned or chaired a meeting, given a presentation or speech. The possession of skills needed for such activities is of course heavily dependent on family background, level of education, and the sort of job one holds. In other words, possession of such skills is significantly correlated with social-economic status. Since these skills are important in political activity, the higher one's social-economic status the more likely one is to become politically active. This has long been known to social scientists who study American political culture. But notably, *Voice and Equality* has also discovered that the acquisition of these skills is significantly correlated with active involvement in a church. The communal participation that takes place in churches helps people learn them. Further, churches enable Americans to develop these skills in a way that is independent of their social-economic status. When looked at nationally and across denominations, religious affiliation is not stratified by socioeconomic status, race, ethnicity, or gender. Rather, opportunities for the development of skills relevant to political participation are accessible in a more equal way to those active in churches than to American society at large. Indeed, most of the other factors that encourage political activism, such as a successful family of origin, a high level of education, and a high-paying job, converge to produce unequal levels of political participation tied to unequal social-economic status. Church participation, on the other hand, provides a counterweight toward the side of more equality in political participation. Thus, the authors reach a provocative conclusion about the United States: "The domain of equal access to opportunities to learn civic skills is the church."[15]

The implications of this finding for discussion of the role of religion in American politics are considerable. Putnam argues that civic participation is declining and that such a decline is traceable to the loss of the social capital of strong civic associations. Verba, Schlozman, and Brady find that political participation is sustained by participation in extrapolitical civic communities and that the churches are among the most important of these communities. The percentage of Americans who are actively involved with religious communities is considerably higher in the United States than in many other developed democracies. Religion has a correspondingly more important influence in American politics. *Voice and Equality* concludes that churches play a compensatory role for the relative weakness of unions and political parties in the United States, another example of "American exceptionalism."[16] On the basis of these studies, therefore, one could conclude that churches play a key role in sustaining the civic involvement that is essential to the health of democracy. One could also conclude that civically strong and politically active churches help "make democracy work," to use Putnam's language. Indeed, it seems that churches play an especially key role in the political empowerment of those with lower social-economic status. Thus, more church activism, not less, would seem called for if more active, more egalitarian representation in democratic politics were judged desirable.

Churches, of course, do not exist simply to encourage active participation in politics. As religious communities they have properly religious ends: worship of God; response to the deepest questions of human beings about the meaning of life, love, work, and death; the nurturing of moral values and virtues that enable people to live in accord with that meaning. Thus, it would be a mistake to assess the vitality of religious communities solely in terms of their contribution to successful democratic political activity. Nonetheless, religious belief has consequences for the whole of human life, not only that part which occurs on Sunday morning. The Catholic Church, for example, stressed the impact of its properly religious mission on public life when the Second Vatican Council stated, "Out of this religious mission itself comes a function, a light, and an energy which can serve to structure and consolidate the human community according to divine law."[17] So, although churches are very different kinds of communities from bowling leagues, they can be expected to have considerable impact on social life. Indeed, the fact that their distinctive identity addresses the meaning of the whole of human existence suggests that they will have social influence that ranges much more widely than communities with more narrowly defined purposes.

Thus, Verba, Schlozman, and Brady are right when they note that religious institutions are not ideologically neutral venues for the development of politically relevant skills. Because of their distinctive identities and missions, churches have significant agendas of their own that influence the issues around which their members are motivated and recruited to become politically active. The range of these issues is large. Today they extend from advocacy for the poor to abortion, on both the prolife and prochoice sides of the debate. *Voice and Equality* suggests that the center of gravity of the religious agenda today is tipped toward more conservative social concerns. It also concludes that different churches have differing effects on the development of the civic skills needed for political activism, with membership in Protestant churches today more positively correlated with the development of these skills than is membership in the Catholic Church.[18] I do not wish here to dispute these suggestions, nor am I competent to do so. It would nevertheless be useful to remember that the involvement of churches in political life has ranged over a wide array of is-

sues in the history of the United States, from abolition, to prohibition, to
the civil rights movement, to opposition to the Vietnam War and the nuclear arms race. It is also relevant that different churches and segments
within churches have played quite different roles in leading their members to civic engagement at different points in American history. For example, immigrant members of the Catholic Church were more heavily involved in the labor movement and urban politics in the first half of the
twentieth century than their Protestant counterparts. The study by Verba,
Schlozman, and Brady could therefore well be complemented by historical inquiry beyond its already ambitious scope.

Even taking these caveats into account, the works of Putnam and of
Verba and his colleagues highlight aspects of the question of religious
involvement in politics that are rarely attended to in contemporary academic debates on the subject. In light of these studies, does it really make
sense to see the presence of religious communities in the public square
as threats to the integrity of democratic political life? Given the correlation between religious and political participation analyzed in *Voice and
Equality*, does it not make more sense to direct our discussions to the *kind*
of political engagement we wish to see churches encouraging rather than
to whether churches should be encouraging such involvement at all? In
light of Putnam's description of the overall decline of civic participation
and its causes, churches seem to play a role that should be encouraged
rather than discouraged. The center of the discussion ought to be how to
achieve wise forms of political engagement by religious communities and
their members.

WHAT KIND OF PUBLIC RELIGION?

Sociologist of religion José Casanova addresses this question by providing several alternative models for the public presence of religion in our
time. Like Kepel, he concludes that religious communities are playing
significantly different roles in social life today than was predicted for them
by theories that identified modernization with across-the-board secularization. As noted above in chapter 1, Casanova distinguishes three possible meanings of secularization: (1) the *decline of religion* in the modern
world, which will continue until it finally disappears; (2) the *privatization
of religion* (i.e., the displacement of the quest for salvation and personal

meaning to the subjective sphere of the self, a displacement that renders religion irrelevant to the institutional functioning of modern society); and (3) the functional *differentiation of the role of religion* from other spheres of human activity, primarily the state, the economy, and science.[19]

Casanova argues persuasively that the first two meanings of secularization are contrary to fact. Worldwide, religion is not declining. In the United States the level of religious belief among the populace has declined somewhat over the past few decades, but it remains notably higher than in earlier periods of American history. Casanova argues that the thesis of the decline of religion is largely based on the experience of modern Western Europe and is not generalizable to other parts of the world. I would add that it is probably not even useful in the Paris of today, where it seems more Muslims attend Mosque on Friday than Catholics attend church on Sunday.

Secularization understood as the privatization of religion is also a factually questionable generalization in light of the religious involvement in public affairs already noted. Whether it is desirable to propose it as a normative objective can be questioned as well. Kepel has argued that the conservative religious movements discussed in *The Revenge of God* arise from the fact that many persons experience a growing malaise about the fragmentation of their social milieu. As sociologists since Durkheim have observed, this fragmentation pushes life-sustaining structures of meaning out of the shared realm of public experience into private zones. All values, especially those rooted in religion, become personal preferences. This seems unsatisfactory to adherents of the conservative religious movements who "complain about the fragmentation of society, its 'anomy,' the absence of an overarching ideal worthy of their allegiance."[20] Such complaints have arisen among the better-educated segments of their societies, especially among those with technical expertise. The adherents of these movements are children of modernity who have rejected the secularist ideology often associated with modernization but who employ the technical fruits of modern instrumental rationality. "They see no contradiction between their mastery of science and technology and their acceptance of a faith not bounded by the tenets of [technical] reason."[21] This latter characteristic makes both the resurgence in the Islamic world and the new Christian right in the United States so effective in advocating their agendas through the electronic media and by other technological means. The pressure to treat religion as a purely private affair may thus be a source of, rather than a cure for, the emergence of fundamentalist religion as a political force. If fundamentalism is normatively objectionable, as I hold it to be, normative recommendations that religion be kept private will be counterproductive.

One normative proposal for keeping religion private sometimes suggested today distinguishes spirituality from institutionalized religion. If modernity fragments social existence and acts as a solvent on meanings that provide purpose in life, perhaps the renewal of personal spiritual experience can knit up the raveled sleeve of society without the divisiveness that often accompanies institutional religious commitment. Once again, however, the empirical data suggest otherwise. Sociologist Robert Wuthnow's survey-based research has shown that, in the United States, people's concern with "spirituality" translates most readily into active civic engagement when this concern is lived out in the context of an organized religious community. When religion or spirituality is understood as a purely private affair between an individual and his or her god, without the mediation of an institutional religious community with a public presence in society, it has little effect on the level of civic voluntarism.[22] In particular, Wuthnow interprets survey data to suggest that religious inclinations have little or no influence on voluntary activity aimed at helping the needy unless one is involved in an organized religious community. When a religious person is involved in an organized church, however, higher levels of piety correlate with higher levels of sustained effort to respond to the needs of the poor and disadvantaged. This suggests that the *kind* of religion one practices is linked with both the level of one's civic involvement and the form that involvement will take. In Wuthnow's view, the spread of individualistic religious styles that separate spirituality from institutional religious commitment is therefore likely to have a dampening effect on levels of civic voluntarism.[23] He also suggests that when individualistic religion does lead to political activism, it is less likely to be the sort of activism concerned with the plight of the poor and the disadvantaged. This may in part explain why televangelism is linked with conservative politics in the United States today.[24] Praying alone, or in front of a television set, may be as apt an indicator of the decline of social capital in the United

States as is bowling alone.[25] If one is seeking to strengthen civic life in a democracy, encouragement of secularization as the privatization of religion does not appear to be a fitting normative objective.

Casanova's third meaning of secularization—the differentiation of religion from the other spheres of public life such as the state—looks more promising, however. Casanova fully supports the modern Western achievements of respect for religious and personal freedom. Thus, he argues that any public role for religious communities must avoid a quest for hegemonic control of social, intellectual, and political life by religion. This raises the questions I take to be central in a consideration of the contribution of religion to civic and political life today. Is it possible for religion to provide a sense of ultimate meaning and salvation that includes the meaning and hope we seek in political, economic, and intellectual activity? Can this happen without religious truth claims becoming legitimations of political authoritarianism and intellectual obscurantism? If this cannot be done, religious efforts to identify and pursue the public rather than the private good will amount to attempts not only to question the sufficiency of modernity but also to negate its achievements.

In earlier chapters, I have outlined some of the philosophical and theological arguments about how this task might be pursued.[26] Here I will stay within the present chapter's purpose of suggesting ways that some discussions of the question by social scientists may lend plausibility to those normative proposals. Casanova in particular has addressed the issue as a social analyst in a way that is particularly helpful. He argues that religious communities can play legitimate public roles in pluralist societies that value freedom in three ways. The first is by entering the public sphere to protect not only the freedom of religion of the church itself but in support of all modern freedoms and rights for believers and nonbelievers alike. Casanova cites the role of the Catholic Church in the process of democratization in Spain, Poland, and Brazil as illustrations of such a role. The second is by entering the public sphere "to question and contest the absolute lawful autonomy of the secular spheres and their claims to be organized ... without regard to extraneous ethical or moral considerations." The United States Catholic Bishops' Pastoral Letters on strategic nuclear arms policy and on economic justice are cited as examples. The third is when a religious community enters public contestation "to protect the traditional life-world from administrative or juridical state penetration, and in the process opens up issues ... to the public and collective self-reflection of modern discursive ethics." He cites the roles of the so-called Moral Majority and the Catholic moral stand on abortion and the right to life as examples, though I would add that these examples seem to indicate more of his aspiration for what the abortion debate could be like than what has in fact transpired in it.[27]

Casanova, in other words, is arguing for an active role of religion in public life on the level of the discourse that occurs in civil society rather than through religious control of the state. Religion can contribute to public life when it relies on civil discourse about the meaning and hope for our common existence rather than on the imposition of such meanings and hopes through the power of the state, the administrative bureaucracy, or the market. Such a proposal is based both on analysis of various possible public roles of religion provided by sociologists of religion today and on a normative vision of the importance of civil society as both the sphere of generating meaning and as a crucial check on the growing power of states, administrative bureaucracies, and markets. It is a theory that has learned not only from the model of the Western revolutions in America and France but also from more recent revolutions in Eastern Europe where the ancien régime was avowedly secularist, even atheist, and from struggles in Latin America, where liberation from economic and authoritarian political forms of oppression has been under way. In both Eastern Europe and Latin America (as well as in the Philippines, Korea, and South Africa), the public role of religion has in significant measure been pursued in ways that exemplify all three of Casanova's potential roles.

Such a role for activist churches is fully compatible with respect for religious freedom. Indeed, it demands it. It rejects what Seyla Benhabib has called "integrationist communitarianism"—the effort to overcome social fragmentation, individualism, and alienation by reorganizing all of social life around a single integrating value scheme that denies or ignores the reality of pluralism.[28] When a religious vision and value orientation is reduced to a political agenda for the whole of public life, with no institutional space left for critique of that religious vision, suspicion of hegemonic intent is quite justified.[29] In the Roman Catholic community, this approach is known as "integralism." It stresses the *unity* of religion, daily life, politics, the sciences, the economy, and the whole gamut of human endeavor. It manifests the deep Catholic instinct to see all things human as potential mediators of the divine presence and grace. This is an instinct rooted in the nature of religion itself as an all-encompassing worldview through which believers enter into relationship with the God who is creator and lord of all that is. It can, however, become perverse when interpreted to mean that all knowledge can be reduced to theology or that all social institutions ought to be extensions of the church. In the words of the eminent theologian Karl Rahner, it can lead to a way of thinking that simply assumes that "human life can be unambiguously mapped out and manipulated in accord with certain universal principles proclaimed by the church and watched over by her in the manner in which they are developed and applied."[30] This integralist or hegemonic approach was firmly rejected by the Catholic Church at the Second Vatican Council, when it affirmed both the civil right to religious freedom for all persons and a legitimate autonomy of secular intellectual disciplines.[31]

Respect for religious freedom, however, does not require either the withering away of the church or the privatization of religion. Religious traditions and communities are among the principal bearers of the cultural sources for our understanding of the human good. They can evoke not only private self-understanding but public vision as well. Both believers and nonbelievers alike have reason to risk considering what contribution religious traditions might make to our understanding of the public good. For a society to try to exclude such visions of the good life from the public simply because they are identified with religion would be to impoverish itself both intellectually and culturally. This would deprive society of one of its most important resources for a more publicly shared self-understanding. Religious communities make perhaps their most important contribution to political life through this engagement in the formation of culture. If they seek to make this contribution through a dialogue of mutual listening and speaking with others in civil society, it will be fully congruent with the life of a free society.

Our options, therefore, are not restricted to self-assertion of group power by religious communities or the privatization of religion. Many of the discussions of the role of religion in public life today are driven by the fear that religion is fundamentally uncivil and that its presence in public life is a threat to liberty. Whether it be Kepel's suggestion that Khomeini and Falwell are paradigmatic of the public role of religion today or John Rawls's frequent suggestion that the wars of religion in the sixteenth and seventeenth centuries are the relevant historical memory, fear of religion as a public force shapes much of the discussion. On the other side of the argument are those who invoke such figures as Abraham Lincoln, Martin Luther King, and Archbishop Oscar Romero of San Salvador, to hold out more hopeful models. For such figures, religious convictions played a formative role in the contributions they made to freedom, equality, and democracy. These contributions were possible because they sought to make them in a way that was governed by the conditions necessary for all genuine conversation and mutual inquiry: pursuit of the truth and respect for the other in an atmosphere of freedom. Dialogue of this kind, rather than high walls of separation, is the key to enabling activist religious communities to make constructive contributions to democratic society today.

Thus, the analysis of the compatibility of public activism by churches with respect for religious freedom will be largely shaped by whether its guiding assumption is fear of abuse or hope for positive contributions by religious communities.[32] In this chapter, I have attempted to lay out a few considerations drawn from social analysis that make it plausible to aspire to positive contributions by the churches to public life. I have not here discussed the ways that religious belief and full respect for the religious liberty of all persons are compatible. A compelling case has been and must continue to be made for such compatibility. Those churches and religious communities that have fully internalized this synthesis of religion and the values of liberty are positioned to make a contribution to democracy that can help overcome the threats to it identified by Putnam. In my judgment, there can be little doubt that democracy in the United States is today in need of considerable help. My hope is that this essay might suggest ways that activist churches might contribute to "making democracy work."

NOTES

1. Amy Waldman, "Why We Need a Religious Left," *Washington Monthly* (December 1995): 37–43; Harvey Cox, "The Transcendent Dimension," *Nation* (January 1, 1996): 20–23.

2. Samuel P. Huntington, "The Clash of Civilizations," *Foreign Affairs* 72 (summer 1993): 22, 25.

3. For evidence of the strong alliance of Catholicism and democracy that has developed since the Second Vatican Council, see Huntington, "Religion and the Third Wave," *National Interest* 24 (summer 1991): 29–42. This article is based on Huntington, *The Third*

Wave: Democratization in the Late Twentieth Century (Norman: University of Oklahoma Press, 1991).

4. Gilles Kepel, *The Revenge of God: The Resurgence of Islam, Christianity, and Judaism in the Modern World*, trans. Alan Braley (University Park: Pennsylvania State University Press, 1994). French original: *La Revanche de Dieu: Chrétiens, Juifs et Musulmans à la reconquête du monde* (Paris: Éditions du Seuil, 1991).

5. Robert Putnam, "Tuning In, Tuning Out: The Strange Disappearance of Social Capital in America," *PS: Political Science and Politics* 28, no. 4 (December 1995): 664–65. See also Putnam, *Bowling Alone: The Collapse and Revival of American Community* (New York: Simon & Schuster, 2000), *Making Democracy Work: Civic Traditions in Modern Italy* (Princeton, N.J.: Princeton University Press, 1993), "The Prosperous Community: Social Capital and Public Life," *American Prospect*, no. 13 (spring 1993): 35–42, "Bowling Alone: America's Declining Social Capital," *Journal of Democracy* 6, no. 1 (January 1995): 65–78. Putnam's definition of social capital follows James Coleman, *Foundations of Social Theory* (Cambridge, Mass.: Harvard University Press, 1990).

6. Putnam, "Bowling Alone," 69–70.

7. Pope Pius XI, *Quadragesimo Anno*, in David O'Brien and Thomas Shannon, eds., *Catholic Social Thought: The Documentary Heritage* (Maryknoll, N.Y.: Orbis Books, 1992), no. 79.

8. Putnam, *Making Democracy Work*, 181.

9. Ibid., 182–83.

10. Sidney Verba, Kay Lehman Schlozman, and Henry E. Brady, *Voice and Equality: Civic Voluntarism in American Politics* (Cambridge, Mass.: Harvard University Press, 1995), 9.

11. Ibid., 3–4.

12. Personal conversation with Kay Lehman Schlozman.

13. Verba, Schlozman, and Brady, *Voice and Equality*, 3.

14. See ibid. esp. pp. 145–49, and chap. 13 on church-based recruitment for political involvement and chap. 14 on motivation for engagement on specific issues, some of which are related to religious belief.

15. Ibid., 320.

16. Ibid., 519–21.

17. Vatican Council II, *Gaudium et Spes (Pastoral Constitution on the Church in the Modern World)*, in Walter M. Abbott and Joseph Gallagher, eds., *The Documents of Vatican II* (New York: America Press, 1966), no. 42.

18. Verba, Schlozman, and Brady, *Voice and Equality*, 320–24, 520–21.

19. José Casanova, *Public Religions in the Modern World* (Chicago: University of Chicago Press, 1994), chap. 1. This account neglects the theoretical richness of Casanova's account, for purposes of simplicity in this context.

20. Kepel, *Revenge of God*, 4.

21. Ibid., 192.

22. Robert Wuthnow, *Acts of Compassion: Caring for Others and Helping Ourselves* (Princeton, N.J.: Princeton University Press, 1991), 156.

23. Ibid., 156.

24. See Jeffrey K. Hadden, "Religious Broadcasting and the Mobilization of the New Christian Right," *Journal for the Scientific Study of Religion* 26 (1987): 1–24.

25. Putnam hypothesizes that television is the prime suspect in his effort to identify the causes of declining civic participation in the U.S. today. See his "Tuning In, Tuning Out: The Strange Disappearance of Social Capital in America," esp. 677–81.

26. In addition to the other chapters in this volume, see Hollenbach, "Fundamental Theology and the Christian Moral Life," in Leo J. O'Donovan and T. Howland Sanks, eds., *Faithful Witness: Foundations of Theology for Today's Church* (New York: Crossroad, 1989), 167–84, "Afterword: A Community of Freedom," in R. Bruce Douglass and D. Hollenbach, eds., *Catholicism and Liberalism: Contributions to American Public Philosophy* (Cambridge: Cambridge University Press, 1994), 323–43; "Virtue, the Common Good, and Democracy," in Amitai Etzioni, ed., *New Communitarian Thinking: Persons, Virtues, Institutions, and Communities* (Charlottesville: University of Virginia Press, 1994), 143–53; "Public Reason/Private Religion? A Response to Paul J. Weithman," *Journal of Religious Ethics* 22, no. 1 (1994): 39–46.

27. Casanova, *Public Religions*, 57–58.

28. Seyla Benhabib, *Situating the Self: Gender, Community and Postmodernism in Contemporary Ethics* (New York: Routledge, 1992), 77.

29. See Benhabib, *Situating the Self*, 76.

30. Karl Rahner, "Theological Reflections on the Problem of Secularization," *Theological Investigations* (New York: Herder and Herder, 1973), vol. 10: 322.

31. See Vatican Council II, *Dignitatis Humanae (Declaration on Religious Freedom)*, no. 2, and *Gaudium et Spes (Pastoral Constitution on the Church in the Modern World)*, no. 36, in Abbott and Gallagher, eds., *The Documents of Vatican II*.

32. See Robin Lovin, "Perry, Naturalism and Religion in Public," *Tulane Law Review* 63 (1989): 1539.

PART THREE GLOBAL ISSUES

10

Christian Social Ethics after the Cold War

The dramatic revolutions in Central Europe in 1989 and the collapse of the Soviet Union have had profound effects on Christian social ethical reflection. This chapter will review a representative sample of the literature that has begun the task of clarifying the impact of these revolutionary events on the ethical agenda. The end of these repressive totalitarian regimes is certainly cause for rejoicing. It raises the issue of what *kind* of non-Communist vision of economic life should be pursued in the future. This question is important not only in the context of Eastern Europe, but in the North Atlantic region and the Southern Hemisphere as well.

Pope John Paul II's encyclical *Centesimus Annus*, issued on May 1, 1991, to commemorate the one hundredth anniversary of Leo XIII's *Rerum Novarum*, addressed the issue at considerable length. Although it would be impossible to discuss all of the topics treated in this lengthy and complex document here, it will be useful to highlight some its main points and selected responses to them.

THE COLLAPSE OF COMMUNISM

A central theme of the encyclical is the failure of "real socialism," a term the pope uses to describe the social systems that prevailed in Eastern Europe and the USSR up to 1989. He presents two sorts of analysis of the reasons for this failure, one more theoretical and the other more practical and historical. On the theoretical level, "the fundamental error of socialism is anthropological in nature." It subordinates the good of the individual person to the functioning of the socioeconomic mechanism. "The concept of the person as the autonomous subject of moral decision disappears." This leads to the destruction of the "subjectivity" of society, by which the pope means a civil society that respects the freedom, initiative, and legitimate autonomy of many diverse communities such as families and the other intermediate groups classically referred to in Catholic social thought under the heading of the principle of subsidiarity. Most fundamentally, "real socialism" has failed because it was atheistic. In denying God, it denied the transcendent dignity of the person. "It is by responding to the call of God contained in the being of things that man becomes aware of his transcendent dignity. Every individual must give this response, which constitutes the apex of his humanity, and no social mechanism or collective subject can substitute for it."[1] State absolutism, in other words, is really a form of idolatry that sacralizes the political sphere and attacks the transcendent freedom and dignity of persons in the process. From there it is but a short step, the pope argues, to a view of class conflict that is "not restrained by ethical and juridical considerations, or by respect for the dignity of others (and consequently of oneself)."[2] The nub of the theoretical critique of "real socialism," therefore, is that its denial of transcendence leads to a denial of authentic humanity.

From a more practical point of view, the encyclical enumerates three factors that especially contributed to the collapse of Communist regimes. The first was the violation of the rights of workers. First in Poland and then elsewhere, working people stood up nonviolently against regimes and ideologies that presumed to speak in their name.[3] Second, the inefficiency of the Communist economic systems became evident. This inefficiency was not simply a technical problem, but was "rather a consequence of the violation of human rights to private initiative, to ownership of property and to freedom in the economic sector."[4] Third, the official atheism of these regimes created a "spiritual void" that deprived youth of a sense of human purpose. This ultimately led many of them, "in the irrepressible search for personal identity and for the meaning of life, to rediscover the religious roots of their national cultures, and to rediscover the person of Christ as the existentially adequate response to the desire in every human heart for goodness, truth, and life."[5] Not only as a theoretical matter, therefore, but very practically as well, the reaffirmation of the transcendent showed the inadequacy of "real socialism."

Before turning to a discussion of the encyclical's vision of the alternative, it will be useful to note some other analyses of the failure of the Communist system in the ethical literature. In February 1990 (and thus more than a year before *Centesimus Annus* was issued), Brazilian theologian Leonardo Boff attended a series of meetings in what was then East Germany to discuss the significance of the events of 1989 for the future of liberation theology. In his reflections on these discussions, he maintains that what failed in Eastern Europe was "command socialism," "patriarchal socialism," or "authoritarian socialism." Following the dictatorial model developed by Lenin, after the Second World War so-called scientific socialism was imposed on Eastern Europe from "outside" and "above" by Soviet troops.[6] The breakdown of this kind of socialism is beneficial for everyone, but this does not mean the end of all socialist models. For Boff, "it is evident that socialism will have a future if it has the capacity to enter into the path of a democracy that is worthy of the name: a popular democracy, structured from below, with the greatest possible participation, and open to the inevitable differences among people." This commitment to popular participation is more basic than efforts to create a society in which all are equal. It must, however, be accompanied by solidarity—"collaboration with others and the joint construction of history." Such participation and solidarity will, in turn, lead to social equality, to respect for differences among people, and, finally, to "communion" among persons.[7] These commitments represent "the true nucleus of utopian socialism."[8] Boff does not present a detailed description of capitalism, though he presupposes that an economic system based on private property and the market is inherently exploitative and "creates so many victims on a world-wide scale."[9] Because of this presupposition, he views capitalism as itself an obstacle to popular democracy. Its "internal logic" leads to inequalities, an asymmetrical relationship between capital and labor, and the formation of monopolies and oligopolies. So even though the collapse of "really existing social-ism" in Eastern Europe means that the socialist vision is "sadly and in purification passing through its 'Good Friday,' " it will yet know its "Easter Sunday."[10]

Max Stackhouse and Dennis McCann proclaim a very different conclu-sion in their jointly issued "Postcommunist Manifesto." Marx and Engels' *Manifesto* began with the words "A specter is haunting Europe—the specter of communism."[11] Stackhouse and McCann turn this sentence up-side down: "The specter that haunted the modern world has vanished. That specter is Communism."[12] This fact has important implications for Christian social ethics. For in their view, much of the modern Christian tradition had identified itself with the failed socialist project: "the Protes-tant Social Gospel, early Christian realism, much neo-orthodoxy, many forms of Catholic modernism, the modern ecumenical drive for racial and social inclusiveness, and contemporary liberation theories all held that democracy, human rights, and socialism were the marks of the com-ing kingdom. For all their prophetic witness in many areas, they were wrong about socialism."[13] They were wrong in believing that capitalism is "greedy, individualistic, exploitative and failing" while socialism is "gen-erous, community-affirming and coming." In fact the truth is quite the op-posite—capitalism is the more cooperative system and socialism the more exploitative. And "no one who has experienced 'really existing socialism' now believes that it was God's design. What we now face is more than a de-lay in the socialist *parousia*. It is the recognition that this presumptive dogma is wrong." The collapse of Communism calls for more than a read-justment in ecumenical social thought. It "demands repentance." This does not mean, however, that Stackhouse and McCann think the churches should embrace the status quo in capitalist societies. Rather they advocate "a reformed capitalism—one that uses law, politics, education and espe-cially theology and ethics to constrain the temptations to exploitation and greed everywhere."[14]

The World Council of Church's *Ecumenical Review* devoted one of its issues to the theme of "Ecumenical Social Thought in the Post-Cold-War Period." Several of the articles move in the same direction as do Stack-house and McCann. Paul Abrecht, who was director of the Church and Society Subunit of the WCC from 1948 to 1983, argues that, for the past twenty years, that body has emphasized the importance of the creation of a "new world economic order." The model of that order was taken to be some form of socialism. Consequently, "the collapse of socialism in Central and Eastern Europe and its disarray throughout the world has shocked those who pinned their hopes on the socialist model."[15] The fact that the WCC was not intellectually prepared to deal with the events of the past few years, Abrecht says, was particularly evident at the world convocation on "Justice, Peace, and the Integrity of Creation," held in Seoul, in March 1990. The report of this conference does not even mention the end of the cold war. "Most important of all, the inability of the convocation to agree on an 'exposition' or interpretation of the present social situation and the causes of injustice and violence in our times resulted in a series of concluding affirmations and covenants so abstract and so generally phrased as to be of little use in guiding Christian social thought and action in the world."[16] Abrecht traces the historical roots of this vacuum to the fact that WCC proponents of revolutionary and liberation models of social change "were more explicit about what they opposed in the present system than about the character of the new one which they envisaged."[17] Abrecht's conclusion on the situation in WCC circles is somber: "After twenty years of 'revolutionary' thought and action on economic and social justice issues, ecumenical thought in these areas is at a dead end. There is no longer a theological-ethical consensus that commands any measure of agreement. Cut off from its historic theological-ethical roots and obliged to recognize that the concept of a revolutionary transformation of the world economic and social order is an illusion, ecumenical social thought faces a crisis of historic proportions."[18] A major reconstruction is called for, which Abrecht does not think will be easily achieved. But the collapse of Communism in Eastern Europe reinforces two key insights of an earlier generation of Protestant ecumenical thinkers: "the interdependence of democracy and social justice" and the ecumenical critique of "Marxism's spiritual and ethical illusions."[19] On these bases, an effort of renewal and self-criticism can begin.

IS CAPITALISM VICTORIOUS?

A number of years ago, Peter Berger argued in *The Capitalist Revolution* that the future will—or at least ought to—belong to capitalism. In a second edition of that book, he admits that the events surrounding the revolutions of 1989 have led to "a certain euphoria among those who have been in favor of capitalism all along" and that "it is nice for a change to be able to indulge in a bit of *Schadenfreude*" over the difficulties being experienced by ideological adversaries.[20] Nevertheless, Berger does not think that the appeal of the socialist idea will entirely vanish, for it has greater mythopoetic power to generate loyalty than does capitalism, especially among the intelligentsia. Some will find a way to sustain a "socialist faith," despite the evidence all around them. They will try to do this by refusing to call a spade a spade. "Since *capitalism* continues to be a negatively charged word in many places, especially among intellectuals, it is often avoided in favor of the less upsetting synonym *market economy*. Conversely, where *socialism* is still a word that uplifts some hearts, it will also be avoided as the term to describe a nonmarket economy; instead reference may be made to *command*, *Communist*, or even *Stalinist* economies." In Berger's view, such distinctions "are semantic games. What is being described is, very clearly, a broad shift from socialist to capitalist models of economic organization."[21] Those who hold out against this conclusion "now appear as people who argue that the earth is flat."[22]

If drawing distinctions between capitalism and market economies are semantic games, *Centesimus Annus* may be fairly accused of playing them. The passage that has received most attention by commentators addresses the question of the significance of the collapse of Communism. John Paul asks whether this means that capitalism has been victorious and should consequently become the goal of the countries of Eastern Europe and the Third World. His response is carefully constructed and deserves quotation at some length:

> The answer is obviously complex. If by "capitalism" is meant an economic system which recognizes the fundamental and positive role of business, the market, private property and the resulting responsibility for the means of production, as well as free human creativity in the economic sector, then the answer is certainly in the affirmative, even though it would perhaps be more appropriate to speak of a "business economy," "market economy" or simply "free economy." But if by "capitalism" is meant a system in which freedom in the economic sector is not circumscribed within a strong juridical framework which places it at the service of human freedom in its totality, and which sees it as a particular aspect of that freedom, the core of which is ethical and religious, the answer is certainly negative.[23]

Further, the pope warns several times that the collapse of Eastern European models of society should not be confused with the victory of what we might call "really existing capitalism." For example, he says that "it is unacceptable to say that the defeat of so-called 'Real Socialism' leaves capitalism as the only model of economic organization."[24] Or again, after discussing the continuing reality of marginalization and exploitation, especially in the Third World, and the reality of human alienation, especially in advanced societies, the pope adds a strong note of warning: "The collapse of the Communist system in so many countries certainly removes an obstacle to facing these problems in an appropriate and realistic way, but it is not enough to bring about their solution. Indeed there is a risk that a radical capitalist ideology could spread which refuses even to consider these problems, in the *a priori* belief that any attempt to solve them is doomed to failure, and that blindly entrusts their solution to the free development of market forces."[25]

What then is the encyclical saying? Rocco Buttiglione has proposed an interpretation of its "complex" answer to the question of whether capitalism has been victorious. It has been reported that Buttiglione participated in the drafting of the encyclical, so his views should be carefully noted.[26] He observes that the word "capitalism" has different meanings charged with different emotions on different sides of the Atlantic and in the Northern and Southern Hemispheres. In the United States, it "implies free enterprise, free initiative, the right to work out one's own destiny through one's own efforts." It is "a thoroughly positive and respectable word," because of its link with a form of widespread entrepreneurship that grew organically in American soil. In Europe, on the other hand, the development of the industrial revolution was often under the control of small groups led by banks with decisive support from the state. In that context, "capitalism" came to connote "the exploitation of large masses through an elite of tycoons who dispose of the natural and historical resources of the land and expropriate and reduce to poverty large masses of peasants and artisans." In Latin America, because of its distinctive history, "capitalism is simply synonymous with social injustice," at least among the intellectuals and a large section of the masses.

Buttiglione suggests, therefore, that there are different kinds of capitalism or at least different meanings to the word. The formal rules of market exchange may be the same in Europe, the United States, and Latin America, but where control of the market is concentrated in the hands of a privileged group, these rules will produce very different effects.[27] In some countries, only a small percentage of the population has the prerequisite skills and resources necessary to gain access to the market. Thus, "they have no choice but to accept whatever conditions are offered them by those who have a monopoly of access to the market." In such a context, Buttiglione suggests, radical change will be needed. "Something just short of a social revolution is needed to create a market: a peaceful revolution of freedom."[28]

This line of argument is surely central in the encyclical. John Paul strongly affirms the efficiency and productivity of market economies. And he endorses entrepreneurship and economic initiative in terms that remind Max Stackhouse of Max Weber's discussion of the "Protestant ethic."[29] At the same time, however, the pope repeatedly stresses that many persons are unable to participate in the marketplace because they lack the resources needed to do so. The following passage is illustrative: "The fact is that many people, perhaps the majority today, do not have the means which would enable them to take their place in an effective and humanly dignified way within a productive system in which work is truly central. . . . Thus, if not actually exploited, they are to a great extent marginalized; economic development takes place over their heads."[30] The pope's argument is here in full agreement with the United States Catholic bishops' statement that "basic justice demands the establishment of minimum levels of participation in the life of the human community for all persons."[31] The lack of such participation, which he calls "marginalization," continues to be present in advanced societies "in conditions of 'ruthlessness' in no way inferior to the darkest moments of the first phase of industrialization." It is the condition in which "the great majority of people in the Third World still live." And at the global level, "the chief problem [for poor countries] is that of gaining fair access to the international market."[32] The pope calls the conditions that lead to such marginalization "structures of sin which impede the full realization of those who are in any way oppressed by them."[33] And he says the church can contribute to an "authentic theory and praxis of liberation" through its social teaching and its "concrete commitment and material assistance in the struggle against marginalization and suffering."[34] It was statements such as these that likely led *The Economist* of London to comment that, though the encyclical supports free markets, "thoroughgoing capitalists cannot take off their sackcloth yet."[35]

RETHINKING PRIVATE PROPERTY

One of the keys to the encyclical's discussion of the need to overcome marginalization is its innovative treatment of ownership, in the long chapter "Private Property and the Universal Destination of Material Goods." Earlier Catholic social thought, both in Aquinas and in the modern period, defended the legitimacy of private property. But this teaching (again in Aquinas and especially since Pius XI) did not regard the right to private property as an unlimited one. The use of privately owned goods was subject to strict limits because the material world was created by God for the benefit of all human beings, not just a few. This is the so-called universal destination of material goods. As John Paul puts it, "The original source of all that is good is the very act of God, who created both the earth and man so that he might have dominion over it by his work and enjoy its fruits (Gen. 1:28). God gave the earth to the whole human race for the sustenance of all its members without excluding anyone." It is only through their intelligence and work, however, that human beings make the earth fruitful. John Paul, echoing Locke and Leo XIII, affirms that persons make part of the earth their own through work. "This is the origin of individual property," but its accumulation is limited by "the responsibility not to hinder others from having their own part of God's gift."[36] This again echoes Locke, who maintained that the natural law limited the acquisition of property by the requirement that there be "as much and as good left in common for others."[37]

It is clear that in Aquinas, Locke, and earlier modern Catholic social thought this line of reasoning envisions private property as initially the ownership of land and natural resources based on individual labor. John Paul's innovation arises from his awareness that this paradigm does not describe the reality of an advanced technological and industrial world. In such a context, the "givenness" of the world of land and natural resources is easily overshadowed by the creativity of human intelligence. Thus, the temptation arises to say that the product of human work comes solely from the activity and initiative of the individuals who do the working. This can lead to the belief that the fruits of industry belong solely to those who actively produced them. This would undercut the limits on the right to private property asserted by the earlier tradition. So John Paul maintains that "a deeper analysis" of the scope and limits of the right to property is called for than that based on a paradigm of agriculture and mining.[38]

This deeper analysis begins with the assertion that "it is becoming clearer how a person's work is naturally interrelated with the work of others. More than ever, work is *work with others* and *work for others*: it is a matter of doing something for someone else."[39] Entrepreneurship based on the knowledge of the needs of others and the development of creative ways of meeting those needs is an important source of wealth in modern society. Such activity "requires the cooperation of many people working toward a common goal." Moreover, the ability to engage in it depends on "the possession of know-how, technology and skill."[40] The possession of these resources today plays a more important role in generating wealth than ownership of land or natural resources. But the pope applies the same moral criteria to the human capital of knowledge and skill that the tradition formerly applied to land: its moral purpose is to serve the needs and well-being of the human community. It will do so when it is organized in ways that lead to "ever more extensive working communities" bound together by "a progressively expanding chain of solidarity."[41] Paralleling the earlier argument that the earth and its natural resources were created by God for the benefit of the whole human community, John Paul argues that human beings as such—with their capacity for creative intelligence—have been created by God for solidarity with others in the economic sphere. The resources of "know-how and technology" are not the purely private possession of anyone. They are meant to be at the service of others. They should be used to open up ways for the vast numbers of people who are marginalized from the market to become active participants in it. Thus, Archbishop Jorge Maria Mejia, who as secretary of the Vatican's Council for Justice and Peace was doubtless closely involved in the drafting of the encyclical, has commented that it presents the principle of the universal destination of material goods in a new way. "Today, therefore, 'the know-how,' 'technology,' and 'skill' (§32) are part of these 'goods' destined for all, but that do not reach everyone and are not enjoyed by all."[42]

This line of argument was anticipated in *Laborem Exercens*, where John Paul wrote that, through work, a person "enters into two inheritances: the inheritance of what is given to the whole of humanity in the resources of nature and the inheritance of what others have already developed on the basis of those resources." In productive activity, persons never act independently. There is always an element of dependence: "dependence on the Giver of all the resources of creation and also on other human beings, those to whose work and initiative we owe the perfected and increased possibilities of our own work."[43]

For example, the small group of high-tech entrepreneurs who founded the Apple computer corporation was dependent on a historical heritage of technological and scientific knowledge given them by others through education. They did not create that corporation simply out of their own resources, even though they began it in the apparent isolation of the garage behind the home of one of the founders. Even highly creative and innovative activity is linked by moral bonds of interdependence with a vast community of other human beings. So *Centesimus Annus* concludes that, if ownership of physical capital or control of "know-how" and "skill" impedes the participation of others in this network of solidarity, it "has no justification, and represents an abuse in the sight of God and man."[44] Put positively, this means that the alternative to the failed Communist system is what the pope calls "a society of free work, of enterprise and of participation." This will be a society with a mixed economy, in which the market is "appropriately controlled by the forces of society and the State, so as to guarantee that the basic needs of the whole society are satisfied."[45]

REFORMING CAPITALISM

Thomas S. Johnson spells out the challenges this involves very pointedly in an essay written for a conference held at the University of San Francisco to commemorate the *Rerum Novarum* centenary. Johnson is a Catholic layman who was president of Manufacturers Hanover Trust Corporation at the time the essay was written. He believes that the collapse of Communism changes the framework for debate about the shape of social and economic life in two interrelated ways. First, the argument over the relative advantages of economic "decision-making by bureaucrats versus an open marketplace has been settled."[46] Second, we have an opportunity to shed the ideological baggage and conceptual rigidities that often encumbered debate during the cold war period. This will enable us "to focus our energy and attention on eliminating the significant faults and inadequacies of capitalism that we know to exist, while at the same time preserving those special properties that imbue the markets with their special genius."[47] Johnson illustrates both the genius and the faults of the market from the example of the city where he works. In New York City, the fruits of the free and competitive spirit abound, "the atmosphere is dynamic, resulting in the best there is to offer, not only in the areas of business and commerce but also in the arts, entertainment, education, and scholarship." At the same time, the city is beset with serious problems: devastating homelessness, drug abuse, crime, decaying infrastructure. Most deeply troubling are those who lack the skills to enter the city's economy: "large groups of people whose spirits have been crushed and who live literally without hope. They are the people who have been left out of the process—the very poor in a city of enormous wealth."[48] The end of Communism thus calls for much more than victory celebrations. It will require the best available thinking by business, political, educational, and religious leaders to identify ways of addressing these devastating problems. The challenge is succinctly put in Johnson's title: "Capitalism after Communism: Now Comes the Hard Part."

Perhaps the most useful contribution of Johnson's essay to this thinking is its stress on the fact that different societies in the capitalist world organize markets in notably different ways. Just a few of the differences he cites can be noted here. In Japan, ownership patterns differ from those in the United States, for in Japan much ownership is in the form of cross holdings by one company in another. There are also significant differences among market systems in the degree to which productive property is owned by the state. For example, before the reunification of Germany, more than fifty percent of the gross national product of capitalist West Germany was produced by state enterprises. In Japan and many Western European societies, there is much greater coordination among companies and the other institutions of society and their governments than in the United States. The role of government in redressing inequalities is also notably different from country to country. It is extensive in Sweden, minimal in Hong Kong. In Johnson's words, the provision of health care and housing in Western Europe "is measurably greater, and arguably fairer, than what is provided in the United States."[49] And this has been accomplished while aggregate growth has on average been greater than in the United States.

Johnson's point is that there is more than one way to organize a market economy. The serious debates of the post–cold war world concern the human costs and human benefits of the various systems of ownership, market structure, and governmental redistribution that are possible. He thinks Christian ethics can make an important contribution to these debates on the basis of several key principles. At a minimum, all human beings should have the "freedom to live a life in which they can choose to follow God's will. At the least, this measure must assure that human beings are removed from bondage—either the literal bondage imposed by a political system or the de facto bondage that results from such a low level of sharing in the wealth that does exist that all hope for progress is extinguished and individual work is always seen as inadequately rewarded."[50] Second, all persons have a responsibility to contribute to the future of their community and to preserve resources for future generations. This has important implications for the tax system and for savings and investment. It is "the responsibility of those who have relatively greater wealth to save and invest more, so that others will be given the opportunity . . . to raise their participation in the economic system in the future."[51] Finally, because in market economies work is increasingly done in large corporate organizations, the structures and activities of these corporations must be evaluated in light of their impact on those who work in them. This means giving careful thought to "ways to include workers as full members of an enterprise, including empowering them to participate genuinely in decision-making."[52]

Johnson's essay was written in the context of the United States for an American audience. Though published just as *Centesimus Annus* was being issued, it provides a helpful framework for interpreting the encyclical's implications in this country. *Centesimus Annus* states that the church "has no models to present" for the precise way socioeconomic affairs should be organized. Such models must be developed in light of the historical situations in different societies. Rather, the pope's intent is to provide an "ideal orientation" based on recognition of the values of the market and enterprise, of the need for these to be oriented to the common good, and of the importance of broadening the possibilities of participation.[53] Neverthe-less, the encyclical goes beyond the restatement of general moral princi-ples and indicates that not all models of a market economy are compatible with its orientation. Johnson's discussion of the diverse forms of market economy is a stimulus to careful consideration of what the encyclical says in this regard.

In the pope's reading of post–World War II history, the spread of Com-munist totalitarianism evoked three different responses in Europe and other parts of the world. The first sought to counter Communism by rebuilding democratic societies, in ways that encouraged economic growth but that avoided "making market mechanisms the only point of reference for social life" by subjecting markets "to social control." Some of the restrictions on the market are "a solid system of social security and professional training, the freedom to join trade unions and the effective action of unions, the assistance provided in cases of unemployment, the opportunities for democratic participation in the life of society." This calls for action by both society and state to protect workers "from the nightmare of unemployment" by seeking "balanced growth and full employment" and "through unemployment insurance and retraining programs." Wages must be adequate for living in dignity, "including a certain amount for sav-ings." And legislation is needed to block exploitation "of those on the mar-gins of society," including immigrants.[54] These limits are some of the elements of the "strong juridical framework" that number 42 of the en-cyclical says are necessary if a free economy is to serve freedom in its totality.

The second kind of postwar response to the spread of Communism is described as a system of "national security" that aimed at making Marxist subversion impossible by "controlling the whole of society in a systematic way" and by increasing the power of the state. This gravely threatens free-dom, and the encyclical unmistakably rejects it. Though no specific re-gimes are named, the pope clearly has in mind those such as Chile under Pinochet.[55]

The third postwar response is called that of "the affluent society or the consumer society." It sought to defeat Marxism by showing that it could satisfy material human needs more effectively than Communism. Accord-ing to the pope, this consumer society shared a reductively material-ist view of the person with Communism.[56] I think the pope is here referring to significant currents in the societies of Western Europe and North America, but I doubt this description gives a full account of what is going on in those countries, nor does he claim this.

It is nevertheless clear that the first of these postwar models is approved by the encyclical, whereas the second and third are rejected. I have written elsewhere that the functioning economic system that most closely resembles what the pope is describing is the social-market economy (*Sozialmarktwirtschaft*) of Germany.[57] An editorial in *Civiltà Cattolica* commented that German and Scandinavian social democratic movements have been notably successful in implementing the objectives outlined by the pope.[58] And in Britain, Frank Turner has written that *Centesimus Annus* "sometimes reads like an unusually well-written Labour manifesto" and is certainly closer to the program of the Labour Party than it is to laissez-faire or libertarian objectives. Turner observes, however, that the democratic socialist parties of Western Europe themselves are often ironically prone to accepting "the primacy of economic criteria and the values of corporate pragmatism."[59] To the extent that they do, they are challenged by *Centesimus Annus* from the Left. Thus, there is considerable room for debate about the specifics of social-economic systems that would be compatible with the ethical teaching of the document. In my judgment, the principles it lays out call for major changes in both the global marketplace and domestic arrangements presently in place in the United States.

THE ROLE OF GOVERNMENT

As noted above, *Centesimus Annus* says that the responsibility for bringing about these changes falls on both "society and the state." This reemphasizes the traditional principle of subsidiarity of Catholic social thought, which rests on the distinction between civil society and the state. This distinction emphasizes that a free society is composed of many freely formed and freely active communities.[60] The idea of civil society has been a central theme in the revolutions of Eastern Europe. Adam Michnik, a Polish intellectual who was a leader of the Solidarity movement, put it this way: In totalitarian regimes, "the State is teacher and civil society is the pupil in the classroom, which is sometimes converted into a prison or a military camp. In civil society, by contrast, people do not want to be pupils, soldiers, or slaves; they act as citizens."[61] Michnik, who is Jewish, says that one of the principal influences on his thinking about the role played by a strong civil society in sustaining democracy was "a priest from Krakow, Fr. Karol Wojtyla."[62] As John Paul II, Father Wojtyla has strongly reaffirmed this role.

At the same time, John Paul repeatedly links the principle of subsidiarity to the ideas of solidarity and the common good. For this reason, as Kenneth Himes has pointed out, the pope's understanding of subsidiarity is clearly different from the laissez-faire view that the market will solve all problems and that the role of government should be as small as possible.[63] In discussing the role of government in promoting the goals of economic justice, the encyclical makes a distinction that should be considered carefully, especially in the United States: "The State must contribute to the achievement of these goals both directly and indirectly. Indirectly and according to the *principle of subsidiarity*, by creating favorable conditions for the free exercise of economic activity, which will lead to abundant opportunities for employment and sources of wealth. Directly and according to the *principle of solidarity*, by defending the weakest, by placing certain limits on the autonomy of the parties who determine working conditions, and by ensuring in every case the necessary minimum support for the unemployed worker."[64] I would interpret this passage in the following way. The indirect role of government in addressing issues such as poverty and unemployment is through macroeconomic policies that stimulate growth and create jobs. These policies create the conditions in which the individuals and the many communities of civil society can freely exercise their initiative and creativity. In Michnik's words, this will enable people to act like citizens, not pupils or slaves. It will enable them to work together and for each other in families, in entrepreneurial activity, and in personalized forms of service and self-help. But if and when this leaves serious problems in place, government should undertake more. For example, legislation regarding working conditions, fair labor practices, and minimum wages are called for. In addition, more direct stimulation of job opportunities, unemployment insurance and other forms of social support will be called for.

In my judgment, this provides a key to understanding what *Centesimus Annus* says about the welfare state, or what it calls "the social assistance state." The pope notes that the range of state intervention to remedy "forms of poverty and deprivation unworthy of the human person" has expanded in recent years. "In some countries," he suggests, this has led to "malfunctions and defects in the social assistance state," which are the "result of an inadequate understanding of the principle of subsidiarity." These defects are the sapping of human initiative and energy through excessive bureaucratization. State interventions to alleviate poverty, the pope says, are "justified by urgent reasons touching the common good"— this is the principle of solidarity—but subsidiarity implies that such interventions are "supplementary" to the primary source of economic welfare, namely, active participation in economic life through work. They are also supplementary to the direct assistance that, if possible, should be provided by families, neighbors, and others who are closest to those in need.[65]

These specifications of when governmental involvement is called for should be kept clearly in view in discussions of the encyclical's relevance to the continuing debate about welfare reform in the United States. It is clear that the encyclical will be embraced by those who argue that recent increases in poverty in this country, especially among children in single-parent families, are due to a welfare dependency in large part *caused* by misguided governmental programs. This was the view of Daniel Patrick Moynihan, who argued that the remedy for poverty is parental self-sufficiency and parental responsibility to contribute to the well-being of their children. Moynihan also argued, however, quoting Judith Gueron, that "the responsibilities of government are to provide the means for parents to become self-sufficient—such as employment services and supports—and to provide income when their best efforts fall short."[66] This is not the place to review the complexity of the welfare debate in the United States, but two additions to what Moynihan has said are crucial. First, poverty is not due simply to welfare dependency. In fact, a substantial majority of those receiving social assistance do so either because employment is simply unavailable or because they lack the skills needed for available jobs. Second, many of the poor in the United States work full time. They are poor simply because their wages are too low. For both of these reasons, the poverty problem has more complex causes than those who blame dependency acknowledge. Efforts to alleviate it will have to be correspondingly complex.[67] The encyclical recognizes this in its call for a blend of individual initiative, voluntary assistance, and both indirect and direct government intervention. It does not offer a blueprint for how these should be combined, but it is a strong call to place discussion of these matters on the public agenda.[68]

CONSENSUS ON THE COMMON GOOD?

The need for a serious discussion of how to deal with poverty in America will highlight one final theme of the encyclical's vision of Christian ethics after the cold war. In the name of subsidiarity, the pope opposes all forms of totalitarianism, but he also warns the West of the opposite danger: the loss of a vision of and commitment to the common good. He writes of "a crisis within democracies themselves, which seem at times to have lost the ability to make decisions aimed at the common good."[69] In advanced societies "the individual is often suffocated between two poles represented by the state and the marketplace. At times it seems as though he exists only as a producer and consumer of goods, or as an object of State administration."[70] This experience leads to distrust and apathy in the face of political and financial power, with consequent decline in political participation and civic spirit. This, I think, is a key element in the pope's critique of "consumerism."

At the most obvious level, a consumer society for the pope is one in which persons organize their lives around the pursuit of material gratification and maximal profit independent of concern for the effects on others.[71] More deeply, it is a society that regards all political, cultural, and religious values as matters of personal preference to be selected cafeteria-style. On this level, a consumer society is one in which the spirit of the marketplace has leached into the sphere of politics, culture, and religion. When this happens, there develops "a tendency to claim that agnosticism and skeptical relativism are the philosophy and the basic attitude which correspond to democratic forms of political life." This further leads to a politics in which the preference of the majority determines all. And this, the pope concludes, is "open or thinly disguised totalitarianism."[72] If a marketplace of exchange based on personal preference becomes the overarching framework in society, therefore, the market itself becomes totalitarian. *Centesimus Annus* raises a strong voice against this tendency. "There are goods which by their very nature cannot and must not be bought and sold."[73] Some of these goods are directly at stake in the marketplace, such as the dignity of working people, the survival of the poor, and the greater participation of developing countries in the global economy. But the pope also implies that the image of the marketplace of ideas is inadequate to portray what is at stake in discussions of how a democratic society should govern itself.

Centesimus Annus repeatedly asserts that democracy and freedom are rooted, not in agnosticism and skepticism, but in commitment to the truth: "obedience to the truth about God and man is the first condition of freedom."[74] This is sure to set many Americans' teeth on edge. Truth-claims in politics, we tend to believe, are the prelude to oppression, not freedom. But we have something very important to learn from the recent experience of Central and Eastern Europe. The Czech philosopher Erazim Kohák has written that the "the entire tenor of Czech dissent, whose most prominent figures are playwright-philosopher Václav Havel and priest-theologian Václav Maly, has been on *life in the truth*.... In word and deed, Czech dissidents have demonstrated their conviction that there is truth, that there is good and evil—and that the difference is not reducible to cultural preference."[75] Kohák acknowledges that these dissidents are marching to a very different drummer than the one heard by the French philosophers Foucault and Derrida and the American Richard Rorty.[76] So is the pope. And like the pope, Kohák asks whether the newly liberated Central European counties should abandon their commitment to living in truth, the importance of which they learned when faced with the lies imposed by apparatchiks, for the "mindless consumerism of the Atlantic basin."[77]

I am uneasy with simplistic uses of the term "consumerism," but a careful reading of *Centesimus Annus* will show that what the term means there is not simplistic at all. It is used to criticize those strands of the culture of North Atlantic nations that have abandoned the effort to achieve a greater solidarity than the market can produce. This solidarity is rooted in the human capacity for self-transcendence and for justice. The pope's insistence that freedom comes from obedience to the truth about one's fellow human beings is similar to John Courtney Murray's insistence that the opening words of the American Declaration of Independence were an affirmation that "there are truths, and we hold them." The encyclical has learned enough from the democratic experience to affirm that the discovery of these truths will come not from theology alone, but from a truly interdisciplinary inquiry, that it demands attention to the practical experience of diverse peoples, and that "many people who profess no religion" will contribute to it.[78] But to this democratic experience, the encyclical makes an indispensable contribution: the need for solidarity and a commitment to the fact that human beings are not for sale, whether they be poor in the advanced societies of the North Atlantic or those who live in the developing countries of the Southern Hemisphere. Those who have been led to believe that *Centesimus Annus* endorses "really existing capitalism" should take a hard look at the text. I hope this survey of some recent discussion of this document will encourage careful reading and subsequent conversation about it, in the spirit of the solidarity and commitment to the common good that permeate the encyclical.

NOTES

1. Pope John Paul II, *Centesimus Annus*, in David J. O'Brien and Thomas A. Shannon, eds., *Catholic Social Thought: The Documentary Heritage* (Maryknoll, N.Y.: Orbis Books, 1992), no. 13. Throughout the English translation of the encyclical, the male gender is used to refer to all human beings. It would be possible to retranslate the Latin into English in a way that uses sexually inclusive language. I have refrained from doing so because the encyclical as a whole reveals an astonishing lack of concern for the economic and social problems faced by women in both advanced and developing countries. After describing the serious economic problems in both kinds of society, the document makes its sole reference to the problems faced by women in a single sentence: "The situation of women is far from easy in these conditions" (no. 33). In my judgment, this is worse than inadequate.

2. Ibid., no. 14.

3. Ibid., no. 23.

4. Ibid., no. 24.

5. Ibid.

6. Leonardo Boff, "La 'implosión' del socialismo autoritario y la teologia de la liberacion," *Sal Terrae* 79 (1991): 321–41, at 322.

7. Ibid., 331–32.

8. Ibid., 327.

9. Ibid., 339.

10. Ibid., 334.

11. Karl Marx and Friedrich Engels, "Manifesto of the Communist Party," in Louis S. Feuer, ed., *Basic Writings on Politics and Philosophy: Karl Marx and Friedrich Engels* (Garden City, N.Y.: Doubleday, 1959), 6.

12. Max L. Stackhouse and Dennis P. McCann, "A Postcommunist Manifesto: Public Theology after the Collapse of Socialism," *Christian Century* 108 (January 16, 1991): cover and 44–47. This citation is from the cover.

13. Ibid., cover and 44.

14. Ibid., 44.

15. Paul Abrecht, "The Predicament of Christian Social Thought after the Cold War," *Ecumenical Review* 43 (1991): 318–28, at 319.

16. Ibid., 324.

17. Ibid., 323.

18. Ibid., 325.

19. Ibid., 326.

20. Peter L. Berger, "Capitalism: The Continuing Revolution," *First Things* 15 (August/September 1991): 22–27, at 23. This is an excerpt from *The Capitalist Revolution: Fifty Propositions about Prosperity, Equality, and Liberty*, with new Introduction (New York: Basic Books, 1991).

21. Berger, "Capitalism," 23.

22. Ibid., 24.

23. *Centesimus Annus*, no. 42.

24. Ibid., no. 35.

25. Ibid., no. 42.

26. Giancarlo Zizola writes that a group headed by Buttiglione (whom he calls a "theoretician of the Communion and Liberation movement") was involved in revising an earlier draft produced by the Vatican Council on Justice and Peace, and that the pope himself made subsequent revisions. "Les revirements d'une encyclique," *L'actualité religieuse dans le monde* (June 15, 1991): 10–11.

27. Rocco Buttiglione, "Behind *Centesimus Annus*," *Crisis* (July/August 1991): 8–9, at 8.

28. Ibid., 9.

29. *Centesimus Annus*, nos. 32 and 34. See Stackhouse, "John Paul on Ethics and the 'New Capitalism,'" *Christian Century* (May 29–June 5, 1991): 581.

30. *Centesimus Annus*, no. 33.

31. National Conference of Catholic Bishops, *Economic Justice for All* (Washington, D.C.: United States Catholic Conference, 1986), no. 77.

32. *Centesimus Annus*, no. 33.

33. Ibid., no. 38.

34. Ibid., no. 26.

35. "God's Visible Hand," *Economist* (May 4, 1991): 42.

36. *Centesimus Annus*, no. 31.

37. John Locke, *Second Treatise on Civil Government*, in *Social Contract*, ed. Sir Ernest Barker (New York: Oxford University Press, 1967), 18. The degree to which Locke took this requirement seriously is disputed. Those who, like C. B. MacPherson, see Locke as a paradigmatic "possessive individualist" think he did not. A recent interpretation that argues

Locke believed in strict limits on property and that his views are closer to Thomas Aquinas than to modern individualism is that of Andrew Lustig, "Natural Law, Property, and Justice: The General Justification of Property in Aquinas and Locke," *Journal of Religious Ethics* 19 (1991): 119–49. To the extent that John Paul echoes Locke, it is Lustig's rather than MacPherson's Locke that is at issue.

38. *Centesimus Annus,* no. 6.

39. Ibid., no. 31.

40. Ibid., no. 32.

41. Ibid., nos. 32 and 43.

42. Jorge Maria Mejia, "Centesimus Annus: An Answer to the Unknowns and Questions of Our Times," *Ecumenical Review* 43 (1991): 401–10, at 406. This issue of *Ecumenical Review* is devoted to articles commemorating the *Rerum Novarum* centenary.

43. John Paul II, *Laborem Exercens*, in O'Brien and Shannon, eds., *Catholic Social Thought*, no. 13.

44. *Centesimus Annus,* no. 43.

45. Ibid., no. 35; emphasis in the original.

46. Thomas S. Johnson, "Capitalism after Communism: Now Comes the Hard Part," in John A. Coleman, S.J., ed., *One Hundred Years of Catholic Social Thought: Celebration and Challenge* (Maryknoll, N.Y.: Orbis, 1991), 240–55, at 247.

47. Ibid., 240–41.

48. Ibid., 241.

49. Johnson, 248 and passim.

50. Ibid., 248.

51. Ibid., 249.

52. Ibid., 253.

53. *Centesimus Annus,* no. 43.

54. Ibid., nos. 15 and 19.

55. Ibid., no. 19.

56. Ibid.

57. David Hollenbach, "The Pope and Capitalism," *America* (June 1, 1991): 591.

58. "Capitalismo Nell'Encyclica 'Centesimus Annus,'" *La Civiltà Cattolica* 142/3383 (1991): 417–30, at 426.

59. Frank Turner, S.J., "John Paul's Social Analysis," *The Month* (August 1991): 344–49, at 347–48.

60. See Michael Walzer, "The Idea of Civil Society: A Path to Social Reconstruction," *Dissent* (spring 1991): 293–304.

61. Erica Blair, "Towards a Civil Society: Hopes for Polish Democracy." Interview with Adam Michnik. *Times Literary Supplement* (February 19–25, 1988), 188ff., at 198.

62. Ibid.

63. Kenneth Himes, O.F.M., "The New Social Encyclical's Communitarian Vision," *Origins* 21 (1991): 166–68, at 167.

64. *Centesimus Annus,* no. 15.

65. Ibid., no. 48.

66. Daniel Patrick Moynihan, "Social Justice in the *Next* Century," *America* (September 14, 1991): 132–37, at 137.

67. For a careful and balanced discussion of this complexity, see David Ellwood, *Poor Support: Poverty in the American Family* (New York: Basic Books, 1988); William Julius Wilson, *The Truly Disadvantaged: The Inner City, The Underclass, and Public Policy* (Chicago: University of Chicago Press, 1987).

68. For a fuller discussion of the issue of poverty in the United States from the viewpoint of an ethic of the common good, see my *The Common Good and Christian Ethics* (Cambridge: Cambridge University Press, 2002), esp. chaps 2 and 7.

69. *Centesimus Annus,* no. 47.

70. Ibid., no. 49.

71. Ibid., no. 41.

72. Ibid., no. 46.

73. Ibid., no. 40.

74. Ibid., no. 41.

75. Erazim Kohák, "Can There Be a Central Europe?" *Dissent* (spring 1990): 194–97, at 195–96; emphasis in original.

76. For Rorty's rejoinder to Kohák, Havel, and Jan Patočka (the philosopher who was the symbolic and spiritual leader of the Charter 77 movement that brought down the Communist regime in Czechoslovakia) on the question of truth, see his "The Seer of Prague," a review of three books by Patočka, one of them edited by Kohák, *New Republic* (July 1, 1991): 35–39.

77. Kohák, 195.

78. *Centesimus Annus*, no. 60.

11

Human Rights and Development

THE AFRICAN CHALLENGE

The place of human rights in social development has been a matter of contention since the proclamation of the Universal Declaration of Human Rights, in 1948. The arguments at the founding of the United Nations were shaped principally by the ideological conflict between advocates of liberal democracy in the West, who argued that civil and political rights were a prerequisite to social development, and the socialists and Marxists of the East, who maintained that economic equality and emancipation of the proletariat were preconditions for democracy. A similar argument with a distinctively African accent was heard again in the 1970s and 1980s in the discussion of the "right to development" proclaimed at the United Nations and in the Organization of African Unity's Charter of Human and Peoples' Rights (the Banjul Charter). Today in the eyes of many in the West, these arguments have been settled by the collapse of the Soviet Union and by the discrediting of African one-party states, symbolized most vividly by the departure of Mobutu Sese Seko from Kinshasa, Zaire, in 1997.

For example, during a ten-day trip to Africa in his second term in office, President Bill Clinton spoke strongly of his conviction that human rights and democracy are linked to economic development. Clinton noted the central role that the idea of human rights has played in the moral conscience of the United States when that conscience has been at its best. He endorsed the continuing relevance of the human rights idea around the world today. In Clinton's words, "Democracy requires human rights for everyone, everywhere, for men and women, for children and the elderly, for people of different cultures and tribes and backgrounds."[1] Clinton also affirmed his belief that human rights and democracy are strongly linked to the expansion of the free market, in Africa as elsewhere. "Democracy must have prosperity. Americans of both political parties want to increase trade and investment in Africa. . . . By opening markets and building businesses and creating jobs, we can help and strengthen each other."[2]

Thus, Clinton's policy for Africa rested on two pillars: democracy and human rights, on the one hand, and markets, trade, and investment, on the other. Free politics and free markets were envisioned as the paths to a more just future and a more developed Africa. This basic policy orientation receives continued support by the administration of President George W. Bush. Indeed, the Bush administration is even stronger in its conviction that markets by themselves are the key to development.

I think, however, that it is a mistake to conclude that the place of human rights in development has been settled once and for all, especially if this is understood simplistically to mean that democratic freedoms plus free markets equal development. The inadequacy of this formula has become particularly evident in the face of the present agonies of the African continent. A preliminary report of a project on Cultural Transformations and Human Rights in Africa, organized by Abdullahi An-Na'im, was correct when it affirmed that "economic, social, and cultural rights are at serious risk of total oblivion in the age of economic liberation and structural adjustment programs in Africa. Yet any human rights paradigm is unlikely to have much significance to Africans if it does not include concern with their fundamental economic, social, and cultural claims and entitlements."[3]

This chapter will outline why I agree with An-Na'im on the inadequacy of an understanding of human rights that does not directly include the economic rights to nutrition, health care, and the satisfaction of other fundamental needs at least to a level required to live in a minimally human way. It will suggest why the individualistic view of human rights charac-teristically found in the United States is inadequate. This individualistic understanding sees a human right through the paradigm of the right to be left alone. Private property, with the emphasis on *private*, is the archetype of all the other human rights. So rights protect my turf from in-cursions into my zone of privacy. Solidarity with others has little formative role on this individualistic concept of human rights. If promotion of hu-man rights is to make a genuine contribution to the development of the poor in Africa, rights will have to be understood in a way that places con-siderably more emphasis on the solidarity among people as a condition for understanding human rights in theory and attaining them in practice. So it will be argued here.

THE IMPORTANCE OF CIVIL SOCIETY

As noted in chapter 8 above, Robert Putnam has used the study of com-parative politics to argue that successful democracies require significant levels of active civic participation by their citizens. This participation is the "social capital" needed to sustain an effective democratic regime.[4] In more classical terms, a high level of social capital is another way of speak-ing about the strength of civil society—the complex web of human rela-tionships that include families, kinship groupings, churches and other re-ligious communities, voluntary associations of varying purposes, labor unions, and political parties. Putnam's argument that strong associational life in civil society is essential to democracy is in harmony with both the civic-republican tradition in political theory and the Roman Catholic tra-dition's "principle of subsidiarity."[5] The bonds of communal solidarity formed in communities of small or intermediate size enable people to act together, empowering them to shape the contours of public life and its larger social institutions, such as the state and the economy. Where civil society is weak or absent, the institutions of democratic governance lack the social base they need to function effectively. In Putnam's words, the strength of civil society is a prerequisite to a democracy that works for the benefit of the people.

Putnam's argument is based on empirical research and analysis of the differences in political activity in northern and southern Italy. His studies showed that Italian regional government worked better in the northern regions of Italy that possessed a stronger civil society. It did not work well in the south, where the communities of civil society were weak. Both state and market function more effectively for the well-being of the people when the people can influence them. And the capacity to exert such influence grows as the bonds of civic life and extragovernmental social solidarities themselves grow stronger. These studies of Italy are highly suggestive as we consider the link between democratization, human rights, and social development in places such as Nigeria and other developing countries in Africa.

AFRICAN UNDERSTANDINGS OF HUMAN RIGHTS

It has become evident that conflicts between competing and sometimes hostile traditions of ethnicity and religion can seriously threaten *both* human rights *and* social development. The horror of genocide in Rwanda and the tragic struggle in Sudan are poignant symbols of the threat. Such conflicts are a challenge to Western liberal views of human rights. Most of the liberal political theory of the West is so deeply individualistic that its only response to communally generated ethnic or religious passion is simply to declare that it should not exist. A more helpful analysis is clearly needed.

This individualistic bias of Western liberalism led a number of African political leaders and academic analysts to be deeply suspicious of "rights talk" in the initial discussions of human rights by African thinkers that began in the 1970s. For example, Nigerian writer Chris C. Mojekwu advocated this line in a 1980 article. In Mojekwu's words, "African concepts of human rights are very different from those of Western Europe. Communalism and communal right concepts are fundamental to understanding African culture, politics and society. One should not make the mistake of thinking that the colonial interlude washed away these fundamental cultures in the society."[6]

Mojekwu's emphasis on communal, rather than individual, self-determination is also prominent in the African Charter on Human and Peoples' Rights adopted in 1981 by the Organization of African Unity, or OAU. The African Charter differs from the United Nations Universal Declaration of Human Rights by calling itself a charter of human and *peoples'* rights. It declares not only that all human beings are equal, but that all peoples are as well. This difference is explained in the preamble to the African Charter, which states that "historical tradition and the values of African civilization . . . should inspire and characterize . . . reflection on the concept of human and peoples' rights." Thus, the charter affirms that *peoples* have the right to self determination, *peoples* have the right to pursue economic and social development according to the policy they have freely chosen, *peoples* have the right to freely dispose of their wealth and natural resources, and *peoples* have the right to economic, social, and cultural development.[7] Accompanying the list of peoples' rights is a list of duties. These include the duty of the individual to serve the national community by placing his or her physical and intellectual abilities at its service and the duty not to compromise the security of the state of which one is a national or a resident.[8]

Rhoda Howard maintains that such support for the communal values of traditional African ways of life can effectively undermine the very notion of the rights of persons. For example, she points out how a number of the authors who defend this view take little notice of the coercive power of communal groupings, including the coercion of women.[9] Further, the duties expressed in the African Charter are so broad and imprecisely defined that the way is opened to a wholesale limitation of rights, eviscerating them of practical meaning.[10] Howard argues, however, that African cultural traditions contain a concept of the dignity of the person that, under the conditions of actual African societies today, can best be sustained through the defense of human rights. This point is reinforced by Timothy Fernyhough's exploration of the actual historical and cultural traditions in a number of African communities. Fernyhough's research has shown that the people of traditional African societies clearly knew how to recognize tyranny when they saw it and how to oppose tyranny when it appeared on the scene.[11]

Nevertheless, there remains an ambiguity in the communalist orientation stressed by advocates of a distinctively African understanding of rights. It is clear that the OAU affirmation of peoples' rights was especially directed against all forms of domination of African peoples by the colonial powers of the West and by postindependence economic powers of the developed world. The right of African peoples to control the natural resources of their lands and the right to development were fundamentally anticolonial assertions; however, when the African Charter affirmed the existence of peoples' rights, it left the meaning of the crucial word "peoples" undefined. Does it mean the people of the existing nation-states of postindependence Africa? The people of a particular ethnic group, whose members are present on both sides of many of the frontiers separating these nation-states? The people of different ethnic groups living side-by-side in the same village or city of one of these nation-states? This ambiguity left a large opening for the emergence of authoritarian rule in postindependence Africa.

The Beninois philosopher Paulin Hountondji points out that the right of peoples to freedom, sovereignty, and historical initiative is unquestionable. It can be traced back to the right of peoples to self-determination affirmed by the French Revolution. Nevertheless, Hountondji challenges the interpretation of peoples' rights as "an absolute right of peoples over the individuals who make them up or, within a people, of the majority over the minority."[12] Such an interpretation rests on a mystified notion of "the people" and has legitimated some of the great tragedies of history. Further, this mystified notion of "peoples' rights" leaves open the question of who interprets the will of the people. In the actual practice of recent African politics, the argument for peoples' rights has most often been invoked by those who are in a position to claim that they themselves speak for the people. It becomes a mask for another much more ominous claim, namely, "I am the people!—le peuple, c'est moi!" Peoples' rights and the critique of Western individualism, through this rhetorical legerdemain, lead to "a mystique of the Leader" or, little less dangerously, to the legitimation of the one-party state.[13] Howard feared the same outcome when she gloomily forecast that the future of African politics might well be a form of "underdeveloped fascism."[14]

Since Hountondji and Howard wrote these analyses in the mid-1980s, there has been a significant decline in appeals to communal or peoples' rights in theoretical discourse about human rights in Africa, just as there has been an incipient move in practice away from one-party states toward democracy in many parts of the continent. The rising support for democracy has even led Goren Hyden to predict that "demands for strengthening the Charter in the direction of greater protection of individual rights—especially those that relate to democratization—will evolve."[15] At least officially, one-party states have been replaced by multiparty systems in Kenya, Zambia, and elsewhere. Also both nongovernmental organizations and international donors are seeking to advance the cause of democracy and good governance on many fronts.

But is this enough to raise our hopes about the future of human rights in African contexts? I have my doubts for two reasons. First, multiparty elections will not be enough to secure human rights when civil society has become as weak as it has in many African countries. The 1997 elections in Kenya were a case in point. Second, the economic or class structure of many African societies have frequently undercut the efforts to strengthen civil society through the structural adjustment programs so favored by the World Bank, the International Monetary Fund, and their backers in the developed world in the 1980s and early 1990s.

On the first point, Hyden is eloquent: "The state-centered approach to development that African countries adopted with full support by the international community after independence has created a situation in which society has been reduced to a desert. Instead of being encouraged to engage in public action for development, Africans have been left to fend for themselves in the informal sector or seek favors by attaching themselves to political patrons who might help them make social or economic gains."[16] With this legacy, clientelism and patrimonialism seem quite compatible with free elections. Jean-François Bayart refers to it as "the politics of the belly." Though this descriptive phrase is drawn from Francophone African idiom, the reality it refers to is by no means confined to areas where French is spoken. For example, it is the form of politics that those who prepared Nigeria's 1976 draft constitution unabashedly defined as "the opportunity to acquire riches and prestige, to be in a position to hand out benefits in the form of jobs, contracts, gifts of money, etc. to relations and political allies."[17]

This leads to my second doubt. When people have so few economic resources that just getting food is their prime task, they are forced into "exchanges born of desperation."[18] They become willing to barter their political support for what little economic gain their patrons might provide them. Or desperate straits lead them to acquiesce in whatever those with political power are willing to concede to them. Those who are not willing to make such bargains face grave consequences, either through the withdrawal of support by their patrons or through repression by those with the guns. And once a pattern of repression has been established, those who presently have the guns stand to lose everything if they lose power. This kind of politics is a desperate zero-sum game, in which the losers lose everything and the winners gain whatever is there for the taking. Such a contest is a self-perpetuating vicious circle. Those in power cannot afford to lose and will be prepared to use all the tools of manipulation to keep power, including the encouragement of group hatred that led to the genocide in Rwanda and that, less dramatically but nonetheless tragically, contributed to the ethnic conflicts in the Rift Valley in Kenya around the 1992 election and again on the Kenyan coast before the 1997 election in that country.[19] The pattern is sadly familiar elsewhere on the continent as well.

Hyden, of course, is aware that the prevailing economic conditions make the advancement of human rights problematic even under the conditions of formal multiparty democracy. He acknowledges that keeping alive the hope for human rights that has arisen in the last decade "depends on how successful African countries will be in solving their economic difficulties and how helpful the rest of the world will be toward Africa."[20] Economic liberalization and the expansion of market-exchange holds out some hope, for in Hyden's view respect for rights and the presence of markets have been positively correlated with each other in the past. Thus, Hyden thinks that structural adjustment programs that seek to expand the scope of free markets "may" help the cause of human rights "if [they are] made to work."[21] True enough. But this is to affirm a tautology: *if* structural adjustment can be *made to work,* we will see progress in good governance, social development, and human rights. The question remains: will opening markets lead to an economic improvement for the poor, an improvement that lessens their readiness to make desperate exchanges in the political domain?

SOCIAL-ECONOMIC RIGHTS AND THE LIMITS OF THE MARKET

This question indicates why the arguments about the relation of human rights to African development are not finally settled. This does not mean that Lenin is about to come forth from his tomb or that state centralism—Soviet or African style—is in any way a viable solution to the problems of

Africa today. It does mean, however, that the social and economic rights contained in the United Nations' Universal Declaration of Human Rights have to be put back on the human rights agenda in Africa.

Perhaps the best way to explain this is to appeal again to my own religious tradition. Pope John Paul II, whom all acknowledge was a major force behind the collapse of the Soviet system, has been a strong advocate of human rights throughout his pontificate. During his 1998 visit to Nigeria, he repeated this theme forcefully: "This moment in Nigeria's history [is] a moment that requires concerted and honest efforts to foster harmony and national unity, to guarantee respect for human life and *human rights*, to promote justice and development, to combat unemployment, to give hope to the poor and suffering, to resolve conflicts through dialogue and to establish a true and lasting *solidarity* between all sectors of society."[22] These words were spoken as the pontiff stood beside the former Nigerian dictator, General Sani Abacha. Abacha had shown his contempt for human rights by hanging opposition leaders such as Ken Saro-Wiwa. This challenge to Abacha made clear that human rights are key to John Paul's vision of Africa's future, just as they were in former President Clinton's.

Note, however, that the idea of *solidarity* has an important place in John Paul's vision of a more just society, particularly in Africa. He affirms that solidarity is a prerequisite for a democratic society characterized by human rights and that the individualism of most theories of the free market is insufficient. The pope has, of course, affirmed the efficiency and productivity of market economies, but he warns against moving from the inadequacy of state centralism to uncritical support for liberal ideologies that see markets by themselves as the solution to Africa's deep problems of poverty, political oppression, and violence. In fact, John Paul II has long held that the market can create problems for democracy and human rights unless it is regulated by norms of justice that emerge from a vision of human solidarity—a vision that we are all in the same boat. For example, during his January 1998 visit to Cuba, the Pope appealed forcefully for human rights and democracy, as he did much earlier in his native Poland when it was still under Communist rule. In Cuba the Pope pointedly stressed that political freedom plus markets is an inadequate formula for a just form of social development. Here is how he put it in Havana in the presence of Fidel Castro:

[V]arious places are witnessing the resurgence of a certain capitalist neoliberalism which subordinates the human person to blind market forces and
conditions the development of peoples on those forces. From its centres of
power, such neoliberalism often places unbearable burdens upon less favored countries. Hence, at times, unsustainable economic programmes are
imposed on nations as a condition for further assistance. In the international
community, we thus see a small number of countries growing exceedingly
rich at the cost of the increasing impoverishment of a great number of other
countries; as a result the wealthy grow ever wealthier, while the poor grow
ever poorer.[23]

In market-based societies, he observes, many persons are unable to participate in the economy because they lack the resources needed to do so.
"The fact is that many people, perhaps the majority today, do not have the
means which would enable them to take their place in an effective and humanly dignified way within a productive system in which work is truly central. . . . Thus, if not actually exploited, they are to a great extent marginalized; economic development takes place over their heads."[24]

This is key to the plight of so many in Africa today: "development takes
place over their heads." They lack the resources needed to become involved in the markets that are the hoped-for engines of economic development. They are also marginalized from genuinely active involvement in
the democratic process because of their economic plight, leaving control
of the political process in the hands of entrenched elites. Political democracy is surely a prerequisite for change in this situation, but political democratization alone is not enough. The last decade's stress on political and
civil rights as preconditions for social development in Africa must be accompanied by rising efforts to secure the minimum economic conditions
needed for people to be politically active. These minimum conditions are
called social and economic rights in the United Nations Universal Declaration. They are not the totality of the "social capital" Putnam sees as a prerequisite for democracy that works, but they are indispensable. That is one
of the reasons why the United Nations called them human rights.

The Nigerian political scientist Claude Ake has noted that the movement for democracy is rooted in the social and economic hopes of African
peoples. Thus, it will not be fulfilled by the institutions of political democ-

racy alone. "It will emphasize concrete economic and social rights rather than abstract political rights; it will insist on the democratization of economic opportunities, the social betterment of the people, and a strong social welfare system. To achieve these goals, it will have to be effectively participative."[25] Ake calls such a vision of social development "people driven democratization." It is a challenge to those reforms that leave elites in a position to continue to dominate both politics and economics. More strongly put, efforts to secure the civil and political rights associated with democratic politics are sure to fail if the political choices of large populations are born of desperation. Such desperation makes them prime targets for leaders willing to exploit the "politics of the belly."

To conclude, African traditional cultures cannot be invoked to negate the importance of human rights in Africa today by those who seek the genuine well-being of the people of the continent. In Simeon Ilesanmi's words, clear-eyed consideration of the relation between human rights and the realities of Africa today calls for "a departure from romanticized traditionalism to an analysis of the totality of African existence: all those institutions that regulate, brutalize, frustrate, and bastardize human lives in Africa."[26] This is a direct challenge to those who would appeal to African traditions to legitimize the continued diminishment of the lives of so many Africans in both the political and economic domains. At the same time, such a consideration of the realities of contemporary African societies strongly challenges the Western bias of the 1980s and early 1990s, which identifies human rights with the liberal freedoms of multiparty democracy and free markets alone. Fortunately, there are some signs that this is beginning to change. For example, the World Bank's efforts to formulate a comprehensive development framework and its 2001 annual *World Development Report* titled "Attacking Poverty" both seek to put the issue of equality back on the development agenda.[27] This change of direction has been sufficient to lead some to argue that today's World Bank leadership has become overly ambitious in pursuit of equality and insufficiently committed to free markets.[28] But these new directions still fall short of what is truly needed. In particular, they fail to describe the meeting of the needs of the economically vulnerable as true human rights. Human rights will play their proper role in social development in Africa today only when they are conceived as the Universal Declaration understood them fifty years ago—as including both civil-political and social-economic rights. Such a

conception of human rights is as much a challenge to Western liberal individualism as it is to some manifestations of traditional African cultures.
This challenge could be a source of hope, were it to become the basis of
new alliances among those concerned with the well-being of developing
countries, particularly the African continent and its people.

NOTES

1. William J. Clinton, "Remarks by the President to the People of Ghana," Accra, Ghana,
March 23, 1998. Posted on the website of the Clinton Presidential Materials Projects,
http://clinton6.nara.gov/1998/03/1998-03-23-remarks-by-the-president-to-the-people-of-
ghana.html [downloaded May 14, 2003].

2. Ibid.

3. Abdullahi Ahmed An-Na'im, Amy Madigan, and Gary Minkley, "Cultural Transformations and Human Rights in Africa: A Preliminary Report," *Emory International Law
Review* 11, no. 1 (spring 1997): 293.

4. Robert Putnam, *Making Democracy Work: Civic Traditions in Modern Italy* (Princeton, N.J.: Princeton University Press, 1993), 167.

5. Pius XI, *Quadragesimo Anno* (1931), in David J. O'Brien and Thomas A. Shannon,
eds., *Catholic Social Thought: The Documentary Heritage* (Maryknoll, N.Y.: Orbis Books,
1992), nos. 79 and 80.

6. Chris C. Mojekwu, "International Human Rights: The African Perspective," in Jack
L. Nelson and Vera M. Green, eds., *International Human Rights: Contemporary Issues*
(Stanfordville, N.Y.: Human Rights Publishing Group, 1980), 92.

7. African Charter on Human and People's Rights, arts. 19–22, in M. Hamalengwa, C.
Flinterman, and E. V. O. Dankwa, eds., *The International Law of Human Rights in Africa:
Basic Documents and Annotated Bibliography* (Dordrecht: Martinus Nijhoff, 1988).

8. Ibid., art. 29.

9. Rhoda E. Howard, "Group versus Individual Identity in the African Debate on Human Rights," in Abdullahi Ahmed An-Na'im and Francis M. Deng, eds., *Human Rights in
Africa: Cross-Cultural Perspectives* (Washington, D.C.: Brookings Institution, 1990),
159–83, esp. 179–80.

10. Rhoda E. Howard, *Human Rights in Commonwealth Africa* (Totowa, N.J.: Rowman
and Littlefield, 1986), 7–8 and chaps. 6 and 7.

11. Fernyhough, Timothy, "Human Rights and Precolonial Africa." in Ronald Cohen,
Goran Hyden, and Winston P. Nagan, eds., *Human Rights and Governance in Africa*
(Gainesville.: University Press of Florida, 1993), 39–73.

12. Paulin J. Hountondji, "The Master's Voice: Remarks on the Problem of Human
Rights in Africa," in Alwin Diemer et al., eds., *Philosophical Foundations of Human Rights*
(Paris: UNESCO, 1986), 319–32, at 328–29.

13. Ibid., 329.

14. Howard, *Human Rights in Commonwealth Africa,* 228.

15. Goren Hyden, "The Challenge of Domesticating Rights in Africa," in Cohen, Hyden, and Nagan, eds., *Human Rights and Governance in Africa,* 264.

16. Ibid., 265.

17. Jean-François Bayart, *The State in Africa: The Politics of the Belly,* trans. Mary Harper (London: Longman, 1993), xvii, citing J. Dunn, ed., *West African States: Failure and Promise, A Study in Comparative Politics* (Cambridge: Cambridge University Press, 1978), 133.

18. Michael Walzer, *Spheres of Justice: A Defense of Pluralism and Equality* (New York: Basic Books, 1993), 100 ff.; see also Arthur Okun, *Equality and Efficiency: The Big Trade-off* (Washington, D.C.: Brookings Institution Press, 1975).

19. Basil Davidson, *The Black Man's Burden: Africa and the Curse of the Nation-State* (New York: Times Books, 1992), chap. 7; see Gérard Prunier, *The Crisis in Rwanda: History of a Genocide* (Kampala: Fountain Publishers, 1995); Human Rights Watch/Africa Watch, *Divide and Rule: State-Sponsored Ethnic Violence in Kenya* (New York: Human Rights Watch, 1993).

20. Hyden, "The Challenge of Domesticating Rights in Africa," 265.

21. Ibid., 266.

22. John Paul II, "Arrival Speech in Nigeria, March 21, 1998," no. 2. Posted on the website of the Holy See, www.vatican.va/holy_father/john_paul_ii/travels/documents/hf_jp-ii_spe_21031998_nigeria-arrival_en.html [downloaded August 3, 2002].

23. John Paul II, "Homily in the José Marti Square of Havana, Sunday, 25 January 1998," no. 4. Posted on the website of the Holy See, www.vatican.va/holy_father/john_paul_ii/travels/documents/hf_jp-ii_hom_25011998_lahavana_en.html [downloaded August 3, 2002].

24. Pope John Paul II, *Centesimus Annus,* in David J. O'Brien and Thomas A. Shannon, eds., *Catholic Social Thought: The Documentary Heritage* (Maryknoll, N.Y.: Orbis Books, 1992), no. 33.

25. Claude Ake, *Democracy and Development in Africa* (Washington, D.C.: Brookings Institution, 1996), 139.

26. Simeon O. Ilesanmi, "Human Rights Discourse in Modern Africa," *Journal of Religious Ethics* 23, no. 2 (1995): 293–322.

27. See Ravi Kanbur and Nora Lustig, "Why Is Inequality Back on the Agenda?" Paper presented at the Annual Bank Conference on Development Economics, World Bank, Washington, D.C., April 28–30, 1999. Kanbur and Lustig oversaw the drafting of the World Bank's *World Development Report 2000/2001: Attacking Poverty* (New York: Oxford University Press, 2001).

28. Jessica Einhorn, "The World Bank's Mission Creep," *Foreign Affairs* 80, no. 5 (September/October 2001): 22–35; Stephen Fidler, "Who's Minding the Bank?" *Foreign Policy* 126 (September/October 2001): 40–50.

12

Faiths, Cultures, and Global Ethics

Since the end of the cold war, the place of religion in world affairs has become a central focus of international politics. In popular discussions, concern with the role of religion in the political and military conflicts of the world is tied to the highly visible role of fundamentalist Islam, especially since the terrorist attacks of September 11, 2001, on the United States. In the academic world, Samuel Huntington's thesis that the future of world politics will be driven by a clash of civilizations shaped by religion has been much debated.[1] Huntington's argument is controversial to be sure, but it, along with a number of other studies, indicates that religion has become a serious topic in the analysis of international politics.[2] Contrary to the title of a book published less than a decade ago, religion can no longer be considered "the missing dimension" of both popular and academic discussions of statecraft.[3]

In light of these developments, the role of religion in forming cultural values has become central in reflection on the ethical dimensions of global politics. Recent trends leading to the globalization of politics and economics have raised many issues of notable ethical importance. They include economic justice for poor countries, including matters of aid, trade, and debt relief; the proliferation and possible use of weapons of mass destruction; the promotion of human rights and response to extreme forms of human rights violation such as ethnic cleansing and genocide; the legitimacy of humanitarian military intervention; response to environmental issues such as global warming; and health-related matters such as the spread of HIV-AIDS. These questions cut across not only the geographic borders of countries, but also the cultural and religious divergences among people. As a result, these urgent global issues have stimulated a lively new discussion of whether religious communities and the cultures they are tied to can find a common moral ground from which to address these issues. Are there ethical standards that reach across the religious and cultural differences that mark our world? In response to this question, a notable body of literature has developed on the possibility of identifying a "common morality."[4] This is not only a question of considerable theoretical interest. It also has important practical ramifications. If such a "global ethic" can be identified, it could serve as a common ground for peaceful approaches to the emergent issues in the political, economic, technological, and environmental domains. On the other hand, if the hope of attaining a global ethic is illusory, the possibility of reaching peaceful resolution to the challenges raised by growing global interdependence will be small. In a globalizing world, therefore, a common global ethic would increase our hope for peace, while the lack of a common ethic would make it likely that we are headed for a clash of civilizations.

There are two main challenges to the possibility of such a common morality or global ethic. The first is the issue of pluralism: in light of the cultural and religious diversity of our world, can we really expect to find shared moral standards that can address the complex social and political questions we face? This challenge is certainly not new. The question of cultural relativism is as old as Socrates' arguments with the Sophists in Plato's dialogues, but the issue takes on heightened significance today as people with diverse traditions become increasingly interdependent because of technological and economic change. The second challenge is that of political realism. Even if we can agree on some minimal set of universally shared moral standards, is it realistic to expect people from diverse nations or cultures to abide by these norms when doing so would carry significant cost to their self-interest? This realist objection to moral appeals in the relations among diverse peoples also has an ancient pedigree, going back through Weber, Hobbes, and Machiavelli to the Sophists, such as Thrasymachus in Plato's *Republic,* and to Thucydides' account of the Peloponnesian War.[5]

The ancient challenges to a universal ethic raised by the plurality of religions and cultures and by the role that self-interest doubtless plays in intergroup politics both have distinctive forms today. This chapter will first explore some of the contemporary challenges to the possibility of a global ethic or common morality raised by religious and cultural pluralism. Second, it will present a constructive argument for movement toward consensus on a global ethic that is modest in theoretical scope but potentially significant in practice. Finally, it will conclude with a brief comment on some political implications of movement toward such a global ethic.

THE CHALLENGE OF CULTURAL AND RELIGIOUS PLURALISM

Much of the recent discussion of a global ethic or common morality has been formulated in terms of an emergent human rights ethic that has been a distinctive development of the post–World War II period. This human rights ethic holds considerable promise as a set of standards on which people from diverse traditions can agree. Indeed, a legal scholar who has traced the history of the drafting of the United Nations' 1948 Universal Declaration of Human Rights has called it a charter for a world made new. Mary Ann Glendon has affirmed that, in the wake of the horrors of World War II, "the mightiest nations on earth bowed to the demands of smaller countries for recognition of a common standard by which the rights and wrongs of every nation's behavior could be measured."[6] The absence of such common standards was seen as one of the sources of war itself. By showing the consequences of the lack of such a standard, the war pointed to the need for common norms to which all nations could be held accountable.

The Universal Declaration of Human Rights thus bases its proclamation of human rights norms on the practical experience of their violation. The Preamble of the Declaration first alludes to the two twentieth-century world wars as evidence of the need for global norms and then affirms human rights as the "foundation of freedom, justice, and peace in the world." It implicitly invokes the Nazi attempt to exterminate the Jewish people when it refers to acts that "outraged the conscience of man-

kind." Such outrages have made the desire for a world where fundamental freedoms are secure the "aspiration of the common people." The
Preamble also refers to the struggle against colonialism that was on the
rise as the Declaration was being written when it states that human rights
must be protected in law if people are not to be driven to rebellion against
tyranny and oppression.[7] The Declaration, therefore, offers a practical,
experience-based case for the plausibility of the claim that "*all* people are
born free and equal in dignity and rights" and that "everyone is entitled
to all the rights and freedoms set forth in this declaration, without distinction of any kind, such as race, colour, sex, language, religion."[8] It neither
presents a technical philosophical argument for a global ethic of human
rights nor seeks to justify its proclamation of human rights by presenting
an argument for their theoretical foundations. Rather, the Preamble appeals to experience when it asserts its universalist claims. The practical rationale sketched in the Preamble reflects the fact that it was not philosophical argumentation of a theoretical nature that led to the drafting of the
Universal Declaration. Rather, it was the negative experiences of war and
what subsequently was named "genocide" that gave rise to a desire to identify practical standards to which all nations could be held accountable.

In the cold war decades following the issuance of the Universal Declaration, however, this experience-based and practical motivation to pursue
common standards was significantly weakened by the strategic competition between East and West. The ideological divide between the two blocs
further deepened the strategic political and military rivalry. The cold war
constituted not only a competition for power, but also a profound intellectual disagreement about the meaning of social life and the best means to
attain it. These philosophical disputes set the democracies of the North Atlantic and the socialist countries of the East in mutual competition. This
ideological rift divided those who believed that keeping individual freedom immune from state interference was the most important social value
from those who held that the fulfillment of basic material needs had primacy. Thus, the cold war competition raised both practical and theoretical
challenges to the idea that human rights could form the core of a common
global morality.

Since the end of the cold war, however, the context for the question of
a common morality has once again changed dramatically. The post–cold
war period has raised new hopes that the promise of a world based on

shared ethical values might be within reach. At the same time, however, it has brought forth new cultural objections to the universality claimed for human rights. The new hopes are evident on several fronts. First and perhaps most significant is the new evidence of worldwide agreement on human rights norms made visible in the 1993 World Conference on Human Rights convened by the United Nations in Vienna. At that conference, delegates of 171 nations, representing 85 percent of the world's population, subscribed to the Vienna Declaration and Programme of Action, which reaffirmed and further developed all the standards contained in the Universal Declaration. Article I, number 1, of the Vienna Declaration explicitly states that "the universal nature of these rights and freedoms is beyond question."[9] Support for this assertion by so many governments shows that in 1993 there was at least verbal support for human rights by representatives of a much higher percentage of the earth's population than was the case in 1948. Many of the countries that supported the Vienna Declaration in 1993 were either colonized or otherwise politically dominated in 1948 and had no voice to either approve or reject the Universal Declaration. The Vienna Declaration, therefore, provides strong support for the argument that human rights are becoming the core of a truly global common morality.[10]

Second, the post–cold war period has also seen significant increases in citizen advocacy of human rights and establishment of institutions for the enforcement of human rights. The astonishing growth in the number of nongovernmental organizations devoted to advocacy for human rights has been noted as one of the most significant developments in international politics in recent years.[11] The development of judicial bodies with at least some power to pursue enforcement of human rights is also significant. These include the International Criminal Tribunals for both Yugoslavia and Rwanda and, more recently, the International Criminal Tribunal that has been permanently institutionalized, despite the refusal of the United States to acknowledge this tribunal's jurisdiction over U.S. citizens. These new emphases on human rights offer a hope that a global common morality can in fact be identified or created. They hold some promise that such a global ethic can help address the tensions of an increasingly interdependent world in a peaceful way.

Despite these hopeful signs, the years since the cold war ended have also witnessed notable countersigns. In particular, those who argue that the human rights norms proclaimed in 1948 are Western rather than truly global have raised questions about the universality of the human rights ethic. Michael Ignatieff has noted three different versions of this cultural argument against human rights and thus against a common morality— Islamic, Confucian, and Western postmodernist.[12] One strand of the Islamic objection is based on Muslim understandings of the limits to legitimate religious freedom. For example, Shari'ah limits the freedom of Muslims to convert to a religion other than Islam. It also places limits on the freedom of non-Muslims in Islamic lands, though it is also true that Islamic law in some ways gives greater protection to non-Muslims than premodern Western law often did to non-Christians. Also, Muslim understandings of the roles of women are not fully compatible with the way gender relations are understood and lived in many Western settings.

In East Asia, a Confucian objection maintains that human rights are too heavily dependent on Western individualism. In particular, the ethic of human rights is seen as in conflict with the communal relationships of reverential respect between parent and child, minister and ruler, husband and wife, older and younger brother, friend and friend that are so important in Confucian societies. The former Prime Minister of Singapore, Lee Kwan Yew, has advanced this view forcefully. Lee suggests that the Western liberal understanding of rights embodied in the UN Declaration is in fact based on the mistaken individualistic view that "everybody would be better off if they were allowed to do their own thing."[13] Lee argues that the Confucian societies of East Asia—China, Japan, Korea, and Vietnam— have not made this error. These cultures recognize that there must be limits on a person's freedom if community well-being is to be achieved. Therefore, these societies cannot fully endorse the human rights ethos of the post–World War II period. As I have noted in chapter 11, some African intellectuals and political leaders make an analogous argument. They state that the strongly communal nature of traditional African religion and culture makes the contemporary human rights ethos culturally inappropriate in the African context.[14]

These challenges to the human rights ethos from outside the West have found receptive ears within the West among advocates of postmodern or postcolonial theory in cultural studies, literary criticism, philosophy, and—to a lesser extent—political theory. These theorists fear that any effort to propose a common morality will amount to a form of Western cultural hegemony and could legitimate political or economic domination.[15]

Despite these objections, the Confucian, Islamic, African, and postcolonial worlds are certainly not of one mind that a global ethic of human rights is a bad idea. As the Vienna Declaration would lead one to expect, there is in fact notable support for a universal human rights ethic among people living in Confucian, Islamic, and African countries. And contrary to the objections to universalism made by Western postcolonial theorists, there is significant support for a human rights ethic among people who were once colonized. This was brought home to me in a vivid way in Kenya several years ago. In a lecture I had outlined some of the objections to the ethos of human rights voiced by several African intellectuals and also by Daniel arap Moi, then president of Kenya. A respondent to my presentation, the attorney heading the independent Kenya Human Rights Commission, expressed considerable relief that I had not supported the argument that human rights necessarily conflict with the culture and social needs of Kenyan society. He asserted that this argument posed a significant threat to the well-being of many Kenyans. In his view, the claim that African communal cultures need to be defended against the imposition of an individualistic Western human rights ethos does not sufficiently attend to the practical economic and political challenges faced by most Kenyans. People like Moi and certain Western advocates of postcolonialist theory could make their argument only because they do not share the struggles faced by many Kenyans. In other words, he turned the charge of cultural narrowness back against those claiming to defend African cultures against Western hegemony. He defended a common morality by appealing to the diverse practical consequences of support for and denial of globally recognized human rights standards. In his view, these practical consequences were more important to the argument about global ethics than claims based on the distinctiveness of African cultures considered in the abstract. This changes the question of whether a common morality of human rights is in full harmony with certain African traditional cultures into a question of whether this ethic will concretely enhance the well-being of the people in these settings.

Similar disputes are present in the East Asian world. Another significant East Asian political leader, Kim Dae Jung, has vigorously rejected

Lee Kwan Yew's claim that the human rights ethos is incompatible with Confucian culture. Kim is a former political dissident and human rights activist who went on to be elected president of the Republic of Korea (South Korea). He argues that no culture is static, including the Confucian cultures of Asia. Under the pressure of contemporary experience, Asian societies are discovering resources within their traditions that support democracy and human rights. For example, Kim cites the duty of Confucian scholars to remonstrate erring monarchs as a Confucian precedent for democratic procedure that antedates the emergence of modern democracy in the West.[16] An indigenous South Asian thinker, Amartya Sen, makes similar claims that resources supporting democratic values and basic human rights can be found in both Indian and Chinese religious and cultural traditions.[17] Of course, Kim and Sen are not scholars of the history of their respective traditions, and their arguments for the compatibility of human rights with Asian traditions may be oversimplified. Nevertheless, there are scholars with historical expertise who maintain that Confucian traditions can be rethought in ways that will sustain endorsement of a global human rights ethic.[18] This should not be surprising, because one of the principal architects of the Universal Declaration, Pengchun Chang, brought Confucian perspectives into the drafting process.[19] It would not be accurate, therefore, to conclude that a conflict between Confucian tradition and human rights makes a common morality of rights impossible. The picture is considerably more complex than this.

This complexity is also present in the Islamic world. There is a serious debate under way among Islamic thinkers about the extent to which human rights norms are compatible with Islamic traditions and whether Islam can develop in a direction that could lead it to affirm a human rights ethic. Resistance to human rights standards as contrary to Islam is certainly a reality in parts of the Muslim world, as the example of the Taliban in Afghanistan has demonstrated in an extreme way, but this resistance is not the whole story either in practice or in theoretical reflection.[20] In practice, several Muslim countries have had women presidents, specifically Pakistan and Indonesia. Although the treatment of women in Pakistan and Indonesia is far from ideal, it does stand in sharp contrast with the treatment of women by the Taliban. On the theoretical level, a number of Muslim intellectuals have been developing careful arguments proposing Muslim grounds for a broad human rights ethic.[21] There is also a significant disagreement among Western scholars about whether the Islamic world is in fact becoming more open or more resistant to the standards broadly associated with Western modernity such as human rights.[22]

In short, the cultural and religious differences of our world have moved to the center of debate about the possibility of attaining a common set of moral standards or a global ethic today. Because the pursuit of a common morality runs the danger of moral and cultural imperialism, some conclude that it should be abandoned. On the other hand, there are notable intellectual and activist movements within the Islamic, Confucian, and African traditions that argue for the value of a global human rights ethic in the context of their own societies. They often do this by proposing that people of their own traditions and societies will be better off if cultural traditions are developed in ways that lead to the affirmation of human rights. Ignatieff calls this "going global by going local." By this he means that the global ethic of human rights becomes more plausible when it can be shown that the local religious traditions and cultures contain elements that support it and that local people will be better off when this ethic gains some social clout.[23]

TOWARD CONSENSUS?

There are, therefore, both grounds for hope and grounds for skepticism about the possibilities for a global ethic. Let us consider several ways that have been proposed for moving beyond the evident reality of pluralism to a broader consensus on human rights as a global ethic.

A first possibility is the pragmatic route to consensus suggested by Ignatieff. He notes that the main stimulus for the development of the human rights ethic has been its effectiveness in giving voice to people's need for protection against abuse and oppression. Thus, Ignatieff suggests that the route to a more widely shared ethos of human rights should be charted in terms of what rights *do* for people practically. Human rights protect people's agency and ability to resist forces that would oppress or harm them. Despite people's fundamentally different understandings of the full meaning of the good life, human rights raise forceful objections to what people agree "is insufferably, unarguably wrong."[24] The duty to respect rights, therefore, is the obligation not to inflict such wrongs on any other human being. A consensus on human rights can emerge from agreement on the harms to which no human being should ever be subjected. Presenting metaphysical arguments for the foundations of human rights is not necessary. Indeed, such arguments may divide, rather than unite, people. Claims about theoretical foundations may actually weaken, rather than strengthen, support for the common morality that the human rights ethos seeks to become. This leads Ignatieff to recommend avoiding any kind of foundational theory for human rights, even such seemingly transcultural values as the dignity, self-worth, or sacredness of human persons. Because we cannot agree on the meaning of the sacred, we should not appeal to the idea that human beings are sacred. And since the idea that humans are sacred is closely linked with the idea that they possess inherent dignity, Ignatieff also recommends avoiding talk of respect for the dignity of persons as the basis of rights.[25] He proposes to replace such arguments with pragmatic appeals to the way a human rights ethos can energize action against harms all people want to avoid. In his view, this will be sufficient to generate the needed consensus on a global human rights morality.

This approach parallels that actually taken by the drafters of the UN Universal Declaration. As was noted earlier, the Declaration was based on practical historical and political experience rather than theoretical understandings of the metaphysical or theological grounding of morality. The drafters were able to reach agreement on human rights norms because of their shared experience of the negative realities of world war and nearly successful genocide, despite their coming from religiously and culturally diverse peoples. Jacques Maritain, who participated in a UNESCO consultation that contributed to the creation of the Universal Declaration, observed that those drafting the Declaration could "agree about the rights but on condition that no one asks us why."[26]

A second possible route to broader support for a global ethic is the development of what John Rawls has called an "overlapping consensus" on the basic moral principles that should govern the most important institutions of society.[27] In such a consensus, people from diverse religions or cultures reach agreement on the standards of justice for the institutions that structure their lives together. They discover within their own particular traditions adequate grounds for affirming a set of basic moral principles that persons from other traditions can also affirm for their own reasons. Rawls has extended his reflection on the shape of such an overlapping consensus in the United States to a global context in his recent discussion of the "law of peoples." The law of peoples aims to set forth the standards of justice and peace for the international relations among peoples from diverse cultures. Rawls argues that it should include many of the principles familiar in international law, such as self-determination of peoples, the duty of nonintervention, and the duty to honor human rights.[28] This overlapping consensus seems to have been realized, at least in part, in the practical agreement reached by the drafters of the Universal Declaration of Human Rights.

Question can be raised, however, about whether Ignatieff's pragmatic reasons are sufficient to sustain consensus on a common morality of human rights and about who actually supports the overlapping consensus Rawls seeks to encourage. As noted above, there are some currents of thought in the Muslim, Confucian, African, and even Western worlds that are reluctant to accept the human rights ethos. Invoking the experience of harm or oppression has so far not led them to join this consensus. The same issue arises with regard to Rawls's hope for an overlapping consensus that is supported by several different traditions, each for its own tradition-based reasons. Because of these continuing dissents, the question inevitably arises whether the partial consensus that has developed is in fact more than a fortuitous convergence occasioned by particularly propitious circumstances. A consensus that arises fortuitously could equally well evanesce if the circumstances that occasioned it were to change. For example, two nations might come to affirm the same standards of behavior toward each other because of a temporary convergence of their self-interests. If a consensus is based on self-interest in this way, subsequent divergence of interests will bring the consensus to an end. Rawls calls this kind of convergence of interests a modus vivendi between the two peoples. It is not a consensus that has genuinely moral weight.[29] In fact, it would likely evaporate if the circumstances and interests of the parties were to change.

The question, then, is whether the practical agreements achieved by the drafters of the Universal Declaration of Human Rights and the signers of the Vienna Declaration were the result of a transitory overlapping of interests or of genuine moral agreement. Ignatieff's pragmatic approach has no way to answer this question, because it comes close to equating interest and moral concern. Rawls's framework of overlapping consensus points to the significant number of people who have agreed that their own traditions support the standards set forth in the major human rights documents. But it should also lead us to note that a number have not so agreed. If we presuppose that movement toward stronger consensus on human rights is desirable, we need to do more than point to the de facto consensus that already exists. We need to present *reasons* why the human rights ethos should become a more truly *common* morality and a more truly *global* ethic. Unless we know the reasons on which the consensus is based, we will not know whether it is a genuinely moral consensus or merely the result of lucky circumstances.

As we have noted, Maritain said that the drafters of the Universal Declaration could agree on the rights to include in their document provided no one asked them why. In this statement, Maritain was referring to the "why" provided by metaphysical or religious reasons and observing that agreement on that level was de facto impossible. He went on to note, however, that agreement on the level of a different kind of "why" was both possible and necessary among the drafters. In his words, the Universal Declaration depended on agreement not on "common speculative ideas, but on common practical ideas, not on the affirmation of one and the same conception of the world, of man, and of knowledge, but upon the affirmation of a single body of *beliefs for guidance in action*."[30] In other words, there can be *good reasons* for conclusions about practical affairs even when their ultimate significance is interpreted differently in diverse religious traditions. It is at least possible to give reasons for affirming that human beings not be tortured, that they not be slaughtered because they are Jews or Armenians or Rwandan Tutsi, that they be allowed to express their religious beliefs and intellectual convictions in freedom, and so forth. Agreement about such practical ideas does not have to be *either* because consensus has been achieved on ultimate metaphysical issues *or* simply because fortuitous circumstances have led to an accidental convergence of incommensurable ways of thinking. There is a third alternative. The consensus could be the result of the common exercise of a shared practical reason. In other words, people whose deeper worldviews have been formed by different religious beliefs or cultural traditions need not disagree about everything because they disagree about God or human destiny. Despite these disagreements about ultimates, it is still possible that they can share practical reasons for endorsing the ethic of human rights. If there is to be a common morality in the midst of religious and cultural pluralism, some such convergence on the grounds of practical reason seems to be a necessity. Otherwise, whatever consensus comes into being will not be a shared morality but only the fortuitous result of a historically accidental set of events.

The question thus becomes whether we can give good reasons why the human rights ethos should both be supported by a particular faith or cultural tradition and why this ethos might sometimes legitimately challenge the present understanding of what a particular faith or cultural tradition requires. The reasons why a particular tradition such as Confucianism or Islam should support the human rights ethos will appropriately include Confucian or Muslim reasons. Unless Confucians and Muslims can give reasons to support the human rights ethic that are endogenous to their own traditions, they will not be able to support this ethic. At the same time, the human rights ethic will raise questions about some of the norms and practices of ancient traditions like Confucianism and Islam (just as they have about Christianity). Thus, if Confucians are to be persuaded that they should support the human rights ethic, they need to be given reasons why they should change or adapt their traditions. They need to be presented with practical reasons that may lead to developments in their religious and cultural traditions. A form of practical reason that is essentially an instrumental calculus of self-interest cannot play this role, for it will either simply reinforce what the group from a particular tradition already believes or challenge the group in ways that lack authentic respect for its traditions. In either case, an instrumental rationality of self-interest lacks what is required to bring traditions together on ground that is genuinely shared.

Moving toward moral consensus on the human rights ethic require addressing three subordinate questions. These can be formulated as follows:

1. To whom are the requirements of the human rights ethos owed, and who has the responsibility to abstain from or take the actions needed to meet these requirements?
2. What are the goods to which people have a legitimate claim and that others are responsible to provide for them? This question can also be put negatively: What are the harms that people have a legitimate claim not to have inflicted upon them and that others are responsible to avoid inflicting?
3. What kind of social and institutional arrangements are needed to make it feasible to respond to these claims and carry out these responsibilities?

Each of these questions highlights a different aspect of the larger issue of whether it is reasonable to assert that a common morality can be identified that might govern global affairs today. The first concerns the beneficiaries and agents of the common morality. It concerns the scope of the community that the common morality aims to govern. In other words, it asks about the "we" that is constituted as a moral community by holding the same moral standards in common. The second concerns the content of the common morality. What, exactly, are the rights and duties that this morality specifies? And the third concerns the social processes and structures that are presupposed when it is asserted that people are linked together in such a moral community. Let us consider these questions in turn.

The Universal Declaration of Human Rights, of course, presupposes that it makes sense to speak of a worldwide human community within which human rights are secured. The terms "all" and "everyone" and "no one" are used repeatedly as the first words in the articles that specify the various human rights. The "everyone" who is the subject of human rights is to be understood without distinctions based on "race, color, sex, language, religion, political or other opinion, national or social origin."[31] Thus, to the question of who possesses human rights, the Declaration's answer is unambiguous: *all* human beings do. The universality of human rights, therefore, aims to relativize all in-group/out-group boundaries when it comes to the protection of the rights it affirms. This is a challenge to all definitions of religious or cultural identity that suggest rights are owed only to the people who possess that identity. Though discrimination on the basis of membership in the identity group may be legitimate regarding some goods, it is not legitimate when those goods are a matter of human rights.

Hans Küng and the 1993 Parliament of World Religions, in which he played a major role, have sought to show that such universality regarding the subjects of human rights can be endorsed by all the major world religions. The Parliament's Declaration Toward a Global Ethic was signed by a number of leaders from most of the world's religions. It affirms that "a common set of core values is found in the teachings of all the religions, and that these form the basis of a global ethic."[32] Küng backs up this claim principally by noting that a version of the Golden Rule can be found in the ethical teachings of all the world religions. He cites versions of the Golden Rule as they appear in a number of religious traditions, including the Confucian ("What you yourself do not want, do not do to another person"), the Jewish ("Do not do to others what you would not want them to do to you"), the Christian ("Whatever you want people to do to you, do also to them"), and the Islamic ("None of you is a believer as long as he does not wish his brother what he wishes himself").[33] On the basis of this appeal to the Golden Rule, the Declaration then concludes, "We must treat others as we wish others to treat us" and that this requires "a commitment to respect life and dignity, individuality and diversity, so that every person is treated humanely, without exception."[34] This approach is cited with approval by a report "In Search of Global Ethical Standards" prepared by a council of former heads of state and chaired by former German chancellor Helmut Schmidt.[35]

The Golden Rule in its various forms is indeed found in most, if not all, of the world's major religious traditions. It stresses the reciprocity of moral obligation and can surely be understood in ways that imply reciprocal duties toward all of one's fellow human beings. It is clear, however, that the religious traditions in which various versions of the Golden Rule appear also contain teachings that sometimes limit its reciprocity to comembers of the community formed by that tradition. Reciprocal concern among neighbors is a certainly a requirement of the Golden Rule. To know what this means in practice, however, one must answer the question put to Jesus regarding the commandment to love one's neighbor as oneself, namely, "Who is my neighbor?" In Christianity, Jesus answered this question in the parable of the Good Samaritan in the universalist manner that Küng's global ethic calls for (see Luke 10:25–37). At the same time, the New Testament also sometimes teaches preferential concern for fellow Christians.[36] In a similar manner, the reciprocity of the Golden Rule in Judaism has often suggested a reciprocity among members of the Jewish community that is in tension with other Jewish teachings, such as those concerning the covenant with Noah as a covenant with the whole of humanity. Similarly, the undoubted universalism of Islam has frequently been taken to call for the incorporation of all people into the Islamic *umma* rather than for the universality of tolerance that the parliament wants to endorse.[37]

The point here is not to reject Küng's effort to show that world religions can become part of a consensus on a global ethic that includes support for human rights. Rather, it is to point out that religious traditions can be interpreted in multiple ways and that this interpretation can lead them to develop in diverse directions. Clearly, Küng and the Parliament of Religions are seeking to lead the world religions to support a global ethic in order to address the realities of the early twenty-first century. I agree with the need to move in this direction, but explanation of why the texts should be interpreted this way is needed if the traditions these texts represent are to support a common morality with genuine conviction.

Reliance on practical reason to interpret texts such as the Golden Rule as requiring reciprocal respect among all human beings might be called the "Kantian" moment in the development of a global ethic that diverse faiths and cultures can support. Such an approach would follow Kant's lead in closely linking the universalizability of moral obligations with the requirement of respect for humanity as such. Kant simultaneously affirmed both the universal reach of moral obligation and the duty to treat every human being as an end and never only a means. He saw both of these affirmations as implications of the effort to be practically reasonable in thinking about moral obligation. Thus, Kant thought it practically reasonable to regard the human race as a moral community with certain reciprocal obligations among all its members. This is at the basis of the cosmopolitan aspects of Kant's political thought.[38]

Similar moves are present in Küng's discussion of a global ethic, where he links the reciprocity of the Golden Rule with the imperative that every person must be treated humanely.[39] This linkage goes beyond simply citing the meaning the Golden Rule has within specific religious traditions. It has been influenced by a form of practical reasoning similar to that employed by Kant, namely, one that associates the universal reach of moral obligation with the intrinsic dignity of persons. There are, of course, well-known problems with Kant's arguments. Nevertheless, some form of practical reasoning that suggests why and how the Golden Rule should be interpreted in a universally inclusive way is needed to provide full support for a global ethics. Let me suggest one way to do this that may have fewer problems than that associated with Kant.

It is the reality of human persons—the kind of beings that they in fact are—that is at the origin of the moral claims human beings make upon one another. Human beings are not things; they possess both self-consciousness and the capacity for self-transcendence. The self-transcendence of a person gives rise to a moral claim that he or she be treated in ways that sustain or at least do not destroy that capacity for self-transcendence. Another person is capable of experiencing that claim precisely because the second person also possesses the capacity for self-transcendence. He or she is not confined within the limits of self-consciousness but can genuinely encounter the other as a fellow person. Thus, one human being *is* a kind of *ought* in the face of another. One person's capacity for self-transcendence makes a claim on another's capacity for self-transcendence. One's ability to know and understand calls out for acknowledgment in the knowledge and understanding of others. One person's freedom places requirements on the freedom of another.[40]

The reciprocal respect among persons called for by the Golden Rule is thus required of a believer not only as a form of fidelity to the believer's religious tradition. It is also required if persons are to be treated as such. To assert this is to make a claim about what is practically reasonable—about what "makes sense" with regard to the way we treat each other and about how moral obligation should be understood.[41] The Golden Rule certainly follows from the way the human condition is interpreted within Confucian, Buddhist, Jewish, Christian, or Muslim traditions. But not only from this. It is also a practically reasonable principle of morality that arises from the human condition itself. Indeed, one can argue that Confucian, Christian, and Muslim traditions affirm the Golden Rule precisely because it expresses the commitment of those traditions to the human good. Further, it means that, if those traditions contain elements that would deny to some human beings the respect that their capacity for self-transcendence requires, those traditions should be changed or developed. The same can be said if it can be shown that a tradition's interpretation of the meaning of the kind of respect due human beings is too narrow. In other words, if this interpretation of the *ought* that arises in the encounter among persons is correct, it will make demands upon all persons and upon all religious and cultural traditions.

The demand that the self-transcendence of human beings receive respect, however, remains a very general expression of what is required by a global ethic. It needs to be made more specific and concrete. The effort to spell out the meaning of respect for human dignity in greater detail might be called the Aristotelian moment in the quest for a global ethic. Aristotle developed his ethics by seeking to identify what the good life is for human beings. A good life has more than one dimension or characteristic. Aristotle suggested that a good life involves a number of diverse kinds of activity, including both intellectual and practical pursuits.[42] In an analogous way, there are multiple preconditions for the realization of genuine dignity in people's lives.

Maritain's experience with the drafting of the Universal Declaration convinced him that people from different religious and cultural traditions can come to practical agreement on more specific requirements of respect for human dignity. These more specific requirements, now known as human rights, come to be known through the reflection of practical reason on historical and social experience. The practical reasoning that leads to the identification of these requirements can begin from the insight that human beings are really different from both beasts and gods and should be treated differently from both beasts and gods.[43] Self-transcendence is a capacity to move beyond the self-enclosed materiality of beasts or things, a capacity that is unique to beings with consciousness or spirit. It is the key index of the distinctive worth of human personhood, and it points to one aspect of how humans can reasonably expect to be treated by each other. We should support one another in undertaking activities of the spirit such as growing in knowledge, exercising freedom, or forming and sustaining personal relationships such as friendship. At a minimum, we should refrain from preventing one another from engaging in these activities of the spirit. At the same time, human self-transcendence is that of a bodily being, and it has material conditions. Human dignity cannot be realized if these material conditions are lacking. Therefore, it can be reasonably affirmed that we have some responsibilities to enable one another to share in the material goods and activities that are among the conditions required for living with dignity. Again, at the minimum we have a duty not to deprive one another of these material basics.

These are affirmations of practical reason that rest on minimal metaphysical presuppositions. Practical reasoning may not lead to full agreement on the total set of activities that are prerequisites for living with basic human dignity. Also, people from different cultural or religious traditions will doubtless seek to explain the origins and full significance of human dignity and what it requires through different narratives, metaphysical theories, or theologies. Despite these differences in interpretation, however, it does not seem impossible that practically reasonable people can agree that human dignity means not being enslaved, politically oppressed, or starving when alternative conditions are genuine possibilities. The quest for a common morality or global ethic is the effort to identify prerequisites of human dignity like these. The drafters of the Universal Declaration believed they had at least made a good start in such an effort. The challenge today, in light of the debates about the influence of religious and cultural pluralism, is to determine whether the list of rights in the Declaration still seems practically reasonable. To dismiss the Declaration's list of rights simply *because* it claims to reach across religious and cultural traditions would be to decide the matter without giving it the practical reflection it deserves.

Lisa Sowle Cahill has observed some notable signs of hope on this score. She points out that, across religious and cultural differences, there are certain basic needs and goods that virtually all people today agree are due to everyone. The UN Millennium Declaration, for example, has set development goals that very few people, including those who stress the significance of cultural differences, would be willing to challenge. These include eradicating extreme poverty and hunger, achieving universal primary education, reducing child mortality, improving maternal health, and combating AIDS, malaria, and other infectious diseases.[44] These Millennium Goals, like many of those set forth in other consensus documents, indicate that there is agreement on at least some basic values across cultures and religious traditions. In Cahill's words, these documents "demonstrate that there are certain basic human needs and goods that are not that difficult to recognize globally."[45] One could add a number of negative proscriptions to the positive prescriptions on which most cultural and religious traditions can readily achieve consensus. These could include the moral prohibition of murder, genocide, torture, enslavement, as well as of less extreme abuses such as political oppression and theft of what rightly belongs to another. Agreement on these matters carries us well along the way toward affirming that many of the human rights affirmed in the Universal Declaration are truly becoming part of a global ethic.

SOME POLITICAL IMPLICATIONS OF A GLOBAL ETHIC

Nevertheless, there remain important differences among traditions that continue to prevent them from achieving full unanimity on all the specific demands of human dignity. For example, although people within most religious and cultural traditions will agree that universal education is a good to be pursued, they have not attained full agreement on how to deal with gender inequalities in education.[46] Similarly, virtually no religious or cultural tradition would explicitly support political oppression. There are clear differences among traditions, however, about the desirability of democracy, especially democracy understood in its Western, liberal form. This is evident, for example, in the position of a well-known Thai Buddhist scholar, activist, and Nobel Peace Prize nominee, Sulak Sivaraksa. Sulak both advocates democracy in Thailand and defends the legitimacy of laws forbidding criticism of the Thai king.[47] Western democrats, especially of the American variety, are likely to regard this as unreasonable and even self-contradictory, because the spirit of democracy is understood to require unhindered freedom of speech, especially freedom of speech that is critical of political rulers. For Sulak, however, Thai Buddhist traditions make democratic respect for the people of Thailand and restraint on criticism of the king compatible. They do not seem practically contradictory as they most likely will for a Western liberal. The cultural and religious traditions of Thailand make it practically reasonable for Sulak to affirm both democracy and laws requiring respect for the king.

Rawls's distinction between liberal peoples and decent peoples can help illuminate what is at stake here. Liberal peoples, as Rawls describes them, support the institutional protections of full political equality to vote and to hold office independent of religion or cultural background, as well as full freedom to exercise religious beliefs in public. They will have full freedom of speech to criticize their rulers in a way that Sulak Sivaraksa finds inappropriate for Thailand. "Decent peoples" will grant all members of their society the right to be consulted and heard in the political process. They may not, however, understand the right to be heard as requiring an unrestricted right to criticize rulers. It might not even require a universal right to suffrage or to hold office. Thus, Rawls can envision what he calls a "decent consultation hierarchy" that sets some restrictions on suffrage or on holding office, perhaps based on religion or culture.[48] The primary case Rawls has in mind here is clearly some form of Islamic republic that seeks to combine both Muslim and democratic values.[49]

It is crucial to note that Rawls thinks that being a "consultation hierarchy" of this sort is compatible with respect for human rights. In fact, for such a society to be considered "decent" in Rawls's terms, it must respect a class of human rights that are particularly urgent. These include "freedom from slavery and serfdom, liberty (but not equal liberty) of conscience, and security of ethnic groups from mass murder and genocide."[50] These rights are taken to be at the very core of a common morality on which all reasonable people can agree, both reasonable Western liberals and reasonable people living in decent hierarchical traditions. In other words, Western Christian, Jewish, and nonbelieving liberals could come to consensus with decent Buddhist nonliberals like Sulak Sivaraksa on the importance of these rights in a global ethic they share.

Rawls is led to draw this distinction between particularly urgent rights and those political rights familiar in Western liberal democracies by a kind of paradox that arises in the commitment to freedom in a multireligious, multicultural context. On the one hand, the reciprocal commitment called for by both the Golden Rule and the consistency of practical reason requires each individual to freely respect the freedom of all other individuals. At the same time, respect for the freedom of individuals calls for respect for their freedom to hold the viewpoints of the traditions they are formed by and embrace. Some of these traditions place higher value on the unity of society as shaped by specific religious and cultural norms than do Western liberal societies. This is the case in Confucian and African societies, as noted above, and it is likely true of most other non-Western traditions as well. Commitment to respect the freedom of such non-Westerners to be who they are, therefore, calls for drawing a distinction between Western liberal versions of freedom and the more urgent freedoms Rawls associates with "decency." In addition, such a refusal to identify human rights with liberal versions of freedom will also enable one to argue that the basic needs and goods the UN Millennium Declaration says should be provided to all persons are in fact due to them by the standards of right. Accepting the limits of liberal understandings of freedom thus not only makes space in a global ethic for non-Western practices, it can also challenge some Western individualistic values associated with the free market that have morally dubious consequences.

The distinction between these basic rights and the rights associated with Western liberalism has significant practical relevance. It is related to the difference between moral norms that we judge should be enforced by law backed by police power and those where we think persuasion is the appropriate way to secure compliance. It is notable that Rawls draws the distinction between liberal societies and decent societies in a book on the *law* of peoples. The urgent rights that he associates with decency are those that must be respected by a state that wants to avoid the status of outlaw. States that do not respect these rights are subject to international condemnation and sanctions. If the violations of these rights are grave, the state that commits the violation may become subject to intervention by the use of force.[51]

A similar issue arises when one disagrees with the moral standards and actions supported by religious and cultural traditions. Respect for the religious and cultural freedom of the diverse communities in our world means that when one does not see the requirements of morality as others do, efforts to persuade those one disagrees with to change is the appropriate approach. Such persuasion should occur in the context of a dialogue conducted in freedom. This is respect for religious and cultural freedom. It might be aimed at persuading Thai Buddhists of the value of constitutional protections of free speech. In a similar manner it might be aimed at challenging those stronger forms of individualism found in American culture that reject economic rights to minimal levels of nutrition or health care. On the other hand, if a community appeals to its religious tradition to justify racism (as did some Afrikaner Christians in South Africa in the apartheid era) or to legitimate denying all education to girls (as did the Taliban in their interpretation of Islam), practical reason justifies raising serious objections. These objections might, as a last resort, go beyond persuasion to the exercise of some form of coercive sanction. Such coercion would be exercised by international courts with genuine enforcement powers, by the use of economic pressure such as the sanctions against the apartheid regime in South Africa or, in the extreme, by military intervention to prevent crimes such as ethnic cleansing or genocide. There are limits to what can be done in the name of religion and culture, even in a global ethic that strongly supports the right to cultural and religious freedom. These limits are set by what we can reasonably conclude are the most fundamental prerequisites of human dignity.

Drawing this distinction between such basic or minimal rights and the list of rights that Western liberals support can help distinguish several practical routes that may be followed in working to implement and institutionalize a global ethic. One might argue, as many Western Christians, Jews, and agnostic liberals are likely to do, that the full guarantees of

Western constitutional democracy, including full equality of all citizens before the law, is a moral implication of both the Golden Rule and of human dignity reasonably interpreted. It would be entirely consistent with this set of beliefs to engage Buddhists like Sulak Sivaraksa, as well as Muslims and Confucians, in arguments that aim to persuade them to support this kind of constitutional democracy. Supporting the ethical appropriateness of such efforts at persuasion should, however, be clearly distinguished from saying that the United States and the European Union should undertake global initiatives to promote democracy worldwide even by the use of force. Forceful promotion and persuasion have very different ethical significance. This difference is most relevant to the way the pursuit of a global ethic is to be understood.

Affirming that persuasion is the preferred route to advancing this global ethic, however, does not mean that persuasion is the only ethically permissible way to do so. To be sure, democratic self-governance is something that people must do for themselves, as Mill pointed out.[52] There is no way to force people to become free. They must be persuaded that the engagement in deliberation and the exercise of freedom that self-governance requires are worth the effort. There are, however, other sorts of cases where external help may be essential to enabling people to become capable of defending themselves and acting on their own. Such may be situations where a people faces ethnic cleansing or genocide, where blacks and coloreds face an apartheid regime backed by the kind of economic and military power that whites controlled in South Africa's apartheid years, or where women and girls face oppression under groups like the Taliban. Here, more than persuasion may be needed. The criteria classically developed for the justice of punishment and for the just use of force will be most relevant in such situations.

Thus, when we discuss the pursuit of a global ethic among global faiths and differing cultures, it will be most important not to confuse persuasion and enforcement when discussing the route toward an effective global ethic. Both persuasion and enforcement will be required if a global ethic is to have an impact on practical global politics. But persuasion and enforcement are not the same, and the former must normally precede the latter. Arguments for universal or global ethical standards are often resisted by claiming that they are implicit if unwitting endorsements of an agenda of cultural hegemony and that they are possible preludes to political domination. In fact, the argument for a global ethic advanced here seeks to persuade the world's great religious traditions and cultures that they should oppose such hegemony in the name of an ethic they can share. In fact, the global ethic argued for here would be prepared to defend people from hegemony or domination, in the extreme case even by military means. Short of such extreme cases where the most fundamental demands of human dignity are clearly being denied, however, movement toward such a global ethic would proceed by persuasion. This is a requirement of the reciprocity demanded by the Golden Rule. It is also an implication of the aspiration to conduct the interrelations among world faiths and cultures in accord with basic requirements of practical reason. It is my hope that the great religions and cultures of our world can support such an ethic both in theory and practice.

NOTES

1. Samuel P. Huntington, "The Clash of Civilizations," *Foreign Affairs* 72 (summer 1993), 22, 25. See also Huntington, *The Clash of Civilizations and the Remaking of World Order* (New York: Simon & Schuster, 1997).

2. See, for example, Gilles Kepel, *The Revenge of God: The Resurgence of Islam, Christianity and Judaism in the Modern World*, trans. Alan Braley (University Park: Pennsylvania State University Press, 1994); José Casanova, *Public Religions in the Modern World* (Chicago: University of Chicago Press, 1994); R. Scott Appleby, *The Ambivalence of the Sacred: Religion, Violence, and Reconciliation* (Lanham, Md.: Rowman and Littlefield, 2000); Mark Juergensmeyer, *Terror in the Mind of God: The Global Rise of Religious Violence* (Berkeley: University of California Press, 2000); Richard Falk, *Religion and Humane Global Governance* (New York: Palgrave, 2001).

3. Douglas Johnston and Cynthia Sampson, eds., *Religion, the Missing Dimension of Statecraft* (New York: Oxford University Press, 1994).

4. These writings include Gene Outka and John P. Reeder, Jr., eds., *Prospects for a Common Morality* (Princeton, N.J.: Princeton University Press, 1993); Hans Küng and Karl-Josef Kuschel, eds., *A Global Ethic: The Declaration of the Parliament of the World's Religions*, trans. John Bowden (London: SCM Press, 1993); Küng, ed., *Yes to a Global Ethic*, trans. John Bowden (New York: Continuum, 1996); Küng, *A Global Ethic for Global Politics and Economics*, trans. John Bowden (New York: Oxford University Press, 1998); Sumner B. Twiss and Bruce Grelle, eds., *Explorations in Global Ethics: Comparative Religious Ethics and Interreligious Dialogue* (Boulder, Colo.: Westview Press, 1998); Jean Porter, "The Search for a Global Ethic," *Theological Studies* 62 (2001): 105–21; Karl-Josef Kuschel and Dietmar Meith, eds., *In Search of Universal Values. Concilium, 2001/4* (London: SCM

Press, 2001); Lisa Sowle Cahill, "Toward Global Ethics," *Theological Studies* 63 (2002): 324–44.

5. For useful studies of this tradition of political realism in international affairs, see Stephen Forde, "Classical Realism," and Jack Donnelly, "Twentieth-Century Realism," both in Terry Nardin and David R. Mapel, eds., *Traditions of International Ethics* (Cambridge: Cambridge University Press, 1992), 62–84 and 85–111; David R. Mapel, "Realism and the Ethics of War," and Jeff McMahon, "Realism, Morality and War," both in Terry Nardin, ed., *The Ethics of War and Peace: Religious and Secular Perspectives* (Princeton, N.J.: Princeton University Press, 1996), 54–77 and 78–92. For a provocative but tendentious discussion of the relevance of classical realism today, see Robert D. Kaplan, *Warrior Politics: Why Leadership Demands a Pagan Ethos* (New York: Random House, 2002).

6. Mary Ann Glendon, *A World Made New: Eleanor Roosevelt and the Universal Declaration of Human Rights* (New York: Random House, 2001), xv.

7. Universal Declaration of Human Rights, Preamble. The Universal Declaration was adopted and proclaimed by the United Nations General Assembly, December 10, 1948. It is available online at the UN website at un.org/Overview/rights.html [downloaded July 11, 2002].

8. Universal Declaration of Human Rights, arts. 1 and 2; emphasis added.

9. World Conference on Human Rights, Vienna Declaration and Programme of Action, adopted 25 June 1993. Text available online at UN High Commissioner for Human Rights website, www.unhchr.ch/huridocda/huridoca.nsf/(Symbol)/A.CONF.157.23.En?OpenDocument [downloaded July 30, 2002].

10. For a study that argues that the Vienna Declaration is a major breakthrough toward the creation of global law based on globally shared norms, see Robert F. Drinan, *The Mobilization of Shame: A Worldview of Human Rights* (New Haven, Conn.: Yale University Press, 2001).

11. See Margaret E. Keck and Kathryn Sikkink, *Activists beyond Borders: Advocacy Networks in International Politics* (Ithaca, N.Y.: Cornell University Press, 1998), and L. David Brown, Sanjeev Khagram, Mark H. Moore, and Peter Frumkin, "Globalization, NGOs, and Multisectoral Relations," in Joseph S. Nye and John D. Donahue, eds., *Governance in a Globalizing World* (Washington, D.C.: Brookings Institution Press, 2000), 271–96.

12. Michael Ignatieff, *Human Rights as Politics and Idolatry*, edited and introduced by Amy Gutmann (Princeton, N.J.: Princeton University Press, 2001), 58–77. See also Ignatieff's article based on this book, "The Attack on Human Rights," *Foreign Affairs* 80, no. 6 (November/December 2001): 102–116.

13. See Fareed Zakaria, "Culture Is Destiny: A Conversation with Lee Kwan Yew," *Foreign Affairs* 73, no. 2 (March/April, 1994): 109–126, at 112. For a later statement that suggests Lee may now hold that East Asian societies may be evolving in ways that will make them more culturally and social receptive to human rights and democracy, see Lee Kwan Yew, *From Third World to First: The Singapore Story, 1965–2000* (New York: HarperCollins, 2000), 487–500.

14. See the writings cited in notes 6–15 of chapter 11.

15. For succinct philosophical/literary statements of this view, see Richard Rorty, "The Priority of Democracy to Philosophy" and "Truth and Freedom: A Reply to Thomas McCarthy," both in Outka and Reeder, *Prospects for a Common Morality*, 254–89; "The Priority of Democracy" originally appeared in Merrill D. Peterson and Robert C. Vaughan, eds., *The Virginia Statute for Religious Freedom* (Cambridge: Cambridge University Press, 1988), 257–82. For a parallel argument by a political theorist see Neta C. Crawford, "Postmodern Ethical Conditions and a Critical Response," *Ethics and International Affairs* 12 (1998): 121–40.

16. Kim Dae Jung, "Is Culture Destiny? The Myth of Asia's Anti-Democratic Values," *Foreign Affairs* 73, no. 6 (November/December 1994): 189–94.

17. Amartya Sen, "Asian Values and Human Rights," *New Republic*, July 14, 1997, 33–40; Sen, *Development as Freedom* (New York: Knopf, 1999), chap. 10.

18. See, for example, Wm. Theodore de Bary and Tu Weiming, eds., *Confucianism and Human Rights* (New York: Columbia University Press, 1998); Wm. Theodore de Bary, *Asian Values and Human Rights: A Confucian Communitarian Perspective* (Cambridge, Mass.: Harvard University Press, 1998). In the second of these volumes (pp. 10–11), de Bary calls for a more nuanced historical approach to the relation between human rights and Asian values than authors such as Sen provide. Nevertheless, de Bary clearly believes that Confucian traditions *can* develop in ways that will support a global human rights ethic.

19. Mary Ann Glendon describes Peng-chun Chang as a "Chinese philosopher, diplomat, and playwrite who was adept at translating across cultural divides" and shows his major role of the drafting. See her *A World Made New: Eleanor Roosevelt and the Universal Declaration of Human Rights* (New York: Random House, 2001), xx and throughout the book. Paul Gorden Lauren calls him "a career diplomat with a strong background in Confucianism and a deep commitment to the values inherent in Asian culture." See his *The Evolution of International Human Rights: Visions Seen* (Philadelphia: University of Pennsylvania Press, 1998), 220.

20. See the report by Amnesty International, *Afghanistan: Making Human Rights the Agenda*, November 1, 2001. Available online at http://web.amnesty.org/aidoc/aidoc_pdf.nsf/index/ASA110232001ENGLISH/$File/ASA1102301.pdf [downloaded May 14, 2003].

21. See Abdullahi Ahmed An-Na'im *Toward an Islamic Reformation: Civil Liberties, Human Rights, and International Law* (Syracuse, N.Y.: Syracuse University Press, 1990); *Reason, Freedom, and Democracy in Islam: Essential Writings of 'Abdolkarim Soroush*, translated, edited, and introduced by Mahmoud Sadri and Ahmad Sadri (Oxford: Oxford University Press, 2000); and Abdulaziz Sachedina, *The Islamic Roots of Democratic Pluralism* (New York: Oxford University Press, 2001).

22. James Piscatori provides an overview of this debate in "The Turmoil Within: The Struggle for the Future of the Islamic World," *Foreign Affairs* 81, no. 3 (May/June 2002): 145–50. This is a review of two different Western readings of what is happening in the Mus-

lim world: Bernard Lewis, *What Went Wrong: Western Impact and Middle Eastern Response* (New York: Oxford University Press, 2002), and Gilles Kepel, *Jihad: The Trail of Political Islam*, trans. Anthony Roberts (Cambridge, Mass.: Harvard University Press, 2002).

23. Ignatieff, *Human Rights as Politics and Idolatry*, 7.

24. Ibid., 56.

25. Ibid., 54, 83.

26. Jacques Maritain, "Introduction," in *Human Rights: Comments and Interpretations*, symposium edited by UNESCO (New York: Columbia University Press, 1949), 9.

27. See John Rawls, *Political Liberalism* (New York: Columbia University Press, 1993), lecture IV, esp. 147 ff.

28. Rawls, *The Law of Peoples* (Cambridge, Mass.: Harvard University Press, 1999), 37.

29. Rawls, *The Law of Peoples*, 44–45, *Political Liberalism*, 146–49.

30. Maritain, "Introduction," 10, emphasis added.

31. Universal Declaration of Human Rights, art. 2.

32. "Declaration Toward a Global Ethic," in Küng and Kuschel, eds., *A Global Ethic*, 14.

33. Küng, "The History, Significance, and Method of the Declaration Toward a Global Ethic," in Küng and Kuschel, eds., *A Global Ethic*, 71–72. See also Küng, *A Global Ethic for Global Politics and Economics*, 97–99.

34. "Declaration Toward a Global Ethic," in Küng and Kuschel, eds., *A Global Ethic*, 14–15.

35. See the writings edited by Küng cited in n. 4 above, and also the report "In Search of Global Ethical Standards," prepared by The Interaction Council, chaired by Helmut Schmidt, March 22–24, 1996, Vienna, Austria, available online at www.asiawide.or.jp/iac/meetings/Eng96ethics.htm [downloaded July 16, 2002].

36. For a careful discussion of this issue of universalism and preference within the Christian community in relation to one important New Testament text, see John Donahue, "The 'Parable' of the Sheep and the Goats: A Challenge to Christian Ethics," *Theological Studies* 47 (1986): 3–31.

37. For a discussion of the tension between universalism and particularism in Judaism, Christianity, and Islam and its implications for human rights, see my "Human Rights and Religious Faith in the Middle East: The Impact of Religious Diversity," in David Hollenbach, ed., *Justice, Peace, and Human Rights: American Catholic Social Ethics in a Pluralistic World* (New York: Crossroad, 1990), 108–23.

38. Needless to say, Kant's moral and political thought is only touched on here. See Kant's different, but related, statements of the categorical imperative in *The Foundations of the Metaphysics of Morals*, trans. Lewis White Beck (Indianapolis: Bobbs-Merrill, 1959), esp. 39, 47. For the statement of his cosmopolitan political orientation see especially *Idea for a Universal History with a Cosmopolitan Intent*, in *Perpetual Peace and Other Essays*, trans. Ted Humphrey (Indianapolis: Hackett, 1983), 29–40.

39. "The Principles of a Global Ethic," in Küng and Kuschel, eds., *A Global Ethic*, 21–24.

40. See William Luijpen, *Phenomenology of Natural Law* (Pittsburgh: Duquesne Uni-

versity Press, 1967), chap. 6, "Justice as an Anthropological Form of Co-Existence," esp. 180. For an approach that is both similar and interestingly different from this, see also Jean-François Lyotard, "The Other's Rights," in Stephen Shute and Susan Hurley, eds., *On Human Rights: The Oxford Amnesty Lectures 1993* (New York: Basic Books, 1993), 135–47.

41. Here, I am influenced by Margaret A. Farley's suggestion that a practically reasonable approach to moral obligation means that it should "make sense" in light of one's best reflection on what human experience reveals about the human condition. See Farley, "Moral Discourse in the Public Arena," in William W. May, ed., *Vatican Authority and American Catholic Dissent* (New York: Crossroad, 1987), 168–86, at 174–75; "Response to James Hanigan and Charles Curran," in Saul M. Olyan and Martha C. Nussbaum, eds., *Sexual Orientation and Human Rights in American Religious Discourse* (New York: Oxford University Press, 1998), 101–109, at 105–106.

42. See esp. Aristotle, *Nicomachean Ethics,* trans. Martin Ostwald (Indianapolis: Bobbs-Merrill, 1962), book 10, chaps. 4–6. This point is developed succinctly by Rawls's discussion of what he calls the "Aristotelian principle," in *A Theory of Justice*, rev. ed. (Cambridge, Mass.: Harvard University Press, 1999), no. 65, 372–80.

43. That human beings are neither beasts nor gods and should be treated accordingly is a presupposition of ethical politics. See Aristotle, *Politics,* book 1, chap. 3 (1253a), trans. Benjamin Jowett, in *The Basic Works of Aristotle,* ed. Richard McKeon (New York: Random House, 1941). Martha Nussbaum takes this as a fundamental presupposition of her "capabilities approach" to ethics in social and economic life. See, for example, Nussbaum, "Human Capabilities, Female Human Beings," in Martha Nussbaum and Jonathan Glover, eds., *Women, Culture, and Development: A Study of Human Capabilities* (Oxford: Oxford University Press, 1995), 61–104, at 73.

44. "UN Millennium Goals," available online at www.un.org/millenniumgoals/index.html [downloaded August 1, 2002]. For fuller development of these goals and some ways to work toward achieving them see "The United Nations Development Declaration," September 18, 2000, online at www.un.org/millennium/declaration/ares552e.pdf [downloaded August 1, 2002], and "Road Map Towards the Implementation of the United Nations Millennium Declaration: Report of the Secretary-General," September 6, 2001, online at www.un.org/documents/ga/docs/56/a56326.pdf [downloaded May 14, 2003].

45. Cahill, "Toward Global Ethics," 337. Probably the most ambitious attempt to outline the goods that all people should have access to and should be able to choose to realize in their lives is that presented by Martha Nussbaum. See, for example, Nussbaum's *Women and Human Development: The Capabilities Approach* (Cambridge: Cambridge University Press, 2000), esp. chap. 1, "In Defense of Universal Values."

46. For a very thoughtful and thought-provoking exchange of views on the relation between support for gender equality and respect for diverse cultural and religious traditions, see Susan Moller Okin, *Is Multiculturalism Bad for Women?* Edited by Joshua Cohen, Matthew Howard, and Martha C. Nussbaum (Princeton, N.J.: Princeton University Press, 1999).

47. See Daniel A. Bell, *Human Rights and Democracy in East Asia* (Princeton, N.J.: Princeton University Press, 2000), 88–89.

48. Rawls, *The Law of Peoples*, nos. 8 and 9.

49. Rawls illustrates what he has in mind through the example of a hypothetical country, Kazanistan. See *The Law of Peoples*, no. 9.3.

50. Rawls, *The Law of Peoples*, 79. This distinction is similar to that drawn by Michael Walzer between minimal or thin rights and fuller or thick ones. See Walzer, *Thick and Thin: Moral Argument at Home and Abroad* (Notre Dame, Ind.: University of Notre Dame Press, 1994).

51. Rawls, *The Law of Peoples*, 81.

52. See the discussion of Mill's position in Michael Walzer, *Just and Unjust Wars: A Moral Argument with Historical Illustrations* (New York: Basic Books, 1977), 87–91.

BIBLIOGRAPHY

Abbott, Walter, and Gallagher, Joseph, eds. *The Documents of Vatican II*. New York: America Press, 1966.

Abrecht, Paul. "The Predicament of Christian Social Thought after the Cold War." *Ecumenical Review* 43 (1991): 318–28.

Ackerman, Bruce. *Social Justice and the Liberal State*. New Haven, Conn.: Yale University Press, 1980.

African Charter on Human and People's Rights, arts. 19–22. In M. Hamalengwa, C. Flinterman, and E. V. O. Dankwa, eds., *The International Law of Human Rights in Africa: Basic Documents and Annotated Bibliography*. Dordrecht: Martinus Nijhoff, 1988.

Ake, Claude. *Democracy and Development in Africa*. Washington, D.C.: Brookings Institution, 1996.

Amnesty International. *Afghanistan: Making Human Rights the Agenda*. November 1, 2001. Available online at http://web.amnesty.org/aidoc/aidoc_pdf.nsf/index/ASA110232001ENGLISH/$File/ASA1102301.pdf.

An-Na'im, Abdullahi Ahmed. *Toward an Islamic Reformation: Civil Liberties, Human Rights, and International Law*. Syracuse, N.Y.: Syracuse University Press, 1990.

An-Na'im, Abdullahi Ahmed, and Deng, Francis M., eds. *Human Rights in Africa: Cross-Cultural Perspectives*. Washington, D.C.: Brookings Institution, 1990.

An-Na'im, Abdullahi Ahmed; Madigan, Amy; and Minkley, Gary. "Cultural Transformations and Human Rights in Africa: A Preliminary Report." *Emory International Law Review* 11, no. 1 (spring 1997): 287–349.

Appleby, R. Scott. *The Ambivalence of the Sacred: Religion, Violence, and Reconciliation*. Lanham, Md.: Rowman and Littlefield, 2000.

Aristotle. *Nicomachean Ethics*. Translated by Martin Ostwald. Indianapolis: Bobbs-Merrill, 1962.

———. *Politics*. Translated by Benjamin Jowett. In *The Basic Works of Aristotle*, 1127–1316. Edited by Richard McKeon. New York: Random House, 1941.

Audi, Robert. "Religion and the Ethics of Political Participation." *Ethics* 100 (1990): 386–97.

Augustine. *The City of God*. Translated by Henry Bettenson. London: Penguin, 1984.

Bibliography

Barber, Benjamin. *Strong Democracy: Participatory Politics for a New Age*. Berkeley: University of California Press, 1984.

Bayart, Jean-François. *The State in Africa: The Politics of the Belly*. Translated by Mary Harper. London/New York: Longman, 1993.

Becker, Ernest. *The Denial of Death*. New York: Free Press, 1973.

Bell, Daniel A. *Human Rights and Democracy in East Asia*. Princeton, N.J.: Princeton University Press, 2000.

Benhabib, Seyla. *Situating the Self: Gender, Community and Postmodernism in Contemporary Ethics*. New York: Routledge, 1992.

Berger, Peter L. "Capitalism: The Continuing Revolution." *First Things* 15 (August/September, 1991): 22–27.

———. *The Capitalist Revolution: Fifty Propositions about Prosperity, Equality, and Liberty*. With new introduction. New York: Basic Books, 1991.

———. "Different Gospels: The Social Sources of Apostasy." *This World* 17 (spring 1987): 6–17.

Berger, Peter L., and Neuhaus, Richard John. *To Empower People: The Role of Mediating Structures in Public Policy*. Washington, D.C.: American Enterprise Institute for Public Policy Research, 1977.

Bernstein, Carl. "The Holy Alliance." *Time* (February 24, 1992): 28–35.

Blair, Erica. "Towards a Civil Society: Hopes for Polish Democracy." Interview with Adam Michnik. *Times Literary Supplement* (February 19–25, 1988): 188 ff.

Boff, Leonardo. "La 'implosion' del socialismo autoritario y la teologia de la liberacion." *Sal Terrae* 79 (1991): 321–41.

Borgmann, Albert. *Crossing the Postmodern Divide*. Chicago: University of Chicago Press, 1992.

Brown, L. David; Khagram, Sanjeev; Moore, Mark H.; and Frumkin, Peter. "Globalization, NGOs, and Multisectoral Relations." In Joseph S. Nye and John D. Donohue, eds., *Governance in a Globalizing World*, 271–296. Washington, D.C.: Brookings Institution Press, 2000.

Buckley, Michael J. *At the Origins of Modern Atheism*. New Haven, Conn.: Yale University Press, 1987.

———. "Christian Humanism and Human Misery: A Challenge to the Jesuit University." In Francis M. Lazarus, ed., *Faith, Discovery, Service: Perspectives on Jesuit Education*, 77–105. Milwaukee: Marquette University Press, 1992.

Burke, Kevin F. *The Ground Beneath the Cross: The Theology of Ignacio Ellacuría*. Washington, D.C.: Georgetown University Press, 2000.

Buttiglione, Rocco. "Behind *Centesimus Annus*." *Crisis* (July/August, 1991):8–9.

Cahill, Lisa Sowle. "Toward Global Ethics." *Theological Studies* 63 (2002): 324–44.

"Capitalismo Nell'Encyclica 'Centesimus Annus.'" *La Civilta Cattolica* 142/3383 (1991): 417–30.

Bibliography

Casanova, José. *Public Religions in the Modern World*. Chicago: University of Chicago Press, 1994.

Clapp, Rodney. "Democracy as Heresy." *Christianity Today* 31, no. 3 (February 20, 1987): 17–23.

Clinton, William Jefferson. "Remarks by the President to the People of Ghana," Accra, Ghana," March 23, 1998. Downloaded from the website of the Clinton Presidential Materials Project, http://clinton3.nara.gov/Africa/19980324-3069.html [downloaded May 14, 2003].

Cohen, Ronald; Hyden, Goran; and Nagan, Winston P., eds. *Human Rights and Governance in Africa*. Gainesville: University Press of Florida, 1993.

Coleman, James. *Foundations of Social Theory*. Cambridge, Mass.: Harvard University Press, 1990.

Coleman, John A. "Religious Liberty in America and Mediating Structures." In John A. Coleman, *An American Strategic Theology*, 209–33. New York: Paulist Press, 1982.

Congar, Yves. *Vraie et fausse réforme dans l'Église*, 2e éd., rev. et corr. Paris, Éditions du Cerf, 1968.

Cox, Harvey. "The Transcendent Dimension." *Nation* (January 1, 1996): 20–23.

Crawford, Neta C. "Postmodern Ethical Conditions and a Critical Response." *Ethics and International Affairs* 12 (1998): 121–40.

Curry, Dean C. "Evangelicals, the Bible, and Public Policy." *This World* 16 (winter 1987): 34–49.

Davidson, Basil. *The Black Man's Burden: Africa and the Curse of the Nation-State*. New York: Times Books, 1992.

Deats, Paul, Jr., ed. *Toward a Discipline of Social Ethics*. Boston: Boston University Press, 1972.

de Bary, Wm. Theodore. *Asian Values and Human Rights: A Confucian Communitarian Perspective*. Cambridge, Mass.: Harvard University Press, 1998.

de Bary, Wm. Theodore and Tu Weiming, eds. *Confucianism and Human Rights*. New York: Columbia University press, 1998.

Descartes, René. *Discourse on Method and Meditations*. Translated by Laurence J. Lafleur. Indianapolis: Bobbs-Merrill, 1960.

Diemer, Alwin, et al., eds. *Philosophical Foundations of Human Rights*. Paris: UNESCO, 1986.

Dionne, E. J., Jr. *Why Americans Hate Politics*. New York: Simon & Schuster, 1991.

Doggett, Martha. *Death Foretold: The Jesuit Murders in El Salvador*. Washington, D.C.: Georgetown University Press, 1993.

Donahue, John. "The 'Parable' of the Sheep and the Goats: A Challenge to Christian Ethics." *Theological Studies* 47 (1986): 3–31.

Bibliography

Donnelly, Jack. "Twentieth-Century Realism." In Terry Nardin and David R. Mapel, eds., *Traditions of International Ethics*, 85–111. Cambridge: Cambridge University Press, 1992.

Dougherty, James. *The Fivesquare City: The City in Religious Imagination*. South Bend: University of Notre Dame Press, 1980.

Douglass, James W. *The Non-Violent Cross: A Theology of Revolution and Peace*. New York: Macmillan, 1968.

Douglass, R. Bruce, and Hollenbach, David, eds. *Catholicism and Liberalism: Contributions to American Public Philosophy*. Cambridge: Cambridge University Press, 1994.

Douglass, R. Bruce; Mara, Gerald R.; and Richardson, Henry S., eds., *Liberalism and the Good*. New York: Routledge, 1990.

Drinan, Robert F. *The Mobilization of Shame: A Worldview of Human Rights*. New Haven, Conn.: Yale University Press, 2001.

Dulles, Avery. "The Gospel, The Church, and Politics." *Origins* 16 (1987): 637–46.

———. "Revelation and Discovery." In William J. Kelly, ed., *Theology and Discovery: Essays in Honor of Karl Rahner*, 1–28. Milwaukee: Marquette University Press, 1980.

Dunn, J., ed. *West African States: Failure and Promise, A Study in Comparative Politics*. Cambridge: Cambridge University Press, 1978.

Einhorn, Jessica. "The World Bank's Mission Creep." *Foreign Affairs* 80, no. 5 (September/October 2001): 22–35.

Ellacuría, Ignacio. "The Crucified People,." In Ignacio Ellacuría and Jon Sobrino, eds., *Mysterium Liberationis: Fundamental Concepts of Liberation Theology*, 580–603. Maryknoll, N.Y.: Orbis Books, 1993.

———. "The Task of a Christian University." In Jon Sobrino, Ignacio Ellacuría, et al., eds., *Companions of Jesus: The Jesuit Martyrs of El Salvador*, 147–51. Maryknoll, N.Y.: Orbis Books, 1992.

Ellwood, David. *Poor Support: Poverty in the American Family*. New York: Basic Books, 1988.

Enquist, Roy J. "Two Kingdoms and the American Future." *Dialog* 26 (1987): 111–14.

Falk, Richard. *Religion and Humane Global Governance*. New York: Palgrave, 2001.

Farley, Margaret A. "Moral Discourse in the Public Arena." In William W. May, ed., *Vatican Authority and American Catholic Dissent*, 168–86. New York: Crossroad, 1987.

———. "Response to James Hanigan and Charles Curran." In Saul M. Olyan and Martha C. Nussbaum, eds., *Sexual Orientation and Human Rights in American Religious Discourse*, 101–109. New York: Oxford University Press, 1998.

Fernyhough, Timothy. "Human Rights and Precolonial Africa." In Ronald Cohen, Goran Hyden, and Winston P. Nagan, eds., *Human Rights and Governance in Africa*, 39–73. Gainesville: University Press of Florida, 1993.

Fidler, Stephen. "Who's Minding the Bank?" *Foreign Policy* 126 (September/October 2001): 40–50.

Finnis, John. "Beyond the Encyclical." In John Wilkins, ed., *Considering Veritatis Splendor*. Cleveland: Pilgrim Press, 1994.

———. *Moral Absolutes: Tradition, Revision, and Truth*. Washington, D.C.: Catholic University of America Press, 1991.

Finnis, John; Boyle, Joseph M. Jr.; and Grisez, Germain. *Nuclear Deterrence, Morality and Realism*. Oxford: Clarendon Press, 1987.

Fisher, Philip. *Wonder, the Rainbow, and the Aesthetics of Rare Experiences*. Cambridge, Mass.: Harvard University Press, 1998.

Forde, Stephen. "Classical Realism." In Terry Nardin and David R. Mapel, eds., *Traditions of International Ethics*, 62–84. Cambridge: Cambridge University Press, 1992.

Friedman, Milton. "The Pope, Liberty, and Capitalism." *National Review*, Special Supplement, 1991, p. S-4.

Gadamer, Hans-Georg. *Truth and Method*. Translated and edited by Garrett Barden and John Cumming. New York: Continuum, 1975.

Gans, Eric. *Signs of Paradox: Irony, Resentment, and Other Mimetic Structures*. Stanford, Calif.: Stanford University Press, 1997.

Geremek, Bronislaw; Varga, György; Milosz, Czeslaw; O'Brien, Conor Cruise; and Rabossi, Eduardo. "Civil Society and the Present Age." In *The Idea of Civil Society*, 11–12. Research Triangle Park, N.C.: National Humanities Center, 1992.

Gierke, Otto. *Natural Law and the Theory of Society*. Boston: Beacon Press, 1957.

Glendon, Mary Ann. *A World Made New: Eleanor Roosevelt and the Universal Declaration of Human Rights*. New York: Random House, 2001.

"God's Visible Hand." *Economist* (May 4, 1991): 42.

Gorbachev, Mikhail S. "My Partner, the Pope." *New York Times*, March 9, 1992, A17.

Greenawalt, Kent. *Private Consciences and Public Reasons*. New York: Oxford University Press, 1995.

———. *Religious Convictions and Political Choice*. New York: Oxford University Press, 1988.

———. "Religious Convictions and Political Choice: Some Further Reflections." *DePaul Law Review* 39 (1990): 1019–46.

Gregory XVI. *Mirari Vos Arbitramur*. In Claudia Carlen, ed., *The Papal Encyclicals*. Vol. 1, 235–41. Raleigh, N.C.: Pierian Press, 1990.

Griffin, Leslie. "The Integration of Spiritual and Temporal: Contemporary Roman Catholic Church-State Theory." *Theological Studies* 48 (1987): 225–57.

Bibliography

Gurr, Ted Robert. "Peoples Against States: Ethnopolitical Conflict and the Changing World System." *International Studies Quarterly* 38 (1994): 347–77.

Gustafson. James M. "The Relevance of Historical Understanding." In *Theology and Christian Ethics*, 177–95. Philadelphia: Pilgrim Press, 1974.

Hadden, Jeffrey K. "Religious Broadcasting and the Mobilization of the New Christian Right." *Journal for the Scientific Study of Religion* 26 (1987): 1–24.

Hamalengwa, M.; Flinterman, C; and Dankwa, E. V. O., eds. *The International Law of Human Rights in Africa: Basic Documents and Annotated Bibliography*. Dordrecht: Martinus Nijhoff, 1988.

Havel, Václav. "Address to a Joint Meeting of the House and Senate of the U.S. Congress, February 21, 1990." *Congressional Record* 136, February 21, 1990, p. H395.

———. *Disturbing the Peace: A Conversation with Karel Hvizdala*, trans. Paul Wilson. New York: Vintage Books, 1991.

———. "The Power of the Powerless." In *Open Letters: Selected Writings, 1965–1990*, 125–214. Selected and edited by Paul Wilson. New York: Vintage Books, 1992.

Hehir, J. Bryan. "Church-State and Church-World: The Ecclesiological Implications." *Proceedings of the Catholic Theological Society of America* 41 (1986): 54–74.

Himes, Kenneth, O.F.M. "The New Social Encyclical's Communitarian Vision." *Origins* 21 (1991): 166–68.

Hollenbach, David. "Afterword: A Community of Freedom." In R. Bruce Douglass and David Hollenbach, eds., *Catholicism and Liberalism: Contributions to American Public Philosophy*, 323–43. Cambridge: Cambridge University Press, 1994.

———. *Claims in Conflict: Retrieving and Renewing the Catholic Human Rights Tradition*. New York: Paulist Press, 1979.

———. *The Common Good and Christian Ethics*. Cambridge: Cambridge University Press, 2002.

———. "The Common Good Revisited." *Theological Studies* 50 (1989): 70–94.

———. "A Communitarian Reconstruction of Human Rights." In R. Bruce Douglass and David Hollenbach, eds., *Catholicism and Liberalism: Contributions to American Public Philosophy*, 127–50. Cambridge: Cambridge University Press, 1994.

———. "Fundamental Theology and the Christian Moral Life," In Leo J. O'Donovan and T. Howland Sanks, eds., *Faithful Witness: Foundations of Theology for Today's Church*, 167–84. New York: Crossroad, 1989.

———. "Human Rights and Religious Faith in the Middle East: The Impact of Religious Diversity," 108–23. In David Hollenbach, *Justice, Peace, and Human Rights: American Catholic Social Ethics in a Pluralistic World*. New York: Crossroad, 1990.

Bibliography

————. *Justice, Peace, and Human Rights: American Catholic Social Ethics in a Pluralistic World*. New York: Crossroad, 1990.

————. "Liberalism, Communitarianism, and the Bishops' Pastoral Letter on the Economy." *Annual of the Society of Christian Ethics*. 1987: 19–40.

————. "The Pope and Capitalism." *America* (June 1, 1991): 591.

————. "Public Reason/Private Religion?" *Journal of Religious Ethics* 22, no. 1 (spring 1994): 39–46.

————. "Virtue, the Common Good, and Democracy." In Amitai Etzioni, ed., *New Communitarian Thinking: Persons, Virtues, Institutions, and Communities*, 143–53. Charlottesville: University of Virginia Press, 1994.

————. "War and Peace in American Catholic Thought: A Heritage Abandoned?" *Theological Studies* 48 (1987): 711–26.

Hooper, J. Leon. *The Ethics of Discourse: The Social Philosophy of John Courtney Murray*. Washington, D.C.: Georgetown University Press, 1986.

Hountondji, Paulin J. "The Master's Voice: Remarks on the Problem of Human Rights in Africa." In Alwin Diemer et al., eds., *Philosophical Foundations of Human Rights*, 319–32. Paris: UNESCO, 1986.

Howard, Rhoda E. "Group versus Individual Identity in the African Debate on Human Rights." In Abdullahi Ahmed An-Na'im and Francis M. Deng, eds., *Human Rights in Africa: Cross-Cultural Perspectives*, 153–83. Washington, D.C.: Brookings Institution, 1990.

————. *Human Rights in Commonwealth Africa*. Totowa, N.J.: Rowman and Littlefield, 1986.

Human Rights Watch/Africa Watch. *Divide and Rule: State-Sponsored Ethnic Violence in Kenya*. New York: Human Rights Watch, 1993.

Huntington, Samuel P. "The Clash of Civilizations." *Foreign Affairs* 72 (summer 1993): 22–49.

————. *The Clash of Civilizations and the Remaking of World Order*. New York: Simon & Schuster, 1996.

————. "Religion and the Third Wave." *National Interest* 24 (summer 1991): 29–42.

————. *The Third Wave: Democratization in the Late Twentieth Century*. Norman: University of Oklahoma Press, 1991.

Hyden, Goren. "The Challenge of Domesticating Rights in Africa." In Ronald Cohen, Goran Hyden, and Winston P. Nagan, eds., *Human Rights and Governance in Africa*, 256–80. Gainesville: University Press of Florida, 1993.

Ignatieff, Michael. "The Attack on Human Rights." *Foreign Affairs* 80, no. 6 (November/December 2001): 102–16.

————. *Human Rights as Politics and Idolatry*. Edited and introduced by Amy Gutmann. Princeton, N.J.: Princeton University Press, 2001.

Ilesanmi, Simeon O. "Human Rights Discourse in Modern Africa." *Journal of Religious Ethics* 23, no. 2 (1995): 293–322.

Bibliography

Interaction Council. "In Search of Global Ethical Standards." Vienna, Austria, 22–24 March, 1996. Available online at www.asiawide.or.jp/iac/meetings/Eng96ethics.htm [downloaded July 16, 2002].

Jackson, Timothy. "Love in a Liberal Society." *Journal of Religious Ethics* 22, no. 1 (spring 1994): 29–38.

John XXIII. *Mater et Magistra*. In David J. O"Brien and Thomas A. Shannon, eds., *Catholic Social Thought: The Documentary Heritage*. Maryknoll, N.Y.: Orbis Books, 1992.

———. *Pacem in Terris*. In David J. O'Brien and Thomas A. Shannon, eds., *Catholic Social Thought: The Documentary Heritage*. Maryknoll, N.Y.: Orbis Books, 1992.

John Paul II. "Arrival Speech in Nigeria, March 21, 1998," no. 2. Downloaded from the website of the Holy See www.vatican.va/holy_father/john_paul_ii/travels/documents/hf_jp-ii_spe_21031998_nigeria-arrival_en.html [downloaded August 3, 2002].

———. *Centesimus Annus* In David J. O'Brien and Thomas A. Shannon, eds. *Catholic Social Thought: The Documentary Heritage*. Maryknoll, N.Y.: Orbis Books, 1992.

———. *Evangelium Vitae*. In David J. O'Brien and Thomas A. Shannon, eds., *Catholic Social Thought: The Documentary Heritage*. Maryknoll, N.Y.: Orbis Books, 1992.

———. "Homily in the José Marti Square of Havana, Sunday, 25 January 1998," no. 4. Downloaded from the website of the Holy see www.vatican.va/holy_father/john_paul_ii/travels/documents/hf_jpii_hom_25011998_lahavana_en.html [downloaded August 3, 2002].

———. *Laborem Exercens*. In David J. O"Brien and Thomas A. Shannon, eds., *Catholic Social Thought: The Documentary Heritage*. Maryknoll, N.Y.: Orbis Books, 1992.

———. *Veritatis Splendor*. Vatican City: Libreria Editrice Vaticana, 1993, no. 5, p. 10.

Johnson, Thomas S. "Capitalism after Communism: Now Comes the Hard Part." In John A. Coleman, S.J., ed., *One Hundred Years of Catholic Social Thought: Celebration and Challenge*. Maryknoll, N.Y.: Orbis, 1991.

Johnston, Douglas, and Sampson, Cynthia eds. *Religion, the Missing Dimension of Statecraft*. New York: Oxford University Press, 1994.

Jonsen, Albert R. "Casuistry." In James F. Childress and John Macquarrie, eds., *The Westminster Dictionary of Christian Ethics*, 78–81. Philadelphia: Westminster, 1986.

Juergensmeyer, Mark. *Terror in the Mind of God: The Global Rise of Religious Violence*. Berkeley: University of California Press, 2000.

Kanbur, Ravi, and Lustig, Nora. "Why Is Inequality Back on the Agenda?" Department of Agricultural, Resource, and Managerial Economics Working Paper 99–14. Ithaca, N.Y.: Cornell University, 1999.

Bibliography

Kant, Immanuel. *Critique of Pure Reason*. Translated by Norman Kemp Smith. New York: St. Martin's, 1965.

———. *Foundations of the Metaphysics of Morals*. Translated by Lewis White Beck. Indianapolis: Bobbs-Merrill, 1959.

———. *Idea for a Universal History with a Cosmopolitan Intent*. In *Perpetual Peace and Other Essays*, 29–40. Translated by Ted Humphrey. Indianapolis: Hackett, 1983.

Kaplan, Robert D. *Warrior Politics: Why Leadership Demands a Pagan Ethos*. New York: Random House, 2002.

Keck, Margaret E., and Sikkink, Kathryn. *Activists Beyond Borders: Advocacy Networks in International Politics*. Ithaca, N.Y.: Cornell University Press, 1998.

Kelsey, David. *The Uses of Scripture in Recent Theology*. Philadelphia: Fortress Press, 1975.

Kepel, Gilles. *Jihad: The Trail of Political Islam*. Translated by Anthony Roberts. Cambridge, Mass.: Harvard University Press, 2002.

———. *The Revenge of God: The Resurgence of Islam, Christianity and Judaism in the Modern World*. Translated by Alan Braley. University Park: Pennsylvania State University Press, 1994.

Kim Dae Jung. "Is Culture Destiny? The Myth of Asia's Anti-Democratic Values." *Foreign Affairs* 73, no. 6 (November/December 1994): 189–94.

Kohák, Erazim. "Can There Be a Central Europe?" *Dissent* (spring 1990): 194–97.

Krausz, Michael, ed. *Relativism: Interpretation and Confrontation*. Notre Dame, Ind.: University of Notre Dame Press, 1989.

Küng, Hans. *A Global Ethic for Global Politics and Economics*. Translated by John Bowden. New York: Oxford University Press, 1998.

———. "The History, Significance, and Method of the Declaration Toward a Global Ethic," 71–72. In Hans Küng and Karl-Josef Kuschel, eds., *A Global Ethic: The Declaration of the Parliament of the World's Religions*. Translated by John Bowden. New York: Continuum, 1993.

Küng, Hans, ed. *Yes to a Global Ethic*. Translated by John Bowden. New York: Continuum, 1996.

Küng, Hans, and Kuschel, Karl-Josef, eds. *A Global Ethic: The Declaration of the Parliament of the World's Religions*. Translated by John Bowden. New York: Continuum, 1993.

Kuschel, Karl-Josef, and Dietmar Meith, eds. *In Search of Universal Values*. Concilium, vol. 2001, no. 4. London: SCM Press, 2001.

Lamb, Matthew. *Solidarity with Victims: Toward a Theology of Social Transformation*. New York: Crossroad, 1982.

Langan, John. "Overcoming the Divisiveness of Religion." *Journal of Religious Ethics* 22, no. 1 (spring 1994): 47–51.

Bibliography

Lauren, Paul Gorden. *The Evolution of International Human Rights: Visions Seen.* Philadelphia: University of Pennsylvania Press, 1998.

Lazarus, Francis M., ed. *Faith, Discovery, Service: Perspectives on Jesuit Education.* Milwaukee: Marquette University Press, 1992.

Lee Kwan Yew. *From Third World to First: The Singapore Story: 1965–2000.* New York: Harper Collins, 2000.

Lewis, Bernard. *What Went Wrong: Western Impact and Middle Eastern Response.* New York: Oxford University Press, 2002.

Lindbeck, George. *The Nature of Doctrine: Religion and Theology in a Postliberal Age.* Philadelphia: Westminster Press, 1984.

Locke, John. *Second Treatise on Civil Government.* In *Social Contract.* Edited by Sir Ernest Barker. New York: Oxford University Press, 1967.

Lonergan, Bernard. "Dimensions of Meaning." In F. E. Crowe, ed., *Collection: Papers of Bernard Lonergan, S.J.*, 252–267. New York: Herder and Herder, 1967.

Lovin, Robin W. "Perry, Naturalism, and Religion in Public." *Tulane Law Review* 63 (1989): 1517–39.

Lubac, Henri de. *The Drama of Atheist Humanism.* Translated by Edith M. Riley. New York: New American Library, 1963.

Luijpen, William. *Phenomenology of Natural Law.* Pittsburgh: Duquesne University Press, 1967.

Lustig, Andrew. "Natural Law, Property, and Justice: The General Justification of Property in Aquinas and Locke." *Journal of Religious Ethics* 19, no. 1 (1991): 119–49.

Lyotard, Jean-François. "The Other's Rights." In Stephen Shute and Susan Hurley, eds., *On Human Rights: The Oxford Amnesty Lectures 1993*, 135–47. New York: Basic Books, 1993.

MacIntyre, Alasdair. *After Virtue: A Study in Moral Theory.* Notre Dame, Ind.: University of Notre Dame Press, 1981.

———. *Three Rival Versions of Moral Enquiry: Encyclopaedia, Genealogy and Tradition.* Notre Dame, Ind.: University of Notre Dame Press, 1990.

———. *Whose Justice? Which Rationality?* Notre Dame, Ind.: University of Notre Dame Press, 1988.

Mapel, David R. "Realism and the Ethics of War." In Terry Nardin, ed., *The Ethics of War and Peace: Religious and Secular Perspectives*, 54–77. Princeton, N.J.: Princeton University Press, 1996.

Maritain, Jacques. *Integral Humanism: Temporal and Spiritual Problems of a New Christendom.* Translated by Joseph W. Owens. New York: Scribner's, 1968.

———. "Introduction." In UNESCO, ed., *Human Rights: Comments and Interpretations*, 9–17. New York: Columbia University Press, 1949.

———. *Man and the State.* Chicago: University of Chicago Press, 1951.

Marx, Karl. "Theses on Feuerbach." In Lewis S. Feuer, ed., *Marx and Engels: Basic Writings on Politics and Philosophy.* New York: Doubleday, 1959.

Bibliography

Marx, Karl and Engels, Friedrich. "Manifesto of the Communist Party." In Lewis S. Feuer, ed, *Basic Writings on Politics and Philosophy: Karl Marx and Friedrich Engels*. Garden City, N.Y.: Doubleday, 1959.

May, William W., ed. *Vatican Authority and American Catholic Dissent*. New York: Crossroad, 1987.

McBrien, Richard. *Caesar's Coin: Religion and Politics in America*. New York: Macmillan, 1987.

McCormick, Richard. "Some Early Reactions to *Veritatis Spendor*." *Theological Studies* 55 (1994): 481–506.

McMahon, Jeff. "Realism, Morality and War." In Terry Nardin, ed., *The Ethics of War and Peace: Religious and Secular Perspectives*, 78–92. Princeton, N.J.: Princeton University Press, 1996.

Meilander, Gilbert. "The Limits of Politics and a Politics of Limited Expectations." *Dialog* 26 (1987): 98–103.

Mejia, Jorge Maria. "Centesimus Annus: An Answer to the Unknowns and Questions of Our Times." *Ecumenical Review* 43 (1991): 401–10.

Miller, William Lee. *The First Liberty: Religion and the American Republic*. New York: Alfred A. Knopf, 1986.

Mitchell, Basil. "Should Law Be Christian?" *The Month* 20 (1987): 95–99.

Mojekwu, Chris C. "International Human Rights: The African Perspective." In Jack L. Nelson and Vera M. Green, eds. *International Human Rights: Contemporary Issues*, 85–95. Stanfordville, N.Y.: Human Rights Publishing Group, 1980.

Mooney, Christopher F. *Public Virtue: Law and the Social Character of Religion*. Notre Dame, Ind.: University of Notre Dame Press, 1986.

Mouw, Richard J. "Understanding the Fundamentalists' Retreat." *New Oxford Review* 54, no. 7 (September 1987): 11–15.

Moynihan, Daniel Patrick. "Social Justice in the *Next* Century." *America* (September 14, 1991): 132–37.

Murdoch, Iris. "Vision and Choice in Morality." In Ian T. Ramsey, ed., *Christian Ethics and Contemporary Philosophy*, 206. London: SCM Press, 1966.

Murray, John Courtney. "The Arguments for the Human Right to Religious Freedom." J. Leon Hooper, ed., In *Religious Liberty: Catholic Struggles with Pluralism*, 229–44. Louisville, Ky.: Westminster/John Knox Press, 1993.

———. "The Declaration on Religious Freedom." In *War, Poverty, Freedom: The Christian Response. Concilium*, no. 15, 3–16. New York: Paulist Press, 1966.

———. "The Declaration on Religious Freedom: A Moment in Its Legislative History," In John Courtney Murray, ed., *Religious Liberty: An End and a Beginning*, 15–42. New York: Macmillan, 1966.

———. "The Declaration on Religious Freedom: Its Deeper Significance." *America* 114 (April 23, 1966): 592–93.

———. *The Problem of Religious Freedom*. Westminster, Md.: Newman Press, 1965, 7, 26–27.

———. "Religious Freedom," In John Courtney Murray, ed., *Freedom and Man*, 131–40. New York: P. J. Kenedy & Sons, 1965.

———. *We Hold These Truths: Catholic Reflections on the American Proposition*. New York: Sheed and Ward, 1960.

Murray, John Courtney, ed., *Freedom and Man*. New York: P. J. Kenedy & Sons, 1965.

Nardin, Terry, ed. *The Ethics of War and Peace: Religious and Secular Perspectives*. Princeton, N.J.: Princeton University Press, 1996.

Nardin, Terry, and David R. Mapel, eds. *Traditions of International Ethics*. Cambridge: Cambridge University Press, 1992.

National Conference of Catholic Bishops. *Economic Justice for All*. Washington, D.C.: United States Catholic Conference, 1986.

Neilsen, Neils. *Revolutions in Eastern Europe: The Religious Roots*. Maryknoll, NY: Orbis Books, 1991.

Nelson, Jack L., and Vera M. Green, eds. *International Human Rights*: Contemporary Issues. Stanfordville, N.Y.: Human Rights Publishing Group, 1980.

Neuhaus, Richard John. *The Catholic Moment: The Paradox of the Church in the Postmodern World*. San Francisco: Harper & Row, 1987.

Neuner, J, and Dupuis, J, eds. *The Christian Faith in the Doctrinal Documents of the Catholic Church*. Staten Island, N.Y.: Alba House, 1982.

Newman, John Henry. *An Essay on the Development of Christian Doctrine*. Garden City, N.Y.: Doubleday Image Books, 1960.

Niebuhr, H. Richard. *The Responsible Self: An Essay in Christian Moral Philosophy*. New York: Harper & Row, 1963.

Niebuhr, Reinhold. *The Nature and Destiny of Man*, 2 vols. New York: Scribner's, 1964.

Noonan, John T., Jr. *The Believer and the Powers that Are: Cases, History, and Other Data Bearing on the Relation of Religion and Government*. New York : Macmillan, 1987.

———. *Bribes*. New York : Macmillan, 1984.

———. *Contraception: A History of Its Treatment by the Catholic Theologians and Canonists*. Cambridge: Belknap Press of Harvard University Press, 1965.

———. "Development in Moral Doctrine." *Theological Studies* 54 (1993): 662–77.

———. *Power to Dissolve: Lawyers and Marriages in the Courts of the Roman Curia*. Cambridge, Mass.: Belknap Press of Harvard University Press, 1972.

———. *The Scholastic Analysis of Usury*. Cambridge, Mass.: Harvard University Press, 1957.

Noonan, John T., Jr., ed. *The Morality of Abortion: Legal and Historical Perspectives*. Cambridge, Mass.: Harvard University Press, 1970.

Nussbaum, Martha C. "Aristotelian Social Democracy." In R. Bruce Douglass, Gerald R. Mara, and Henry S. Richardson, eds., *Liberalism and the Good*, 203–52. New York: Routledge, 1990.

Bibliography

―――. "Human Capabilities, Female Human Beings." In Martha Nussbaum and Jonathan Glover, eds., *Women, Culture, and Development: A Study of Human Capabilities*, 61–104. Oxford: Oxford University Press, 1995.

―――. "Human Functioning and Social Justice: In Defense of Aristotelian Essentialism." *Political Theory* 20 (1992): 202–46.

―――. *Women and Human Development: The Capabilities Approach*. Cambridge: Cambridge University Press, 2000.

Nussbaum, Martha C., and Glover, Jonathan, eds. *Women, Culture, and Development: A Study of Human Capabilities*. Oxford: Oxford University Press, 1995.

Nye, Joseph S., Jr., and John D. Donahue, eds. *Governance in a Globalizing World*. Washington, D.C.: Brookings Institution Press, 2000.

O'Brien, David J., and Thomas A. Shannon, eds. *Catholic Social Thought: The Documentary Heritage*. Maryknoll, N.Y.: Orbis Books, 1992.

Okin, Susan Moller. *Is Multiculturalism Bad for Women?* Edited by Joshua Cohen, Matthew Howard, and Martha C. Nussbaum. Princeton, N.J.: Princeton University Press, 1999.

Okun, Arthur. *Equality and Efficiency: The Big Tradeoff*. Washington, D.C.: Brookings Institution Press, 1975.

Olyan, Saul M., and Martha C. Nussbaum, eds. *Sexual Orientation and Human Rights in American Religious Discourse*. New York: Oxford University Press, 1998.

Ombletts, John. "Activists Get Their Training at Church." *Boston College Biweekly* (March 26, 1992): 5.

O'Neill, Onora. *Bounds of Justice*. Cambridge: Cambridge University Press, 2000.

O'Riordan, Sean. "Toward a Decisional Model of Church." *Furrow* (November 1991): 607–15.

Outka, Gene, and Reeder, John P., Jr., eds. *Prospects for a Common Morality*. Princeton, N.J.: Princeton University Press, 1993.

Perry, Michael J. *Love and Power: The Role of Religion and Morality in American Politics*. New York: Oxford University Press, 1991.

―――. *Morality, Politics and Law: A Bicentennial Essay*. New York: Oxford University Press, 1988.

―――. "Neutral Politics?" *Review of Politics* (fall 1989): 479–509.

―――. *Religion in Politics: Constitutional and Moral Perspectives*. New York: Oxford University Press, 1997.

―――. "Religious Morality and Political Choice: Further Thoughts—and Second Thoughts—on Love and Power." *San Diego Law Review* 30, no. 4 (fall 1993): 703–27.

Piscatori, James. "The Turmoil Within: The Struggle for the Future of the Islamic World." *Foreign Affairs* 81, no. 3 (May/June 2002): 145–50.

Bibliography

Pius XI, *Quadragesimo Anno*. In David J. O'Brien and Thomas A. Shannon, eds. Maryknoll, N.Y.: Orbis Books, 1992.

Plaskow, Judith. *Sex, Sin, and Grace: Women's Experience and the Theologies of Reinhold Niebuhr and Paul Tillich*. Washington, D.C.: University Press of America, 1980.

Plato. *Republic*. In *The Collected Dialogues of Plato*. Edited by Edith Hamilton and Huntington Cairns. New York: Random House, 1961.

――――. *Theaetetus*, 155d. In *The Collected Dialogues of Plato*. Edited by Edith Hamilton and Huntington Cairns. New York: Random House, 1961.

Pope, Stephen J. "Expressive Individualism and True Self-Love: A Thomistic Perspective." *Journal of Religion* 71 (1991):384–99.

Porter, Jean. *Natural and Divine Law: Reclaiming the Tradition for Christian Ethics*. Grand Rapids, Mich.: Eerdmans, 1999.

――――. "The Search for a Global Ethic." *Theological Studies* 62 (2001): 105–21.

Prunier, Gérard. *The Crisis in Rwanda: History of a Genocide*. Kampala: Fountain Publishers, 1995.

Putnam, Robert. "Bowling Alone: America's Declining Social Capital." *Journal of Democracy* 6, no. 1 (January 1995): 65–78.

――――. *Bowling Alone: The Collapse and Revival of American Community*. New York: Simon & Schuster, 2000.

――――. *Making Democracy Work: Civic Traditions in Modern Italy*. Princeton, N.J.: Princeton University Press, 1993.

――――. "The Prosperous Community: Social Capital and Public Life." *American Prospect*, no. 13 (spring 1993): 35–42.

――――. "Tuning In, Tuning Out: The Strange Disappearance of Social Capital in America." *PS: Political Science and Politics* 28, no. 4 (December 1995): 664–65.

Rahner, Karl. "Theological Reflections on the Problem of Secularization." In *Theological Investigations*, vol. 10. New York: Herder and Herder, 1973, 318–48.

――――. "Toward a Fundamental Theological Interpretation of Vatican II." *Theological Studies* 40 (December 1979): 716–27.

Ramsey, Ian T., ed. *Christian Ethics and Contemporary Philosophy*. London: SCM Press, 1966.

Ramsey, Paul. *War and Christian Conscience*. Durham, N.C.: Duke University Press, 1961.

Rawls, John. "The Idea of an Overlapping Consensus." *Oxford Journal of Legal Studies* 7 (1987): 1–25.

――――. "The Idea of Public Reason Revisited," In *The Law of Peoples with "The Idea of Public Reason Revisited."* Cambridge, Mass.: Harvard University Press, 1999, 152–56.

――――. "Justice as Fairness: Political not Metaphysical." *Philosophy and Public Affairs* 14 (1985): 223–51.

——. "Kantian Constructivism in Moral Theory." *Journal of Philosophy* 77 (1980): 515–72.

——. *The Law of Peoples*. Cambridge, Mass.: Harvard University Press, 1999.

——. *Political Liberalism*. New York: Columbia University Press, 1993.

——. *A Theory of Justice*, rev. ed. Cambridge, Mass.: Harvard University Press, 1999.

Reichley, A. James. *Religion and American Public Life*. Washington, D.C.: Brookings Institution, 1985.

Rico, Hermínio. *John Paul II and the Legacy of Dignitatis Humanae*. Washington, D.C.: Georgetown University Press, 2002.

Rorty, Richard. *Contingency, Irony, and Solidarity*. New York: Cambridge University Press, 1989.

——. "Postmodernist Bourgeois Liberalism." In Robert Hollinger, ed., *Hermeneutics and Praxis*, 214–21. Notre Dame, Ind.: University of Notre Dame Press, 1985.

——. "The Priority of Democracy to Philosophy." In Merrill D. Peterson and Robert C. Vaughan, eds., *The Virginia Statute for Religious Freedom: Its Evolution and Consequences in American History*, 257–82. Cambridge: Cambridge University, 1988.

——. "The Seer of Prague." *New Republic* (July 1, 1991): 35–40.

——. "Truth and Freedom: A Reply to Thomas McCarthy." In Gene Outka and John P. Reeder, Jr., eds., *Prospects for a Common Morality*, 254–89. Princeton, N.J.: Princeton University Press, 1993.

Rosenblum, Nancy, ed. *Liberalism and the Moral Life*. Cambridge, Mass.: Harvard University Press, 1989.

Sachedina, Abdulaziz. *The Islamic Roots of Democratic Pluralism*. New York: Oxford University Press, 2001.

Saiving, Valerie. "The Human Situation: A Feminine View." In Carol Christ and Judith Plaskow, eds., *Womanspirit Rising: A Feminist Reader in Religion*, 25–42. New York: Harper & Row, 1979.

Sen, Amartya. "Asian Values and Human Rights." *New Republic* (July 14, 1997): 33–40.

——. *Development as Freedom*. New York: Knopf, 1999.

Shute, Stephen, and Susan Hurley, eds. *On Human Rights: The Oxford Amnesty Lectures, 1993*. New York: Basic Books, 1993.

Smolin, David M. "Regulating Religious and Cultural Conflict in a Postmodern America: A Response to Professor Perry." *Iowa Law Review* 76 (1991): 1076–77.

Sobrino, Jon. *The Principle of Mercy: Taking the Crucified People from the Cross*. Maryknoll, N.Y.: Orbis, 1994.

Soroush, 'Abdolkarim. *Reason, Freedom, and Democracy in Islam: Essential Writings of 'Abdolkarim Soroush*. Translated, edited, and introduced by Mahmoud Sadri and Ahmad Sadri. Oxford: Oxford University Press, 2000.

Bibliography

Stackhouse, Max L. "John Paul on Ethics and the 'New Capitalism.'" *Christian Century* (May 29–June 5, 1991): 581.

Stackhouse, Max L., and McCann, Dennis P. "A Postcommunist Manifesto: Public Theology after the Collapse of Socialism." *Christian Century* 108 (January 16, 1991): cover and 44–47.

Stahl, William A. "The New Christian Right." *Ecumenist* 25 (1987): 81–87.

"Symposium: The Role of Religion in Public Debate in a Liberal Society." *San Diego Law Review* 30, no. 4 (fall 1993): 643–915.

Taylor, Charles. *Sources of the Self: The Making of the Modern Identity*. Cambridge, Mass.: Harvard University Press, 1989.

TeSelle, Eugene. "The Civic Vision in Augustine's *City of God*." *Thought* 62 (1987): 268–80.

Thomas Aquinas. *Summa Theologica*. 5 vols. Translated by the Fathers of the English Dominican Province. Allen, Tex.: Christian Classics, 1981.

Tierney, Brian. *The Crisis of Church & State, 1050–1300*. Englewood Cliffs, N.J.: Prentice-Hall, 1964.

Tracy, David. "Catholic Classics in American Liberal Culture," In R. Bruce Douglass and David Hollenbach, eds., *Catholicism and Liberalism*, 196–213. Cambridge: Cambridge University Press, 1994.

———. *Plurality and Ambiguity: Hermeneutics, Religion, Hope*. San Francisco: Harper & Row, 1987.

Troeltsch, Ernst. "The Ideas of Natural Law and Humanity in World Politics." In Otto Gierke, ed., *Natural Law and the Theory of Society*, 201–22. Boston: Beacon Press, 1957.

———. *The Social Teaching of the Christian Churches*. 2 vols. Translated by Olive Wyon. New York: Harper Torchbook, 1960.

Turner, Frank, S.J. "John Paul's Social Analysis." *The Month* (August 1991): 344–49.

Twiss, Sumner B., and Grelle, Bruce eds. *Explorations in Global Ethics: Comparative Religious Ethics and Interreligious Dialogue*. Boulder, Colo.: Westview Press, 1998.

UNICEF. *State of the World's Children*. Oxford: Oxford University Press, 1996.

United Nations General Assembly. *Universal Declaration of Human Rights*. December 10, 1948. Available online www.un.org/Overview/rights.html [downloaded July 11, 2002].

United Nations Millenium Development Goals. Summary of "The United Nations Development Declaration." Available online www.un.org/millenniumgoals/index.html [downloaded August 1, 2002].

United States Catholic Conference Administrative Board, "Political Responsibility: Choices for the Future." *Origins* 17 (1987): 369–75.

Vatican Council II. *Dignitatis Humanae*. In Walter M. Abbott and Joseph Gallagher, eds., *The Documents of Vatican II*. New York: America Press, 1966.

Bibliography

―――. *Gaudium et Spes. The Pastoral Constitution on the Church in the Modern World*. In Walter M. Abbott and Joseph Gallagher, eds., *The Documents of Vatican II*. New York: America Press, 1966.

Verba, Sidney; Schlozman, Kay Lehman; and Brady, Henry E. *Voice and Equality: Civic Voluntarism in American Politics*. Cambridge, Mass.: Harvard University Press, 1995.

Waldman, Amy. "Why We Need a Religious Left." *Washington Monthly* (December 1995): 37–43.

Walzer, Michael. "The Idea of Civil Society: A Path to Social Reconstruction." *Dissent* (spring 1991): 293–304.

―――. *Just and Unjust Wars: A Moral Argument with Historical Illustrations*. New York: Basic Books, 1977.

―――. *Spheres of Justice: A Defense of Pluralism and Equality*. New York: Basic Books, 1993.

―――. *Thick and Thin: Moral Argument at Home and Abroad*. Notre Dame, Ind.: University of Notre Dame Press, 1994.

Weber, Max. "Science as a Vocation." In *From Max Weber: Essays in Sociology*. Translated and Edited by H. H. Gerth and C. Wright Mills. New York: Oxford University Press, 1958.

Weigel, George. *Tranquillitas Ordinis: The Present Failure and Future Promise of American Catholic Thought on War and Peace*. Oxford: Oxford University Press, 1987.

Weil, Simone. *Waiting for God*. New York: Harper & Row, 1973.

Weithman, Paul J. "Rawlsian Liberalism and the Privatization of Religion." *Journal of Religious Ethics* 22, no. 1 (spring 1994): 3–28.

Wilkins, John, ed. *Considering Veritatis Splendor*. Cleveland: Pilgrim Press, 1994.

Wilson, William Julius. *The Truly Disadvantaged: The Inner City, The Underclass, and Public Policy*. Chicago: University of Chicago Press, 1987.

Wolfe, Alan. *One Nation After All: What Middle-Class Americans Really Think about God, Country, Family, Racism, Welfare, Immigration, Homosexuality, Work, the Right, the Left, and Each Other*. New York: Viking, 1998.

―――. *Whose Keeper? Social Science and Moral Obligation*. Berkeley: University of California Press, 1989.

World Bank. *World Development Report 2000/2001: Attacking Poverty*. New York: Oxford University Press, 2001.

World Conference on Human Rights, *Vienna Declaration and Programme of Action*. 25 June 1993. Text available online at UN High Commissioner for Human Rights website www.unhchr.ch/huridocda/huridoca.nsf/(Symbol)/A.CONF. 157.23.En?OpenDocument [downloaded July 30, 2002].

Wuthnow, Robert. *Acts of Compassion: Caring for Others and Helping Ourselves*. Princeton, N.J.: Princeton University Press, 1991.

————. *The Restructuring of American Religion: Society and Faith Since World War II*. Princeton, N.J.: Princeton University Press, 1988.

Zakaria, Fareed. "Culture Is Destiny: A Conversation with Lee Kwan Yew." *Foreign Affairs* 73, no. 2 (March/April, 1994): 109–26.

Zizola, Giancarlo. "Les revirements d'une encyclique." *L'actualité religieuse dans le monde* (June 15, 1991): 10–11.

INDEX

Abacha, Sani, 226

Abrecht, Paul, 198–99

Ackerman, Bruce, 109

activism, political, 157–58, 185–86, 187–88. *See also* citizen participation and politically active churches

Africa. *See* human rights and development in Africa

African Charter of Human and Peoples' Rights, 218, 221–23

Ake, Claude, 227–28

American politics and religion, 75–96; and Augustinian interpretations, 87–88; casuistry and, 95–96; Catholic contributions to, 82–84, 94–96, 98n62; churches' indirect engagement, 89–90; churches' participation in policy process, 90–91; and civil law and morality in pluralistic society, 91–94; common good and, 82–84, 93–95; practical moral reason and, 83–84, 94–95; rethinking Catholic Church's social role and, 88–96; U.S. Constitution and, 90, 92–93. *See also* Catholic community and American politics; Christian right

An-Na'im, Abdullahi, 219–20

Aristotle, 84, 161, 247–48

Audi, Robert, 123n59

Augustine, 10, 41, 60, 87–88, 161

Barber, Benjamin, 113

Barth, Karl, 110

Bayart, Jean-François, 16n2, 224

Benhabib, Seyla, 187

Berger, Peter, 199–200

Bhagavad Gita, 68

Boff, Leonardo, 197–98

Borgmann, Albert, 19–20, 23, 43

Brady, Henry, 158, 179–83

Buckley, Michael, 67

Bush, George W., 219

Buttiglione, Rocco, 201–2

Cahill, Lisa Sowle, 249

Calvin, John, 10, 80

capitalism and market economy: *Centesimus Annus* and, 200–203, 207–9; collapse of communism and, 197–98, 200–201, 205–9; common good and, 207–8, 212–14; communism and, 197–98, 200–201, 207–9; consumer society and, 212–14; different societies' organization of, 206–7; and post–cold war Christian social ethics, 197–203, 205–9, 212–14, 227–28; and postwar models of market economy, 208–9

The Capitalist Revolution (Berger), 199–200

Casanova, José, 4–5, 183–84, 186–87

Castro, Fidel, 226–27

casuistry, 95–96

Catholic community and American politics, 81–88; casuistry and, 95–96; Catholic contributions to American public life, 82–84, 94–96, 98n62; and church in paradoxical relationship with the world, 85–86; common good and,

Index

Christian social ethics, 207–8, 210–14; and Rawls's "method of avoidance," 149–50, 161–62; and religion's influence on civil society and culture, 149–50, 158–59, 160–65; tolerance and, 149–50, 161–62; and virtues of the social inquirer, 50–52

Communism, collapse of: capitalism and, 197–98, 200–201, 205–9; *Centesimus Annus* on, 196–97, 200–201, 207–9; and new idea of civil society, 155–56; and post–cold war Christian social ethics, 196–99, 200–201, 205–9; and public conversations about human good, 163, 173n32

Confucianism in East Asia, 236, 237–38, 243, 244–45

conscience, freedom of, 131–34

Constitution, U.S., 90, 92–93, 102–3

Cuba, 226–27

"Cultural Transformations and Human Rights in Africa: A Preliminary Report" (An-Na'im et al.), 219

Curry, Dean C., 79–81

Czechoslovakia, 163, 173n32

Davidson, Basil, 16n2

democratization in modern world history, 125–27, 129, 186

Descartes, René, 41, 55

development. *See* human rights and development in Africa

"Development in Moral Doctrine" (Noonan), 25

Dewey, John, 53n18

dialogic universalism, 10–16

Dignitatis Humanae (Declaration on Religious Freedom) (Vatican Council II), 89, 109, 131–32, 135–40, 143. *See also* Vatican Council II and conciliar arguments about religious freedom

Dionne, E. J., 160

Dougherty, James, 88

Dulles, Avery, 34, 88–89

East Asian Confucianism, 236, 237–38, 243, 244–45

Eastern Europe: alternative models for public role of religion in, 187; capitalism and, 200–201; collapse of communism and, 155–56, 163, 196–99, 200–201; dissidents and commitment to truth, 213; John Paul II on, 22–24, 200–201; and new idea of civil society, 155–56, 209–10; and public conversation about human good, 163, 173n32

Edwards, Jonathan, 110

Einstein, Albert, 11

Ellacuría, Ignacio, 66–67, 68

Enlightenment, 8–9, 10–11, 17n14

ethical dimensions in global politics. *See* global human rights ethic

Evangelical Protestantism, 83, 109, 167. *See also* Christian right

Falwell, Jerry, 76, 77, 78–79

feminist theology, 63

Fernyhough, Timothy, 222

Finnis, John, 34

The First Liberty: Religion and the American Republic (Miller), 82

Friedman, Milton, 128

Gadamer, Hans-Georg, 37n44

Gandhi, Mohandas, 67–68

Gaudium et Spes (Vatican Council II), 9, 12, 84, 88–89

Geremek, Bronislaw, 155

Glendon, Mary Ann, 233

global human rights ethic, 231–54; addressing the practical reasons for, 242–43; Aristotelian moment in quest for, 247–48; and challenge of political realism, 232–33; and challenges of plu-